THOSE WHO SHOULD BE SEIZED SHOULD BE SEIZED

THOSE WHO SHOULD BE SEIZED SHOULD BE SEIZED

CHINA'S RELENTLESS PERSECUTION OF UYGHURS AND OTHER ETHNIC MINORITIES

JOHN BECK

THOSE WHO SHOULD BE SEIZED SHOULD BE SEIZED
First published in 2025 by Melville House
Copyright © 2024 by John Beck
All rights reserved

First Melville House Printing: February 2025
Distributed by Penguin Random House LLC,
1745 Broadway, New York, NY 10019 USA.
www.penguinrandomhouse.com

Melville House Publishing
46 John Street
Brooklyn, NY 11201
and
Melville House UK
Suite 2000
16/18 Woodford Road
London E7 0HA
mhpbooks.com
@melvillehouse

ISBN: 978-1-68589-179-4
ISBN: 978-1-68589-180-0 (eBook)

Library of Congress Control Number: 2025951305

Designed by Beste M. Doğan
Printed in the United States of America

1 3 5 7 9 10 8 6 4 2

A catalog record for this book is available from the Library of Congress
The authorized representative in the EU for product safety and compliance is Easy Access System Europe,
Mustamäe tee 50, 10621 Tallinn, Estonia. gpsr.requests@easproject.com

AUTHOR'S NOTE

This book is the result of reporting carried out across six years in Turkey, Kazakhstan and the United States. It recounts the memories of the people who lived these events, as told to me over many hundreds of hours of interviews. It also includes fragments of contemporary archive material. Details were fact checked and cross referenced wherever possible and some names have been changed to preserve anonymity.

THOSE WHO SHOULD BE SEIZED SHOULD BE SEIZED

1

We say China is a country vast in territory, rich in resources and large in population; as a matter of fact it is the Han nationality whose population is large and the minority nationalities whose territory is vast and whose resources are rich.

—Mao Zedong

I t was always her mother's voice that dragged Saira from sleep. "Open your eyes," she would call through to the children's room. "Get yourselves out of bed. You know the early bird catches the worm."

The house would smell of brewing tea and fresh bread or warm golden *baursak* dough balls if they were lucky because her mother rose hours before them to mix and knead and boil and steep. Saira would emerge bleary and reluctant with her brother and sisters. She would eat and she would wash. Then she would pack jotters and pencils into her yellow school backpack and begin the anxious and interminable wait for her parents to leave for work.

She waited in the main room of the house, hiding her nerves as they said goodbyes and watching from the quickly attained window as the backs of their heads disappeared down the road.

There were usually only moments before she had to leave for school so she moved fast. Through to her parents' room and straight to the heavy wooden chest of folded clothes, sheets and blankets pushed up against the wall. Her parents imagined themselves unobserved and busied themselves with the not-quite-silent opening and shutting of it in the evenings but Saira was too sharp for them and she always saw. She would negotiate the chest lid herself and reach down through layers of wool and coarse cotton until her fingers met the cool resistance of a book cover. The book would go into her backpack beneath her school supplies and she would step out onto the road in turn.

School was forever the same. A playground full of overexcited children, the rote drudgery of history and math and Chinese language classes. Break times came and Saira's classmates would chase each other in screaming circles as part of some pointless game while she found a spot on her own. Under a tree with the sun shining between the leaves and birds singing in the branches if the weather was right but a classroom corner would do when the rain or snow blew keen off the mountains. She would settle herself, take the book from her bag and read. Mouthing new words as she found them and doubling back for difficult passages.

Home again and Saira placed the book back in its hiding place and eased the chest lid down on top of it to preserve the secret of her own reading within her parents'. It was that secrecy that had so puzzled her when aged seven or eight she first noticed angular shapes inside jackets or under arms and the great care taken to keep them from the world. She had not betrayed herself by asking her parents anything but brooded on why they used such caution when there were books at school that no one ever bothered locking away.

Unendurable curiosity had drawn her to her parents' room whenever they were out of the house and eventually to the chest. She only dared quick glimpses at first, wondering at the illustrations and tracing the Arabic script that ethnic Kazakhs in China like them still used even though the Soviets had replaced it with Cyrillic in Kazakhstan itself. Then would come a footstep heard or imagined and she would close the lid and spring away.

She had returned often to the books. There were never many in the house and sometimes none but new ones appeared and others vanished with the visits of village neighbors and of family. They usually ended up in the chest but her parents had various other spots in their bedroom out of sight and easy reach of a child. Up on a high shelf. Under their mattress. Saira could not spend long in her parents' room without risking discovery so to study them properly she had devised her routine. In the evenings she would position herself somewhere with a view of the door to her parents' room and mount watch while she did homework. She was often rewarded by a peripheral glimpse of her mother or father concealing something and would note where it was for retrieval the following morning.

She cherished and nurtured her secret. And in it she found worlds so unlike her carefully managed surroundings. The books were written by Kazakhs and were about Kazakhs who had lived not so long before. In *Botagoz* by Sabit Mukanov, she came to know life in the steppe during the cruel final days of the Russian Empire through a courageous girl who joined the uprising against the Tsarists. In Gabit Musrepov's *Ulpan*, she followed a young woman who was married off to a much older husband and rose to a position of power usually held only by men that she had to fight to defend after her husband's death.

Through the settings and details that framed these stories Saira learned of how many Kazakhs had come to live in the 640,000 square miles of mountain, valley, desert and steppe that formed China's Xinjiang Uyghur Autonomous Region before it had even been called that. There were those who had been displaced by soldiers of the

Russian Empire and those who fled in the early 1900s to escape attempted conscription. There were more who followed when the Soviets tried to force them from Islam and their nomadic pastoral existence to live in atheist efficiency on the collective farms. And there were more still who came after because these successive calamities and exoduses along with pitiless livestock and grain requisitions finally festered into years of famine.

None of that was in the Party-mandated school curriculum on the glorious revolutionary history that birthed the People's Republic of China. Saira did well anyway when tests came around, as she did in everything except mathematics, which she hated, and physical education, which she hated most of all. There was an hour of PE in the yard every afternoon. The children would form up into lines for games, running or clumsily synchronized calisthenics intended to prime their bodies to strive for the good of the nation. It was always boring and always hard so Saira would do her best to hide herself in some overlooked corner and carry on reading.

She would be told off if a teacher discovered her and if the scolding was particularly severe, she would cry. Once she ran to her grandmother, who lived across the street from her in a house made the old way of interlinked logs pressed in with mud, and explained the injustice she had suffered with tears still wet on her face. "They made me do exercises," she said. "They shouted at me and all I want to do is read."

Her grandmother always smarted at the slightest affront directed at Saira and hurried off to the school. Their village was small and Saira's grandmother had known all the teachers when they were themselves young girls. She cursed at them with no regard for their new positions and told them what was to be done. The other children would exercise and Saira would be left alone in the classroom with her books. The teachers wished to avoid further berating and they agreed.

Saira's parents worked long hours. Her father sold meat for the government and meat, like sugar, milk powder, eggs, cooking oil, cloth, bikes and sewing machines, could only be had via ration coupons and long waits. Her mother tended to the sick and elderly and was often out late. So Saira's grandmother helped raise her and taught her much about life and family and the bad times that had gone before.

Saira did not remember the bad times. She had been born in June 1976 just as they were coming to an end and grew up instead in a golden era, as her grandmother, her parents and most of the other adults around continually reminded her. Golden because Kazakhs in Xinjiang could make a bit of money from tending their crops and rearing their animals and could do it as they thought best without worrying about Red Guards or Party cadres taking their produce away. "You're luckier than you know," they would tell Saira. "You must appreciate the good days and the policies that have made things this way because the new leader gave them to us and one day he could take them away."

It was difficult to imagine how things had been. A few years earlier Chairman Mao Zedong had been everything, her grandmother told her. He was the Great Leader, the Great Commander, the Great Helmsman and the Great Teacher. It was his words, thoughts and orders that formed the fabric of their lives and his likeness that watched over them ceaseless, all-powerful, red, bright and shining.

On posters and billboards he strode thickset and tall at the head of crowds of workers and peasants, their rapt, happy faces bathed in his luminescence. He surveyed fields and factories, battleships and blast furnaces. He addressed mass gatherings of immense size. His disembodied head radiated sunbeams over flags and upraised arms clutching scarlet-bound copies of his quotations.

On the wall of nearly every home hung his smooth-skinned and benevolent portrait. And if it did not then anyone living there might be denounced as counter-revolutionaries. Back then it was as if Mao had mesmerized the whole country, Saira's grandmother told her. They really believed that only he could lead them and provide for them. That without his word they would not even have bread. If a woman in the village gave birth, she said, it was traditional to celebrate by slaughtering a sheep. Because the government owned everything, that was not a decision that could be made alone and it was first necessary to go to the enormous billboard of Mao that supervised the village and talk to him. So the father of every new baby would walk over there to explain and ask permission to kill one of the herd. Then they would take a sheep to the man who butchered the animals and let him know that it was ok because he had talked to Mao.

That was when there were sheep. Before that had been the hunger, her grandmother said. Real, cruel hunger like she hoped Saira would never feel. Some days there was nothing, no food at all, and people would not say hello when they saw each other in the street but ask if the other had eaten yet. That was the time too of the war on sparrows, she said. The sparrows that stood accused of eating the grain from the fields and the fruit from the trees. Orders came directly from Mao that the birds must be eradicated. Not only in their village or its Altay region or Xinjiang but in all of China. So that was what the people started doing. Destroying the nests, killing the chicks, shooting the adults on the wing and at roost. They did it in the village too, even though the arrival of a sparrow in a house was well-known to portend fortune and happiness and killing them meant there would be none of either. It was soon proven true because without the sparrows to prey on them, great swarms of locusts gathered and stripped what was left from fields and branches. Of course, Saira's grandmother said, there had been no question of blaming Mao or even asking whether it had been the right thing to do. That would have revealed signs of ideological impurity that would not go unpunished.

On September 9, 1976, a little more than two months, after Saira was born, her grandmother kneaded, filled, folded, pinched and steamed a few meals' worth of *manti* dumplings and took some extra to a neighbor's place. She found them gathered around their low round dining table crying in unrelenting despair. Crying because the radio had announced with deepest grief that Comrade Mao Zedong, the esteemed and beloved Great Leader of their party, their army and the people of all nationalities of their country, the Great Teacher of the international proletariat and the oppressed nations and oppressed people, Chairman of the Central Committee and the Military Commission and the Honorary Chairman of the National Committee, had passed away at ten minutes past midnight that morning. Saira's grandmother sat with her neighbors, and she cried too. She could not imagine what they were to do and how they would be able to look after themselves. She joined the whole village in their ordered week of national mourning and 1,500 miles away in Beijing, a million people wreathed the Great Hall of the People, filing past a glass case containing Mao's body on a white-shrouded bier, his eyes closed, his remaining hair combed neatly back and the five-star red flag pulled up to his chest.

The announcement had also ordered that the unity of the Party should be maintained and Chairman Mao's revolutionary line and policies continue to be carried out resolutely. So Party leaders in the village ordered that learning and recitations of his teachings carry on. They redoubled it, eternalizing his spirit through mass repetition. Saira's grandmother went to the village meeting with everyone else and they stood with their right arms raised in the air and their fists clenched and they repeated Mao's words. The village leaders kept them at it until Saira's grandmother's arm grew sore and so tired that she no longer had the strength to hold it aloft and had to support it with her left. Some of the people around her who saw her standing there with one arm holding the other thought that must be the way things were supposed to be. They did the same until one of the village leaders saw them, shouted at them and docked Saira's grandmother three days of wages.

Further back, times had also been bad and were more confusing still to Saira when she heard about them. Her father's family were pastoralists who had tended animals in the steppe for generations. Her father's father had settled around what became her village in Altay and his brother settled in another further west. One day her grandfather visited his brother and his brother talked of the smooth green hills around them. "Go," he said, "fetch your horses, the grazing is so much better here." Her grandfather looked around him and agreed then went home to pass the night. He set off again in the morning with his animals and came upon soldiers of the People's Liberation Army along the way. The soldiers stopped him and demanded to know where he thought he was going and why he was trying to leave China. He tried to explain himself but they turned him around and told him there was a border there now and none could cross it.

What had been to the brothers open land was now impermeably split between China and the Kazakh Soviet Socialist Republic. They had that morning become unknowing citizens of different states. States that allowed international travel to nearly no one. Saira had almost no recollection of her grandfather because he died when she was three years old but her family said that when he did, it was with a heart full of sadness and yearning to see his brother. Saira's grandmother would always wonder aloud at the life her brother-in-law had passed. He had surely married but how many children had he had? Was it possible that he was alive even then?

The Party had designated Saira's other grandfather a class enemy so those days had been bad for him too. His family's fields had once been worked by a thousand peasant households. The Land Reform Law seized it all and cadres set to ridding the exploiting classes of counterrevolutionary thinking through struggle sessions, beatings, jail, labor camps and sometimes death. Authorities made the family move into a house shared with three others and confiscated all their money and jewelry apart from some earrings, bracelets and a Quran that Saira's grandfather bagged up and buried under a pile of rocks. He was at least spared detention or execution but not the ritual humiliation that was his due. Cadres and villagers scrawled his crimes across him, put a tall paper hat on his head and a string of potatoes around his neck and led him tied behind a donkey through the streets of the village as jeering children pelted him with stones.

By the time Saira was eleven there were around a thousand families in the village. Most were Kazakhs but a few were Uyghurs and Saira did not notice much difference because Uyghurs were Turkic like them and Muslim like them. People lived mostly as Saira's grandparents had. Tending to their animals and planting and harvesting the wheat fields. She loved it there. Around them was countryside of the most beautiful kind with valleys and hillsides deep in long grass where come spring, the globeflowers emerged gold from their beds of sawtoothed emerald alongside delicate lilacs and the yellow hearts of daisies. Occasional rivers split it all, rushing from the higher ground then sedately feeding lakes that shone iridescent turquoise when the sun caught them. Southwest were the mountains. Always visible, always ice-topped no matter the season.

The houses were built close together and everyone knew each other. So when someone cooked up something delicious like her grandmother's manti, they took some next door or down the road. If a neighbor lent another money, they did not think about signing a formal contract as might be done in a bigger town or city. There was never any need. They kept to traditions because the reforms known as the Four Modernizations that the new leader, Deng Xiaoping, had set in motion not only abolished the collective farms and allocated land back to the people but also allowed minorities to dress once again in clothing that reflected their heritage and follow cultural and religious practices that had long been restricted.

Not that Saira's relatives were particularly religious. Her parents did not pray five times a day or often at all but she still grew up sure of the existence of one God and creator in a house where there was never pork and rarely alcohol. Some of the other families in the village were less strict and drinking was common enough but usually when someone died they were still given an Islamic burial and the year's big celebration was not the Lunar New Year like the Han Chinese but Eid al-Adha.

Saira always knew that before anything else she was Kazakh. Her grandmother made sure of it. They would sit in that old house with its one large room and curtained-off sleeping areas and her grandmother would tell her of their distant ancestors in the Merkit, a tribe of warriors so fearsome that they battled Genghis Khan. And their more recent ancestors, her grandmother said, were from the six tribes that made up the Middle jüz grouping and had been among the hundreds of Kazakh families who resettled in Altay.

Her grandmother told her many other things. Often things that she said would be useful to Saira once she was older. Like how to tell if someone could be trusted. "If they don't look you in the eye," she would say, "if they keep looking every way but at you, it's because they are a liar. If they sit all hunched forward with their head tilted down, stay away from them too. And watch out for women with thin, curled lips. They're always gossips. When it's time for you to look for a husband, notice a man's shoes. They give him away. And notice his sleeves. If they're too long, don't choose him. If his trousers are not ironed, he's lazy. You can tell a lot from a man's hands as well, particularly the size of his fingers compared to his palms. If they're equal, he is practical, sensible. Skewed one way, and he's good-spirited. Skewed the other, and he's mean. As for short men, they are usually good in business."

When the Han Chinese started coming to the village, Saira's grandmother told her to be wary. They came because another of Deng's new policies was that Xinjiang should be developed. That meant opportunities to make money from the endless tracts of fertile earth there and the coal, gas, oil and rare metals under it. So there were more olive-clad soldiers with peaked caps and red on their collars and there were workers from the inland provinces building houses in the area and working on new government projects. Some of them brought children and the children appeared at school. Saira and her classmates knew nearly no Chinese then but they all talked and played together, shouting at each other in cheery incomprehension. The Chinese children were fascinatingly different, especially the girls. Saira and her friends were proud of their long hair and usually wore flowing skirts and dresses. The new girls had bobs and their legs emerged from hemlines far shorter. "Don't look at these girls, don't try to be like them," her grandmother would warn her. "They came because the inland parts of the country are so populated that it's no longer enough for them. You are from different nations, different cultures. You are not Chinese, you're Kazakh, you're Merkit."

The two adult populations left each other mostly alone as far as Saira could tell and coexisted in habitual segregation. Points of strain and of resentment did surface as the Chinese began to build on and exploit what Kazakhs thought of as their land without regard for the way things had been. New restrictions were introduced specifying where cattle could roam or setting winter grazing grounds aside for some official purpose. She was vaguely aware that further away in the Kazakh regions there had been conflict between local farmers and the Xinjiang Production and Construction Corps. The *bingtuan*, people called it, a paramilitary development organization that settled Han in Xinjiang whole communities at a time to work its colossal farms, mines and construction projects. There were still never major disputes in the village and after the bad times, the cost of progress seemed bearable.

The newcomers lived the way they had at home and that changed the way the Kazakhs were with each other. Formal contracts stating the terms of repayment started to be drawn up when money was borrowed and there were so many new houses that the village became a town and neighbors did not always know each other well anymore. Saira's Chinese got better and she started to understand the things that the Han children said about them and that some of the adults said too. That Kazakhs were wild and uncivilized and did not know how to live in the new China.

Perestroika brought cross-border trade and there was more still when Kazakhstan gained its independence from the Soviet Union in 1991. Saira was fifteen and there were still no passports for people like them but salesmen from Kazakhstan started coming to the village hawking all kinds of goods. Saira's grandmother was losing her hearing by then and she would yell at any she saw. "Please, do you know a certain man living just across the border?" she would ask, naming her brother-in-law and describing what she remembered of him. "Is he there? Is he alive?" But the traders had been raised as Russian speakers and thought little of these villagers who had lived in another country entirely and spoke Kazakh with an accent. They replied briefly, negatively and in Russian or they did not reply at all.

Saira continued to read and devoured all she could find. There was joyous verse from Mukaghali Makatayev. There was the novelist and playwright Mukhtar Auezov. And there was the great Abai Qunanbaiuly, who more than seventy years earlier had been among the first Kazakhs to abandon the oral traditions relied on by generations of their nomadic ancestors and entrust his poems to ink and paper. Not all of it was old. Saira came back often to *Qylmys* (*Crime*) by Qazhyghumar Shabdanuly and that had only been published in 1982. He too was an ethnic Kazakh living in China and he wrote on the oppression of Kazakhs there and with arresting lucidity on the life of a political prisoner, as he himself had been for twenty-two years in a Tarim Basin detention camp.

She came to know about the laws prohibiting ownership of books not authorized by the government and sold in licensed bookstores. That books on Kazakh and Uyghur culture and history could be considered evidence of banned political activities or of separatist thought. It even happened to Shabdanuly again. He had intended *Qylmys* to consist of four volumes. The second was published in 1985, but he was arrested before the third and fourth could be and given a thirteen-year jail sentence in Urumqi, Xinjiang's regional capital. That was why Saira's parents had always been so careful. It was not enough to keep her from reading. She just made sure to hide the books that needed to be hidden as far as she could from the eyes of the state and the dutiful citizens who might report them.

2

National separatism and illegal religious activity are the chief threats to the stability of Xinjiang. The main problem is that international counter-revolutionary forces led by the United States of America are openly supporting the separatist activities inside and outside of Xinjiang. The outside national separatist organizations are joining hands and strengthening the infiltration of Xinjiang sabotage activities with each passing day . . .

Take real measures to train a large number of Han cadres who love Xinjiang and who will stick to the basic theory, principles and guiding policy of the Party to correctly implement the ethnic and religion policies of the Party and then relocate them to Xinjiang . . .

Take strong measures to prevent and fight against the infiltration and sabotaging activities of foreign religious powers. Restrict all illegal religious activities. Severely control the building of new mosques. Mosques built without permission from the government have to be handled according to registration methods of practicing sites of religion. Relocate or replace quickly people who are hesitant or support ethnic separatism. Give leadership positions in mosques and religious organizations to dependable, talented people who love the motherland. Stop illegal organizations such as underground religious schools, kung-fu schools and Koran studies meetings . . .

Tightly control the media market. Books, journals, audio and video tapes which twist the history and inspire ethnic separatism and illegal religious ideas should be prohibited and confiscated without exception; the involved personnel have to be investigated.

—Document No. 7: record of the Standing Committee
of the Communist Party of China Politburo special
session convened March 1996 to discuss the
"Xinjiang question" Classification: Top Secret
via Human Rights Watch

Adiljan stood among the naked boughs of the apricot and cherry trees and his breath hung in the bright air. He could hear the gunfire. The shouts too, the sirens and the engines. He ached to know what was happening but the high concrete wall of the yard blocked any glimpse outside and his mother had forbidden him from leaving the house at the first sign that anything was wrong. Fourteen then, he would not defy her. Soon the television and radio and the loudspeaker-mounted police trucks forbade it too and declared an emergency curfew for unspecified security reasons. There was nothing but to wait while the stories flitted between the houses and yards, finding their way through the neighborhood where people could not.

When they reached Adiljan they said that early that morning hundreds of Uyghurs, mostly young and mostly men, had gathered in different parts of the city to demand that they be allowed to celebrate their identities just as the Han majority were. They equipped themselves with homemade banners and communal chants and Adiljan heard that some stripped to the waist despite the cold to show that they had no weapons. Ranks of armed police charged to meet the slogans and exposed skin. They lashed out with batons, loosed snarling, dark-snouted dogs and brought up water cannons to spray icy arcs into the crowds.

The gatherings persisted and some among the crowds turned to attacking shops and burning cars so the police levelled their guns and bodies fell. The protests were snuffed and snuffed once more but flared in squares and alleys and suburbs. Police reinforcements arrived. Anti-riot squads, troops clambering out of olive trucks with squat submachine guns in their arms. They dealt still harsher violence. Some were said to have executed detainees right there in the streets.

Knowing exactly what was happening was by then nearly impossible because, as well as the curfew, the airport and station were closed. The entire city cut off.

Hundreds were arrested, perhaps more. Children too and those who had not taken part in the protests at all but had just been watching or passing by. The city's jails were soon full and the overflow taken to neighboring provinces. People who had seen it said the police had marched detainees into the snow-covered grounds of a sports stadium and hosed them down. Then they made some of their soaked and shivering charges take off their shoes and socks and run barefoot for cruel amusement. After two hours the ones with frostbite were taken to hospital and the rest to prison. The worst frostbite cases turned gangrenous and doctors amputated toes, fingers, feet and hands.

When the trains and intercity buses were moving again, the number of dead depended on who you asked. Uyghurs thought it was at least two hundred and possibly as many as a thousand but they could not check the hospitals and morgues to find out exactly. It had been, they said, a massacre. The government and its compliant media spoke only of an incident and put the dead at precisely ten.

This was just one more piece of Adiljan's world that went by a different name depending on who was talking about it. There was the city with its wan blocks punctuated by chimneys and radio masts, its streets crowded with neon and billboards and the strung-out northern suburbs where he lived with his mother and brothers. Chinese authorities called it Yining but to him and to other Uyghurs it was always Ghulja. Then there was Xinjiang itself, where Uyghurs had lived for so many centuries. Some Uyghurs used a name for it that was forbidden in books or newspapers. The name of the Islamic republics that had briefly existed before the foundation of the People's Republic of China. They called it East Turkestan and they remembered its flag of sky blue with a white star and crescent.

Adiljan knew all about that. He knew how Xinjiang had been incorporated into the PRC in 1949. Illegally some Uyghurs believed. And he knew about how the *bingtuan* and broader state-sponsored migration of Han Chinese had grown the Han population there from 6 percent to more than 40 percent by the late 1970s. Before Adiljan's father divorced his mother and moved to Aksu province, he had made sure that Adiljan knew too about the Cultural Revolution and how the terror wrought by Red Guards to wipe out Old Ideas, Old Culture, Old Customs and Old Habits had involved shuttering mosques, abusing imams and burning piles of Qurans and religious books in the streets. During the famine, he said, Adiljan's grandfather had starved to death on a collective farm.

Things had been better for a while, then worse, and then better again. The years before the protests had been the time of the *meshrep* gatherings in Ghulja, when Uyghurs came together in mutual celebration and expression of their culture and identity. They would often begin sitting cross-legged on carpets laid out in courtyards or back rooms to eat and talk and recite stories and poetry. Usually the musicians among them would pick up tämbürs and dutars and begin to pluck out muqam melodies and after a while dancers would step forward to whirl ever-faster into the gathering night. There were more conservative meshrep organizers who incorporated readings from the Quran or the public chastening of those who had erred by drinking or smoking or neglecting prayer. And there were others who did not. The Party had allowed and even encouraged meshreps at first because that was easier than dealing with the ills that troubled the city's marginalized Uyghur communities like drinking, drug abuse, gambling and the discrimination that made finding work so difficult.

In 1996 the "strike hard" anti-crime campaign had begun. Vast, indiscriminate and all over China. In Xinjiang and in Tibet it was accompanied by a further crackdown on anything that authorities considered to be encouraging ethnic split-ism and separatist thought. That ended the Party's indulgence for meshreps and expressions of identity that did not align precisely with its own. The groups were abruptly banned from meeting and their organizers arrested. One meshrep leader was beaten so severely in custody that he died and police still refused to release the body to his family.

Then meshrep attendees were taken as well and so were religious students. 1997 began and a stifling unease settled over Ghulja's Uyghur districts. January 10 was the first day of Ramadan so practicing Muslims wanted to focus on fasting and prayer and time with their families. The raids continued and the timing made them smart all the more. The last untenable insult came when police descended on a group of women who had gathered to pray at one of their homes and arrested them. That had triggered the protests.

The killing did not end there. On February 25, there was a series of bombings in Urumqi. Three devices packed with ball bearings, screws and nails exploded on buses, leaving nine bodies among the blood and panic and shattered glass. Another bomb of the same composition failed to detonate at the city's main railway station. Uyghur groups outside China claimed responsibility.

The crackdown that followed was worse and enforced by more

truckloads of soldiers. Arrests again and denunciations by Party loy-
alists of Uyghur neighbors and petty enemies. Then came the trials.
The biggest were held publicly and involved several prisoners at once.
Convictions were assured thanks to the lengthy and improbable confessions the police had extracted in advance and the punishment often
death or at least a sentence spanning decades.

The only way to help a relative among the detained was to gather
a bribe. One so large that it took everything most families had and
more on loan. That worked sometimes so a son, brother, husband or
father was quietly freed after one-sided negotiations. The same money
might also be exchanged for the same promises only for a loved one to
be sentenced like the others.

East Turkestan, the Cultural Revolution. That was one thing for
Adiljan. A past nearly impossible to picture when there was always
food in the shops and reforms underway. Coming of age during the
massacre and its aftermath made the difference in treatment between
Uyghurs and Han clearer than it had ever been to him. It hardened
his Uyghur identity around him and marked the beginning of the time
that he thought of as his awakening.

He saw anew everything that the Party had tried to take away
from them. The Uyghur history erased from their curriculums. The
land given to the new migrants. The systematic theft of their right to
shape their own futures. He made furtive purchases of secondhand
books from marketplaces in the center of town, the kind of books
that were not permitted. He read and learned and read until he had
amassed a small collection on the shelves of his bedroom. Many of
those books touched on Islam and the role faith played in the lives of
the Turkic peoples that stretched from Xinjiang to Eastern Europe.

Adiljan was brought up in what he considered to be a normal Uyghur family. Culturally Muslim but not in a way that anyone in it spent much time thinking about. His reading made him surer that religion itself was the central part of the identity that authorities were trying to eradicate. High school finished and he used some of his newly free time to start going to the local mosque. That was permitted but the Party controlled attendance and sermons carefully.

It was only Friday prayers at first. He would walk to the mosque and perform his ablutions at the courtyard fountain. Washing his right hand then his left. Rinsing his mouth and his nose. Washing his face, his forearms, his head, his ears and his feet. He knelt shyly with the other men inside. He moved as they moved and spoke when they spoke and he grew accustomed to it. He went more often and fell in with a circle of boys around his own age and men a little older. They would meet to read and study the Quran together and to learn and recite the hadith. In their company Adiljan grew convinced of the correctness of a strict interpretation of Islam.

He stopped shaving his cheeks, chin and neck as the Prophet instructed. It was not much of a beard, just a few soft hairs, but to him it represented his awakening. His friends did the same and they stood out for it with the kind of open nonconformity that authorities disliked. One look at them and people knew exactly what names they would use for people and places and events.

That was why the police first came for him. It was not long before his eighteenth birthday and the day was slipping past without money or distraction. He left the house after lunch and soon ran into four friends he knew from mosque. They walked together to nowhere in particular until one of the large police vans with the sliding side doors passed them and unhurriedly pulled over ahead. Dark-uniformed officers walked towards them and they were unhurried too. There had been a surge of arrests over the past few months but usually the police would raid houses in the middle of the night so that neighbors would not know what was happening and all the confused family could do was uselessly beg. "Get in please," the police told them, "we have things to ask you." There were no handcuffs or shouting or official warnings of arrest but Adiljan and the others did as they were told and sat quietly in the back of the van until the door slid open again at the local police headquarters. The officers who hustled them inside were a mix of Han and Uyghur but the Han were in charge. They ordered Adiljan and his friends down to a holding area then took their wallets and anything else from their pockets and lined them up to start barking questions. What were they doing there in the street? Where had they been going? How did they know each other? The others told the police that they did not know each other well and had only said *salam* to each other and walked together a while. Adiljan told them that too. "We were friendly with each other," he said, "because we all had beards."

The policeman questioning them got angry when he heard that. He slapped and kicked the first of them and carried on down the row one at a time and they could do nothing but sink their chins to their chests and wait for it to pass. Then it was down to a holding cell lined with thin metal bunk beds. They sat down there and made and broke eye contact but said little. A while later the officers began calling them one at a time by name and shoved and swore at whoever it was even if they came willingly so the others all saw. Each was taken for a couple of hours at least then came back quiet and cowed but nodding in reply to the others' whispered inquiries.

Adiljan was shoved insulted down the corridor too. His group at the mosque had discussed the possibility of something like this happening to them and agreed that if it did, it would be a test of their faith and of their will. He badly wanted not to be scared but his heart beat hard. They stopped in front of a heavy door and one of the officers swung it open. There was a chair inside under a bright overhead light and it was a peculiar kind of chair. Its frame and seat were metal and there was a hinged apparatus at the front that could be swung in on the person sitting there like a lunch tray. Except that the tray could be locked into place, had adjustable metal fastenings on top and extended down to a horizontal metal bar at the bottom. There was a footrest too and two more metal fastenings on the front legs. It was the first time he had seen one but Adiljan knew it immediately. People called them tiger chairs and there was at least one in most police stations.

The officers pushed him down under the light and into the seat and closed and fastened the hinged section so the bar on the bottom pushed into his thighs. They pulled his hands through the fastenings on the tray top then tightened the metal around his wrists. They tightened the lower fastenings around his ankles and he was trapped. If he hunched forward the little he could it eased some of the strain from his wrists but that was all. Panic rose in him and he breathed deep until it subsided.

One of the Han officers began the interrogation. He asked about Adiljan's family, about people he knew and about a man he did not. He asked if he attended religious gatherings and whether he preached when he did. He wanted to know too what books he read and owned. Adiljan had imagined his faith would give him the strength to defy them but he told them what he thought they wanted. He did not preach, he said. That was true. He did not go to many gatherings, just to the mosque. That was mostly true. He read only normal books from book stores. There he lied. The officer asked again about his beard. It was like a woman's pubic hair, he said. Why would he want to look like that?

He sat hunched under the spotlight, and the metal pressed on his bones. Blood pooled in the backs of his thighs, his buttocks grew dull and it was nearly impossible to move to relieve it. He endured but it started slowly, that's what people who had experienced the tiger chair said. And sometimes they kept you in there for days so the way it constrained your movement became agonizing.

Another officer stepped forward and asked the same questions. Adiljan's family, his relationships, the man he did not know, his religious habits, his books. He tried to answer as before, but it was not exact enough and there were more questions about the inconsistencies they found. One of them slapped him across the head every time he gave an answer they did not like.

A third officer began the same questions again until at last there were no more and they unfastened his wrists and his ankles then swung back the hinged section of the chair so the blood came coursing back through him. In the cell he nodded to the ones who had sat in the chair and the ones still to experience it.

He slept on a bare bunk mattress among the snores and mumblings of the others. In the morning officers called only him and cuffed him then took him out to the van from the day before or another like it. They drove a short way and stopped at what he realized was his home. He craned around as the police went through the metal gate and disappeared behind the high concrete wall. He could see nothing of what happened inside and wondered if his brothers had been home and had dared to say anything. If his mother had screamed or protested the intrusion and whether the officers had insulted or mistreated her. They came back after a short while and in their arms they carried his books. It took them two trips, and he felt sick knowing that when they looked through them they would see that these were not at all the normal kind.

The police put him back in the cell with the others and stacked the books out of sight. "Look," he heard one of the officers say about the pile. "This asshole has been lying to us and he'll soon regret it."

The next interrogation was worse. They locked him in the chair again but this time the questions were about the books and that made it much harder to give the right answers. There was one book in particular that had them worried. It discussed the collective Islamic community around the world and the need for unity within it.

One of the policemen held it up and asked what the main idea of the book was. Adiljan told him that it was to treat each other well and live together as if they were part of one large family.

"What are you planning when you come together with all the Muslims?" the guard asked, and he was shouting. "Why do you want to unite them?" Adiljan and his friends, he said, were poisoning the minds of others with thoughts of Islam. Adiljan had nothing to say to that that they liked either and they slapped and kicked him and hit him with batons and he just bent further down in the chair and tried not to cry out.

One of the senior officers told Adiljan that this was his last chance to escape his incorrect choices and his problematic thoughts. "You are young," the man said and bent closer, "but you should know that there are two kinds of viruses that no one can cure. One is AIDS, and the other is being a religious student."

Some of the Uyghur officers came and spoke to him the following day. They were kinder and seemed to understand him. They said that they felt sorry for him and his friends because they'd had problems of their own with the government before joining the police but that they had looked at some of his books and found in them harmful content.

The police took them all to a detention center that afternoon. That was not good news. Usually nobody was held in a police station for more than fifteen days. A center could mean a month or more and perhaps a trial. The place was underground too and each of them was held in a separate cell. Three blank walls and one of just bars. No more than four or five square meters in all. Adiljan was no longer beaten or interrogated but sitting on his iron cot, he heard blows and slaps from other rooms and the occasional cries of men who could not withstand their pain.

Two weeks passed and the guards told him and the others that they were going to be released. A rush of relief. They must not have found anything serious enough to send them to prison. The guards gathered them together in one room and said that they would each be fined 1,000 yuan and that before they would be allowed to go they would have to shave off their beards. They pointed towards the corner where there was a sink and an electric beard trimmer. Adiljan looked at the others and hurt tainted his relief. The oldest, toughest and most devout of his friends set their jaws and began to protest.

"So you won't do it?" the guards asked.

"No," one of Adiljan's friends said. The guards must have been expecting it because several of them grabbed him, dragged him to the ground and pinned him on his back. One of them to each limb. Then another guard produced a set of dark metal claw pincers. The kind used to pull nails from wood. He bent down and gripped a clump of beard in the pincers and ripped it out and he did not stop until the cheeks and chin and neck of Adiljan's friend were bare and spotted with blood.

Adiljan shaved in the sink and left a small pile of scraggly hairs on the porcelain. "Shave like everyone else, don't read books like these and we won't see you back here," one of the Uyghur guards said to him. And he was free to go home to his mother and his brothers and his room with its empty bookshelf.

He soon heard of many other youths who had been arrested too and that the ones who had been defiant during questioning or who had admitted things he had not were given jail sentences. The thought of it scared him but he was not ready to yield to the Party. His friends emboldened him and he let his beard grow back, resumed his religious studies and waited for his turn to come again.

3

Amnesty International is gravely concerned about the growing number of executions and the use of the death penalty as a tool of political repression in the XUAR [Xinjiang Autonomous Region]. It is also concerned that many of those executed are reported to have been sentenced to death after summary proceedings, in violation of international fair trial standards.

The XUAR is the only region of the People's Republic of China where political prisoners have been executed in large numbers in recent years. The unrest in the region and the continued use of the "Strike Hard" anti-crime campaign to target "separatism" have resulted in a growing number of executions of Uighurs. As elsewhere in the PRC, the death penalty is also applicable for a very wide range of offences, including many nonviolent offences such as theft, economic and drug-related crime.

Since January 1997, Amnesty International has recorded at least 210 death sentences in the region, of which 190 were executed shortly after sentencing— the real figures are believed to be higher. Almost two thirds of the cases recorded were publicly reported by Chinese official sources. The vast majority of those sentenced to death and executed were Uighurs.

These figures indicate that the ratio of death sentences to the population is several times higher in the XUAR than elsewhere in China. The execution rate vis a vis the number of death sentences appears also to be higher.

**—Gross Violations of Human Rights in the Xinjiang Uighur
Autonomous Region, Amnesty International, March 31, 1999**

T ursunay's father always joked that she should have been named after the hillock that rose dull and rocky along the road north from their village. The day she was born, August 10, 1978, her mother's labor pains began and heavy clouds closed in from the mountains. A warm summer rain fell on the pastures and the trees and the fields, swelling the river and pelting the roof of their house. There was no doctor, nurse or midwife in the village and the nearest clinic was in a bigger settlement a few miles away. So Tursunay's father harnessed their bony horse to the carriage he used to carry supplies to the fields and crops into town. He helped her mother out onto the carriage then he seated himself in front and drove the horse as hard as he dared along the softening mud road.

The rain fell heavier, the carriage slowed and Tursunay's mother's contractions grew closer together. They had made it only as far as the hillock when her mother, who had already borne three sons and one daughter and so knew what she was doing, said the baby was coming. Tursunay's father reined in the horse by the roadside, unhooked the traces and helped her mother down then heaved the cart over and upside down for a shelter. There was a woman named Sabira that the family knew who lived just near there and Tursunay's father ran a little way towards Sabira's house calling for her to come and help. Sabira was not home or did not hear so he doubled back and it was him that delivered Tursunay into that patch of dry under the planks of the upturned cart with the sky emptying itself all around them.

It sounded like a fairytale to Tursunay and so seemed a fitting start for a life lived in what she believed a fragment of heaven. Their village was named Keziletale and was in a rural stretch of a Xinjiang county about ninety miles from the Kazakh border that Chinese speakers called Xinyuan but Tursunay and other Uyghurs knew as Künes. On the village's eastern side was a long, jagged range of mountains that fed a stream tumbling down not far from Tursunay's house.

The ground to the west sloped into trees, farmland and then the Tekes River slipping north towards the Ili delta.

Their house stood apart from the others on top of a rise. Its white-washed walls sturdy amid the green slopes with clean white curtains hanging from the windows. Inside was space enough for all the children, including the girl and boy that followed Tursunay in more conventional births. There were bedrooms, a kitchen, the raised earthen *supa* with its cushions and pillows where they ate and rested and a separate dining room for when they had guests. There was electricity but for drinking water the children were sent down the path to the stream, taking turns to carry a yoke slung across their backs with a bucket hanging on each side of it.

The yard was always neat. In front was her mother's beloved flower garden, so assiduously planted, watered, weeded and propagated. There were lilies and cyclamen like colorful butterflies and peonies blooming brief and wonderful with their fragrant pink flowers. Figs sprouted straight from terra-cotta pots and vines climbed the trellises around the area where they lounged on wooden daybeds come summer. The children helped with the garden. Simple things at first and when they got older, they laid down stones on paths and split bricks to upend the halves in repeating triangles bordering the flower beds.

Her parents grew vegetables too. Tomatoes, onions, cucumbers. All of it fresh and delicious and ready to eat after just a rinse. Even when they had nothing else, her mother could always make a salad to serve guests along with their mugs of salty milk tea.

Their fields were a little way below. Around ten acres of mostly wheat and sunflowers kept from parching through the warmer months because her father had brought specialists in from the desert Turpan

Depression, where the *karez* well system kept agricultural areas fertile, to dig and divert and channel the water. The cows slept in the open near the house and the calves snorted and grunted their way through the night from a pen. Once Tursunay had started at the elementary school down in the village, her mother would hurry her out of bed early each morning and tell her to take the herd to pasture before she left. The cows knew their way. All Tursunay needed to do was shoo them three hundred feet or so and they would lope uphill and start cropping the grass while she set off in the other direction. The plaintive bleating of the hungry calves always brought them back in time for milking.

The chickens also lived wild and roosted wherever they wanted, ignoring the nesting boxes Tursunay's mother made. When it came time to gather the eggs, Tursunay and her sisters and brothers would fan out to pick through the long grass and peer under bushes, gathering them in their arms a couple at a time or in a clutch of twenty from some new hiding place. If there were too many for them alone then they shared with friends in the village and relatives in Ghulja more than two hours' drive to the northwest.

Those Ghulja visits always required planning. Only one bus left Keziletale each day and it ran from the township of Qarabora half an hour from the village. Anyone who had business in town had to be waiting by the roadside early to catch it and could only return when the bus retraced its route later in the evening. So Tursunay's early years passed mostly in Keziletale delineated by the passing seasons. Spring was when her father harvested last year's wheat then harnessed the plow to the horse and carved dark furrows for the seed of the crop to come. Summer and the wheat and sunflowers swayed yellow and gold and it was too hot to do nearly anything but lie on the carpets and cushions around the daybeds. Then it was again harvest time and her father and brothers would pile the cart with sacks of wheat and sunflower seed and make the slow journey to Qarabora to have it processed into flour and oil.

Come autumn the berries ripened out on the mountain slopes and Tursunay's mother would send her and the children out to gather them with the same buckets and yoke they used to collect water. The berries were sweet and delicious and the children would eat as they gathered, filling the pails and their stomachs, staining their faces and their fingers a stubborn purple. Those they brought back her mother would stew into great steaming pots of jam that lasted all winter. Snow would already be creeping down from the mountains then and soon lay everywhere. In the house they pressed close to the metal kitchen stove and kept it fed with logs. Everything was more beautiful still then and when Tursunay and her brothers and sisters were sent to fill the pails, her mother would make sure they did not take a sled with them because she knew that they would only play and ignore their chores. On the way to the stream, they would usually see the other children sledding. They would leave the yoke by the side of the path then take off their jackets and sit on them to slide down the frozen slopes, screaming and shouting and climbing breathlessly back up, not caring at all whether their jackets ripped or lost a button. They would return home shivering and red-cheeked as night fell, with the pails still empty and Tursunay's mother would scold them. "My God," she would say, "you've forgotten the water again."

Theirs was one of only a few Uyghur households in the village. Most of the others were ethnic Kazakhs. Tursunay's father was

Uyghur, but he had been born in Kazakhstan and moved to Xinjiang only when he was four years old. He talked often of the family left behind. There was a brother and a sister who he had not seen since the day he left. He talked often of his plan to visit them one day when things were quieter and it became possible to secure a passport. The family always spoke Uyghur at home, but the elementary school taught in Kazakh and it was the only one for miles. Both languages were Turkic and as a young girl Tursunay slipped unconsciously between them as she talked and only disentangled themselves if someone stopped or corrected her. She once tried to arrange a meeting with a Uyghur cousin by asking her to meet at the *kópir* (bridge), and the cousin said, "That's a *köwrük*," and went home and told Tursunay's aunt and the other children that Tursunay was a Kazakh who spoke a language the rest of them didn't understand.

Tursunay had not liked that. She knew that they had much in common with the Kazakhs but they were still different and Uyghur culture felt unique and special. You could tell a Uyghur home from the outside just by the way they decorated the place, she thought, the white curtains and the beautiful gardens. The yards of the Kazakh houses in her village seemed untidy by comparison and unadorned.

The differences between them and the Kazakhs were nothing compared to the differences she noticed in another settlement nearby where mostly Han families lived. It seemed so alien in look, in atmosphere and even in smell. The walls of the houses were often just bare brick or earth and the yards looked neglected. Her parents warned her to stay away from the place and wild stories circulated among the Uyghur children about their Chinese neighbors. The one that scared Tursunay most was that a little girl once disappeared from Keziletale and search parties eventually found her at a crazy old man's place as he boiled a huge pot of water in preparation for cooking her.

Time began to intrude on Tursunay's heaven. Her older siblings married and moved away and though they sometimes visited on the new motorcycles they had bought, the house was not as lively. She grew up too and by her fourteenth summer was looking forward to life as a high school student. Then her mother fell badly enough sick that she could no longer do much work. Tursunay was the only unattached child old enough to earn money and her parents sat her down and told her she needed to drop out of school then move to Qarabora and apprentice as a seamstress.

She picked up her new trade quickly enough in the unaccustomed noise and bustle of the town. Soon she had learned to thread a needle and work a sewing machine. To cut and seam and hem. To straight stitch, back stitch and bar tack. It was not how she had imagined her life but she got good at it and by 1997 was working from her own little shop and things were busy. Then her father died and she went home for a time to be with her family. Even in her grief, everything looked as peaceful and as lovely as it always had but she thought of her father and the relatives in Kazakhstan that he had always talked of but never visited and decided she would get a passport and do what he had been unable to.

4

Tang said following the September 11 Incident, the anti-terrorism issue has become the focus of the international community. Holding the Security Council's foreign ministerial meeting on the anti-terrorism issue is conducive to strengthening and promoting the international struggle against terrorism. Tang said that China has also been facing the threat of terrorism. "East Turkistan" terrorist forces have long been trained, financed, and supported by international terrorist groups. They are responsible for several terrorist activities in China's Xinjiang Region and other countries, doing harm to the innocent. "East Turkistan" is out and out terrorism and part of international terrorism and should therefore be resolutely countered.

Tang said that China is consistently against all forms of terrorism, and has taken administrative, juridical, economic, and security measures against it. China has completed domestic legislative procedures for its accession to the international treaty against terrorist explosions not long ago, and will sign the international treaty against financing terrorism soon. We have also strengthened anti-terrorism consultation and cooperation with the relevant countries.

**—Chinese Ministry of Foreign Affairs Summary of
Chinese Foreign Minister Tang Jiaxuan's remarks at the UN Security
Council Anti-Terrorism Meeting of November 12, 2001.**

I t was 2001 when Saira first mentioned leaving for Urumqi to her mother. She was twenty-five and hated living the way they had to. At the end of eleventh grade she had graduated high school looking forward to studying literature and earning herself the best of things. Beautiful clothes, good food, a mobile phone. Then a few months later her father died of an unceremonious, unexpected heart attack that broke the family and forced them to move to a smaller place on the east side of the village. Saira's ambitions were necessarily abandoned. Her mother began making traditional robes, skirts, scarves and headscarves for bridal outfits and folk dancers and Saira helped her.

They worked by hand in the house, using a needle and sila-hook to shape embroidered designs in silver and gold and scarlet and turquoise, then affixing arrays of beads and jewels. Saira began at eight in the morning. Her mother would already have been long at it and would give her a cup of tea, six pieces of sugar and three pieces of bread to last the day. They would work through until well after dark, gazes fixed on the needle points and thread ends until they could not see much beyond them.

They barely made enough money to get by. Instead of beautiful clothes, Saira wore castoffs from relatives. A new phone would have been an impossible expense. She stitched, looped and threaded her days and she pondered a way out. Sometimes she heard that life was better in Urumqi, 250 miles south-southeast across mountains and wild desert and many miles more by road. She had never been and the way people talked it seemed like a foreign country but the thought came to her often. She started to glimpse herself a success there. Educated and well-dressed. Sending money home to provide for her mother and sisters. She decided she would go and never considered that she might fail.

She went to convince her mother of her case. They would never make enough money the way they were going, she said. In Urumqi people were doing business and traders were coming from all over to buy and sell goods. She was young and spoke good Chinese so she could work there and eventually learn how to do business herself. Eventually she could earn enough to build a house of their own.

Her mother was uncertain.

"My daughter," she said, "I have no money to send you and we have no relatives there either. How will you live?"

"Find me 200 yuan," Saira said. "I will make it with that."

Her mother borrowed the 200 from her own sister and a little more to buy Saira a phone that was scratched and beaten up but functional enough. There were no trains or airports nearby then. Only the long-haul buses that crossed Xinjiang crammed with bags and boxes and passengers. Saira bought a ticket, packed a suitcase and piled on apprehensive and excited. They drove south around the mountains, stopping every so often for fuel and bathroom breaks until the city rose gray and massive ahead of them and the bus's passage grew halting in the snarled traffic.

She stepped out into air that smelt of smoke and saw a skyline like none she had ever seen. Towers of twenty or thirty gleaming stories topped with domes and spires and viewing platforms then cranes hauling up the skeletons of more to be clad and glazed. Between stood radio masts and factory stacks spewing smog that blurred the ridge of distant mountains. Down at street level were broad expressways many lanes wide where vans, buses, scooters and taxis passed hurriedly around each other sounding persistent horns. The pavements and overpasses thronged with tides of people breaking then merging around each other and the white-painted trunks of occasional trees.

Saira used most of the money she had left on a room that was small and shared with two other women about her age. Then she headed out to hunt for work and the city rushed at her again. There were faces from

everywhere and voices too. There was life and enterprise crammed anywhere it would fit. You could buy snacks and cigarettes from booths
under overpass stairs or steamed buns from behind smudged glass windows or sticks of greasy mutton pieces cooked on charcoal grills next
to a cluster of plastic stools. You could call someone from a landline
telephone placed out on a table. You could watch packed lines of older
men playing xiangqi on nine-by-ten grid markings worn faint by years
of sliding pieces or you could join the jaded crowds gathered around
street performers swinging sledgehammers at bricks balanced on each
other's chests and clambering into precarious human towers.

All around were advertisements. Images of rice wine, phone cards
and skin cream looming massive from facades and billboards. Neon
signs that outshone the stars when night came. Occasionally Saira
saw flashes of incredible wealth. She took in the beautiful dresses and
sleek cars without envy but resolved that she would learn how to one
day have that for herself.

Her job search took her straight to the market stalls and she moved
between them looking for something that would fit her. A woman
would be hawking flatbreads at one and a man varieties of socks at the
next. There were folded quilts, baskets, dutars, stacked trays of eggs,
brooms, sacks of walnuts and underwear.

Saira introduced herself to traders and at last a woman selling
locally made fabrics thought she might be in need of Saira's language
skills and background. It did not pay well and was soon repetitive but
it was better than dressmaking and Saira worked hard at it. One day
she had a customer from Kazakhstan, a woman of around fifty. Saira
knew from her clothes and the way she carried herself that she was
making good money. They chatted in Kazakh and the woman made

her a proposition. "Listen," she said, "don't just stand at this stall for the rest of your life. I'm visiting from Astana for ten days to buy goods and I need a translator. Come and work with me."

"But you're only here a short time," Saira said. "After you leave, I'll be left with no money."

"Just be honest with me as we work," the woman said, "and as soon as I go I'll send you more customers and I promise you'll be busy." Saira did not think long before agreeing and the woman did as she had said she would. Her friends and contacts in Astana began calling Saira when they came to Urumqi and Saira earned herself a good reputation with them. The woman returned too and she suggested an addition to their arrangement. Saira would buy goods on her behalf and take a 10 percent commission.

Saira was good at that as well. At spotting quality products and running down bargains. As she worked she always remembered the things her grandmother had taught her. If ever someone did not look her straight in the eyes or sat too hunched over, she would make an excuse to avoid doing business with them. If someone's sleeves were too long or their trousers crumpled or they acted as if they were important but wore cheap, scuffed shoes, she avoided them too. Short men, she felt confident about buying from.

So it went and she was never cheated. Customers in Astana wanted homeware like curtains and bedspreads and crockery. And they wanted traditional clothing too. Saira bought it all and arranged to have it shipped on to Kazakhstan. She had no bank account then so whenever she was paid, she kept a bit of the money for her daily necessities and stuffed the rest in her suitcase under her clothes when her roommates were not looking.

She got to know the city. Its layout and its rhythms, the overflowing energy forcing its borders outwards each year. She knew the bus routes and the train station and how to deal with taxi drivers. She walked the narrow backstreets and mosques of the old Uyghur quarter and the broad avenues with new apartment blocks and glass-fronted offices. She recognized the outlines of the mountain ranges. The Tian Shan to the south then the Bogda Shan rising east. It was them that kept the city alive by feeding meltwater down to farmland through irrigation canals that traced the karez system of two thousand years earlier.

The air never stopped smelling of smoke but she grew used to it. Urumqi was one of the most polluted places in all the country, in all the world some people said. It was because of the metal and cement works towards the edge of town, where flue gas streamed white from the stacks as the city churned the materials of its own transformation. It was because of the spoils being scraped from the vast coal fields. A fire had been burning under the earth for decades at one of them. Hidden flames eating their way through millions of tons of coal, venting toxic clouds and leaving only cinders where the seams ran so the ground sometimes subsided and took buildings, livestock, people with it. And it was because of the burning trash that smouldered in empty lots or belched from the slim chimneys of industrial incinerators and settled back down as a film of ash.

A good wind would carry the worst of the smoke and effluvia off but often there was not one and it seeped into dusty skies to gather into a sulfurous yellow-brown shroud. As the winter set in it grew worse still because coal was the only way to stay warm. Temperatures stayed well below freezing until March and the flue gas drifted icy in the frail sunlight. When it snowed, the falling flakes gathered the ash then settled and coated everything in filth. Blow your nose and the snot was black. Wear light clothes outdoors and you would never get the stains out.

Two million people officially lived in Urumqi. Others were likely there unregistered and more were always arriving. Han were still encouraged by the government to come and people from minority backgrounds made the journey with the hope of earning the sort of money they could never have in their hometowns and villages. The government-sponsored migration had worked so well that official statistics put the Han population at nearly 75 percent. About 13 percent were Uyghur and there were other mostly Muslim minorities like Hui and Kazakhs and Uzbeks and there were ethnic Mongolians as well. There were businesspeople, lawyers and marketing professionals, factory workers and Party officials. There were drug users and alcoholics too, thieves and prostitutes. There were good people and the worst kind and if you found yourself in the wrong company, you would soon be in trouble. That meant so much more for Saira to consider than in the village where it now seemed impossible to her that anyone had the slightest thought beyond a simple day's work and going home to their family.

The Uyghurs in Urumqi, Saira noticed, were not like the Uyghurs she had known before, whom she could mostly identify from looking at but who kept essentially the same habits as the Kazakhs. The headscarves women in the village wore were of gayly patterned traditional fabrics but some of the Uyghur women in Urumqi wore dark hijabs. A few were completely veiled. In the old quarter's residential districts where the streets grew so narrow it was difficult for a car to pass, she would see crowds of young girls already with their hair covered and boys in their *doppas*, the traditional rounded skullcaps. She made more Uyghur friends and business partners and she asked them about their community and their lives. How was it, she wondered, that some seemed to have many more children than the One Child Policy would allow? The policy made certain allowances for minority groups but they knew of some families who had children beyond any allowance and never registered them. They said it was with the hope of populating an independent East Turkestan but those unregistered children could not enroll in state education so instead attended unofficial religious schools in apartment basements.

It seemed sometimes as if Uyghurs experienced the city in concurrent but entirely separate worlds to the Han and interacted only if there was some pressing need. Many Uyghurs spoke only basic Chinese, and almost no Han understood any Uyghur at all, including the government officials assigned there. Walk into a Uyghur restaurant or cafe, and the TV would be tuned to the Uyghur-language channel of Xinjiang Television or there would be a VCD of a Turkish or central Asian soap opera on. Nowhere on the menu would be the pork found in so many Han Chinese dishes.

Even the time of day was different. Urumqi officially ran on Beijing Time, along with the rest of China but they were so far west that the sun was sometimes not up until nearly ten. So there was also Xinjiang Time and it was two hours behind like in Kazakhstan. The Han usually preferred to adhere to government time and structure their days around it. Uyghurs usually did not, unless they had a state job. Things often synched up so shops or offices were open over the same periods but it still meant that conversations with strangers required clarifications or assumptions based on the way the other looked. Xinjiang Television broadcast in Chinese, Uyghur, Kazakh,

Kyrgyz and Mongolian and its own timekeeping varied by channel.

Saira moved between Urumqi's Han and Uyghur communities and she saw the splits and the slighting remarks made easily about the other as she did. Han spoke of unwarranted privileges extended to Uyghurs. The higher social welfare spending, the chance to have more children, the affirmative action policies and subsidies that they often called reverse discrimination. And despite that, they would say, Uyghurs remained ungrateful for everything done for them and did not even bother to learn the national language. They called Uyghurs lazy, violent, prone to crime and said they insisted on following a faith backwards and uncivilized.

These prejudices extended inevitably into the working world. Uyghurs expected discrimination based on the way they looked, their names and their accents but sometimes it would be right there in the job advertisement. HAN ONLY. Employers would ask for proof of Mandarin language ability, even if it was not required for the role. Or they would list excuses as to why positions were unsuitable for Muslims, like an inability to provide halal food. It was not just the private firms. State-owned banking and healthcare operations had done the same. The *bingtuan* was responsible for a large share of Xinjiang's economic output and about 90 percent of its workers were Han.

Saira started to see what had happened to so many of the young people, men mostly, who had come there from majority Uyghur cities like Kashgar or Hotan seeking a future beyond tending crops and herding animals. Uyghur university graduates had huge difficulties finding work in Urumqi. What hope was there for the rest with no qualifications and little Chinese? They found that the new apartments and the glass-fronted office buildings were not for them. Instead, they jostled for crushing shifts carrying, digging or pushing then slept on some temporary patch of flophouse floor and could do nothing but watch the city's promise and riches pass them by.

That was why there was so much crime, Saira thought. She understood it because people needed bread and shelter. And that was why some of them were lost to the extinction of a syringe or bottle. She saw the resentment that Uyghurs held for the Han, who were to them occupiers taking their resources, their land, their jobs and even their music, which was the one Uyghur thing some Han people did seem to like. When Han started moving into parts of the city that Uyghurs thought of as theirs, that resentment grew. It grew again when government regulations impinged on their segregated lives through pushes to control religious practices or expressions of identity. Those regulations had been getting worse since the attacks in the United States that happened not long after Saira arrived in Urumqi and what they called the War on Terror had begun. Chinese authorities said a Uyghur group named the East Turkestan Islamic Movement was allied with al-Qaeda and so must be destroyed. They talked often about the incident in Ghulja and the insurgents and separatists that they said had been arrested there. So there were new security measures, and thousands of imams were taken off for re-education.

Saira started seeing more security forces, all different kinds. The navy-uniformed civilian police, the paramilitary police in their white APCs and camouflage uniforms, and sometimes soldiers crowded into their olive trucks.

Months of work and Saira knew that her money must be building up. She did not spend much and was selective with her luxuries. Often she made herself choose just one of the things she wanted. Books usually won out. She would go to pick up a new lipstick, then decide to make do with what she had and buy a recently published novel or something older she had been meaning to read.

There came a day when Saira's two roommates were both out of town. She pulled out her suitcase, lifted the clothes and started counting her money. She kept counting long after she expected to stop and she had begun to feel dizzy. More than 30,000 yuan lay in front of her. About what two men could expect to earn a year in steady jobs. She called her mother on her battered phone. "Mom," she said, overwhelmed "we got rich."

"You did it, my daughter," her mother said. "You did it." And she was overwhelmed too. She asked if Saira could send some of it back so that she could start having the house built they had talked about but Saira did not know how. "Call your cousin," her mother said, speaking of a woman who had moved to a bigger city too. "She can tell you how to open a bank account." Saira did and soon she had wired money home.

She did not wire it all. When her roommates were back, she took them out and bought them new clothes and told them she would rent them a new place together. A bigger one with its own bathroom. "Don't worry about the cost," she told them, "I'll cover it. And anyway, I'm making good money. If there is too much work for me, I'll give it to you too." She bought herself clothes as well and more books. Kazakh authors and poets and more expensive works by foreign writers.

Saira built on her success and began to run operations on her own now that she knew how it all worked. She kept on building, employing others and branching out until she was where she had seen herself when she first left for Urumqi. So she began to think of her discarded ambitions too. The most important of them had always been a university education. A degree in literature. She could not spend all her time in classrooms when there was so much to do but she was sure that she would already have read all the key texts and the writing on them too. She arranged a meeting with a faculty head at the University of Xinjiang. She brought him a gift and treated him to a dinner while she made her case. "I already know the contents of the course," she told him. "I studied it all before coming here. All I want is to be able to sit the exams, and if you let me, I'm confident I'll pass them." In the face of her charm, her conviction and her generosity, he agreed.

That was around the time that she started writing for local newspapers. Short articles first on authors and poets and newly released or newly translated books. A while later came verse of her own that touched off the joy of self expression. She joined a society of writers and began holding poetry evenings with reading and recital that she hoped would connect young people with the literary history of their own cultures and of others.

In books she also saw a business opportunity. Some Kazakh titles were not available in China and the ones that were had often been altered to abide by Party censorship rules. She thought up a way around it. A customer or friend arriving from Kazakhstan would bring a copy of a book with them. Then a team of mostly university students she had assembled would retype the unaltered text from Cyrillic into Arabic script to be sold as a PDF. It was the kind of rule-bending that was still permitted in Xinjiang but it was only possible with literature or poetry. Anything in direct opposition to their Party-defined reality would have had consequences.

Saira learnt more about Uyghur literature and publishing. Historical epics also made up much of the Uyghur canon because writing the truth under the veil of fiction had been a way to diverge from Xinjiang's official history without the certainty of punishment. It had not always worked and their novelists, poets and historians had been jailed for their work like Qazhyghumar Shabdanuly was. The tolerance authorities had for them was so low that in 2002 they burnt thousands of books on Uyghur craft techniques, history and culture.

She moved through a varied circle of intellectuals, entrepreneurs and other self-made successes. Many of them had spent time studying abroad and would bring her mementos. Like the Mongolian student who came back from Istanbul and presented her with a pair of beautiful earrings inlaid with a star and crescent for the Turkish flag that soon became her favorite.

She became well-known enough that Kazakhs looking to do business often sought her advice or blessing for the projects they planned. There were suitors too. Men who wanted to date her or who talked of marriage. She was interested in none of them, she had better things to do with her time.

Saira loved the life she had built for herself. So when her brother was killed in a car accident in 2005, she grieved terribly and hurried home to spend time with her mother and her sisters but soon she was apologizing that she could not stay too long. There were so many things that she had to be doing back in Urumqi.

5

The government published in December 2003 a 'terrorist list' of organizations, such as the World Uighur Youth Congress, that it viewed as terrorist entities. However, there is no clear evidence that most of these advocate violence. Many Uighurs continued to receive long prison terms and to be executed for separatist or terrorist activities.

Even cultural or religious popular events may fall foul of the 'War on Terrorism' in Xinjiang. The Xinjiang Party Secretary issued instructions to all local authorities from February 2002 to crack down on 'separatist techniques', one of which was 'using popular cultural activities to make the masses receptive to reactionary propaganda encouraging opposition', permitting the intimidation, arrest and detention of Uighur cultural and human rights activists, and even poets writing about a blue pigeon, as occurred in 2005.

— **State of the World's Minorities 2006, Minority Rights Group**

The passport office staff had come to know Tursunay well and they were always the same with her. There were no questions about what she wanted when they saw her walk in one morning cradling her reams of paperwork. They said simply that it wouldn't do, that it was impossible and told her to leave. As usual she lost her temper with them and their blank denials.

"Look," she said, and she was starting to shout. "I'm following procedure so at least do your job. Why don't you ask me even a single thing? Why am I here, where do I want to travel? You just take one look at my face, see that I am Uyghur and tell me to leave. It's not fair, and it's not just, but I'm going to fight it. I'll do whatever I must to get my passport."

They had her kicked out and that was as usual too.

It was 2008 and the repeated defeats had taken almost any remaining hope from her but she had thought so often and so hard of Kazakhstan and of finding her relatives there that she kept going back to the office.

This time there was a man waiting there as she stalked out. She knew him. Halmirza was his name, a doctor. He was slight, shorter than her and a good bit older and his hair stood on end all over his head. He had come into her shop the previous year to get a pair of trousers pressed and they had fallen into talking. Halmirza was a Chinese citizen but he was an ethnic Kazakh and had been born in Kazakhstan too. In fact, he said, he had recently bought land there and was thinking of moving back and applying for citizenship. That was something the diaspora could do relatively simply through a Kazakh government scheme. *Oralman,* authorities called them, returnee. Thousands had since Kazakh independence but it was not always an easy decision because neither Kazakhstan or China allowed dual nationality.

Tursunay had told him that her father had come from Kazakhstan as well and had relatives there that she had never met but would like one day to find.

"You should go there and search for them," Halmirza had said. "Family is important. Anyway you should see the world when you can. People round here never want to go to other places or other countries but they really should."

"How am I supposed to go and do that?" Tursunay had asked. "I have nothing. No passport, no visa."

Halmirza had told her that he had helped others sort out the invitation letters from Kazakhstan that were required as part of the passport and visa application process so perhaps he could do the same for her. Tursunay took him up on it and they had met up to arrange things but it had still not been enough to get her application accepted.

Halmirza was at the passport office to sort out paperwork for his mother and his sister. He asked if Tursunay had her passport yet and she told him about the office staff.

"You should not fight with them," he said. "If you fight, they will never do anything for you." He told her to wait a moment and he went inside to talk to them on her behalf.

He came back a few minutes later and relayed a conversation that had not gone much better. He had asked one of them why they were treating Tursunay like that when all she wanted was a passport. "So long as I'm here," the officer had said to him, "I'm never going to issue a passport for her." The only way, the officer said, would be if she were to get married to someone born abroad, like Halmirza, and bring in the marriage certificate. Maybe then, the officer said, he'd think about it.

Halmirza smiled when he told Tursunay that bit, as if to dismiss the comment, and she saw that he liked her. She thought that he seemed nice too. Kind with a good job and background and a family that he cared for but she had not realised until then that he was single.

She had heard before that a Kazakh spouse made the passport application process easier and she thought of it again when she next saw Halmirza. They had come to understood each other pretty well by then and she decided that she would go through with it. They married June of 2008 in Qarabora and took the certificate to the passport office. Staff at last accepted Tursunay's application but said it would take time to process. Maybe a year or more. She waited and Halmirza spoke to her of Kazakhstan. Its glorious mountains and endless steppe, its delicious food and boundless hospitality. "You must see Almaty, just wait until you visit," he would say, telling her of the wide streets, leafy parks and shining towers of Kazakhstan's biggest city. She had only intended to look for her family there but he suggested finding themselves work and staying a time.

Neither her or her mother owned a phone so she heard little from home then but the next time she took the bus back to Keziletale. her mother had news for her. It seemed that the son of a local official thought the valley as lovely as they did. Or at least thought it a lovely opportunity to make money. He wanted to turn it into the kind of place that tourists would visit and planned to do it by damming the Tekes and creating an artificial lake. Authorities had apparently agreed to the plan and delegations of officials had begun visiting the people living in the valley. They had gone to the Han villages first and held meetings to persuade residents to give up their land. In exchange they offered modern apartments in the city. Apartments with power and plumbing that were close to jobs and hospitals and schools and were worth significantly more than their current houses. It seemed as if the Chinese families would be happy to take them up on the offer.

Officials came to Keziletale too but when they talked of compensation the sums were significantly smaller. Tursunay's mother and the other villagers had complained. They said they had heard what their Han neighbors had been offered and they asked why it should be so much less for the Uyghurs and the Kazakhs. Most of them had refused to move out at all. The officials had told them that the work would be going ahead and the area flooded whatever they chose, so they had better accept. Tursunay had not believed it possible that the valley would flood. She put it out of her mind and got back to her sewing machine.

Things were busy so it was months before she found time to visit again. She boarded the bus as usual and the driver followed the familiar way out of town past red-roofed houses and fields delineated by tree-lines and irrigation channels. Then the road skirted the mountains and curved to meet the Tekes and entered the jagged mouth of the valley. Closer, closer and then two or three miles short of the village, something new. A massive structure of gray concrete cutting across the river, swelling the upstream water far beyond its banks. Tursunay looked out appalled as the bus continued unperturbed along the shores of the new lake. Then the village was ahead and she saw that the waters had already crept up to take some of the lower-lying houses. Theirs still stood clear up on the rise.

Her mother cried when she arrived and they looked out at where their neighbors had lived. Some of them had disobeyed orders to move out, her mother told her, and the authorities had arrived with vans and batons to evict them. They had not given some even the chance to retrieve their belongings before they took them away. Parties of officials had visited Tursunay's mother again but she had scorned them. They had offered only 40,000 yuan for the house and all of the land. 40,000 against the years she and Tursunay's father had spent building a home and a life for the family. It would not buy even a single apartment.

She had demanded that they offer at least enough to house her children. They had told her only that the utilities would be cut off soon and that she should let them know when she had decided to sell.

One man said that if she persisted in being so stubborn then she would surely die alone there.

They did as they had warned and cut off the electricity. Then after a time the rising water ruined the well system so that the fields and the crops started to dry up. It was not right, Tursunay's mother said, not just, but she still trusted the Party and reasoned that this had likely all been done only on the orders of local officials. If they let the regional government know what had happened then they would surely offer more reasonable compensation.

Two of their old neighbors tried lodging an appeal before any of Tursunay's famiy got around to it. Their petition was ignored and eventually led to them being arrested.

Tursunay began going home more often. The water was a little higher each time and her mother more desperate. Thieves had begun ranging the area along the main road and livestock and bikes were no longer safe. Her mother said she could no longer sleep properly for fear the water would finally reach the house and flood inside as she lay there in the dark.

Tursunay tried to calm her mother and told her she was safe for now and that they could appeal and find her somewhere better to live. She bought a mobile phone, and she took pictures documenting the damage done to their land. "What is the use in doing that?" her mother asked, her faith in the Party used up. "They have no shame, and they sentenced our neighbors for even trying to stop them. I don't want you to end up in jail too."

One afternoon in 2009 Tursunay visited with her brothers and they talked of the same things as always. Her mother was particularly upset and said she felt one of her headaches coming on and needed to go to bed. Tursunay set off to buy her medicine but one of her brothers called as she was on her way home and said their mother had fainted. She was still unconscious when Tursunay made it back and would not wake up to take the medicine so they got her to the nearest hospital. She did not wake up there either and twenty days later, she died. Brain bleeding, doctors said, and Tursunay knew that it was because of the pressure she had been living under, because of the authorities and because they were Uyghur.

After they had buried their mother, Tursunay decided to fight their case and went to Künes officials to appeal.

"The compensation is so much less than you offered others," she told them. "It's not fair."

"If it's not fair, it's not fair," they said, "but that's how much we can offer you, and we can't do anything else."

She argued and she tried again many times over. None of it did anything and she began to feel like there was nothing much for her there anymore. So she let herself be drawn in to Halmirza's plans for Kazakhstan. He wanted to open a clinic there and said that if he did that there would be need for help. Tursunay gave up her shop and began attending nursing classes in Ghulja to prepare for her place in that new life.

6

The Chinese government and the Communist Party handled the July 5 riot in Xinjiang Uygur Autonomous Region "decisively and properly," said a senior official
from the Communist Party of China on Friday, July 17.

"The CPC and government have always advocated social stability, the socialist
legal system, national unity, as well as the interests of the people," said He Guoq-
iang, a member of the Standing Committee of the CPC Central Committee Political
Bureau.   **— Xinhua, July 17, 2009**

The air had not much cooled from the day's eighty-five-degree
peak as Saira made her way home through uniform blocks and
tree-lined avenues on the evening of July 5, 2009. She reached
her first-floor apartment in Urumqi's south around six, greeted her
housemates and sat down in front of the television without bothering
to change into house clothes or take off her favorite earrings with the
Turkish star and crescent. Xinjiang Television's Kazakh service was
on and she watched it for a while. The channel's hulking headquarters
was two streets over from their place and she liked that it was close
enough that she could see the roof from her window and glimpse the
thousands who worked there hurrying in and out at shift change.

There was nothing much interesting on and Saira thought instead
of dinner. She felt like cooking but found little to do it with in the
kitchen so she put her shoes on again and walked to the nearest mini
market, a Chinese place. She moved between the few other shoppers
in the fluorescent glare, filled her basket and took her place in line.

There was a Han couple in front of her. A woman several months pregnant and surely not far from term with a man who must be her husband. Saira watched them unheeding, absorbed in thoughts of work and the meal to come. She heard but did not process the murmurs around her and the raised voices outside that were distant but growing closer. Then the queue evaporated and there was only the Han woman behind the till telling Saira abruptly, loudly, to go, to leave now.

The woman must not want to serve her for some reason, Saira thought, and she grew angry and tried to argue back. The woman did not listen and kept telling her to go, go, go. Shooing her away with bemusing and increasing agitation. Only then did Saira notice the noise out on the street. She looked through the door of the market and saw chaos.

A crowd of Uyghur men were gathering around the market entrance carrying sticks and knives and bottles with rags stuffed into their necks. The men were shouting things Saira could not catch and chanting the takbir. "*Allahu akbar*," God is great. Only a few people were still in the market. Saira, the woman behind the till, the Chinese couple from the queue and one or two others. They all shied back towards the rear wall.

Then the men were shouting right into the shop. "Muslims come out," they called. "Muslims come out."

Saira thought they were going to attack anyone who left and she stayed terrified where she was. Then a wide-eyed Uyghur girl of no more than eighteen was saying something to Saira and she was looking at Saira's earrings. "Sister," she said, "let's go," and she grabbed Saira's hand and pulled her into the street. The men opened a path, the girl pulled Saira through it and some of the men began taking cigarette lighters from their pockets. They touched their butane jets to the rags at the necks of those bottles and hurled the bottles hastily at the market front so they bloomed into orange flame.

Saira lost control of herself and any understanding of what was happening. She and the Uyghur girl could only stand holding each other's hands and stare at the blaze consuming the place where they had stood so recently and so normally. They looked around at each other after a moment and they started laughing. The wild, hysterical laughter of shock and of relief. It doubled them over.

The girl came to herself before Saira. "Sister," she shouted again. "Sister, we have to go. Where is your house?" Saira turned and pointed and then she looked back towards the shop. The crowd had thinned out and at their feet she saw the pregnant woman who had stood in front of her in the queue. There was a slash, a knife cut, right across her stomach. Blood was flowing from inside her but no one was doing anything about it and the woman's husband was just standing staring down at her as the market burnt behind them and the men moved on to the next Chinese business.

The Uyghur girl shook Saira and they ran. They ran as fast as they could towards the corner where her apartment was. They had to stop again before they reached it, limbs burning, lungs grasping at the air. And then they were laughing again as helpless as before. Dazed and appalled at herself, Saira remembered her grandmother had once told her that if ever you cannot stop laughing then you should look at your fingernails and repeat *Bismillah*, in the name of God. "Bismillah, Bismillah, Bismillah." She did it, and the girl did it too and she felt able to think again.

Saira did not speak Uyghur properly, neither the girl Kazakh but they could understand each other well enough. She really was young and as terrified as Saira. "Don't be scared of me," the girl said. "I wasn't there to join in, I was just going to visit a classmate and it all started. Please take me to your house." Saira took her and they ran the rest of the way and through the main door and clammy and trembling into her apartment.

Her two roommates had heard the breaking glass, the chants and screams and they were pressed to the edges of the room with their eyes on the window. Saira locked the door behind her and then she shut the curtains too because anyone could see right in from the street. She was calmer now and she remembered another thing her grandmother had told her. That during times of violence in Xinjiang, the family would hang thick cloth up over the windows so that if an explosion or gunshot shattered the pane then the shards would not pepper the room. She told her roommates and they scrambled past each other to find blankets and hung them over the window as well.

The terrible clamor continued outside, moving closer, closer, then abating again. They kept themselves low and ended up sitting with their backs to the wall and their knees up at their chests, checking their phones to try and find out what was happening. Saira kept glancing at the Uyghur girl and then cringing when footsteps and shouts passed by their shield of fabric and glass. She could think only of the pregnant Chinese woman lying there bleeding and the image appeared unbidden behind her eyelids. Who could do something like that to someone else? Perhaps the girl actually had been there to join them. They were her people outside.

Saira's roommates were looking sideways at the girl too and she had obviously realized it. She might think they were after her and attack them with some idea of self-defense. Saira got up and went to the kitchen. She opened the cutlery drawer and took the sharp knives out and she emptied the knife block too. Then she went and hid them all in her bedroom. That way they would all feel safer.

Still she was nervous. She turned to the girl again. "You saved me," she said, "and I'm so grateful, so please don't hurt us. But can you sit on the other side of the room, and we'll stay on this one?"

"Please don't worry," the girl said. "I'm not a rioter. I knew something might happen but not anything else about it. I just saw your earrings and knew you were Muslim. I'd never hurt you."

She did as Saira had asked anyway and they sat like that as the skies darkened on the other side of the curtains, the street lamps came on and their faces faded to pale shadows. They did not dare turn on a light because sometimes the shouts and ragged, horrible screams were right outside the window.

Everything cut out around ten. Power, phone signal, wi-fi. Then they heard the shooting. The snap of automatic gunfire echoing between concrete. The yelled orders of trained men and the roar of diesel engines. "Oh God," the girl said, "they are killing our Uyghurs."

They faced each other unseeing in the darkness for hours more and Saira could hear the sharp intakes of breath at something particularly loud or close outside. She knew the night could not last forever and she clung to that but again came the image of that pregnant woman and her rent stomach. Perhaps only those Turkish earrings had saved her from something similar. She tried to remember the rest. Their flight from the market, how long they had been standing there as it burned. It was all a mess, her memories fragmented and imperfect.

The long yearned-for dawn emboldened them as it seeped into the room. They moved hesitant from the apartment to the stairwell and climbed up all the way to the fifth floor then out onto the roof. In the gentle light they saw the night's carnage beneath them. The bodies of Chinese and Uyghurs were splayed out in the road amid great smears of clotting blood. Han-owned storefronts were blackened and cars burnt to their bones. Strewn everywhere were the glimmering shards of wind-shields and window panes. Police were moving their way from the end of the street accompanied by paramilitaries and soldiers with trucks that had canvas strung over the beds. The police and soldiers were picking up bodies and dumping them into the covered truck beds all on top of each other but it looked as if they were only taking the bodies of Uyghurs and leaving the Han where they were. Other crews followed behind, washing blood from the streets with high-powered hoses.

The girl was sobbing. "Only a few Uyghurs did this," she said, "but all Uyghurs will be punished for it." It seemed to Saira that she was probably right.

An old Hui man who lived in the building and who Saira knew well enough to greet in the stairwell came up behind them, gray and serious. "Hey," he said, "come inside. If they catch you on camera up here you will all be in trouble." He was right too.

Back downstairs and Saira tugged open a gap in the curtains and the sheets and recoiled nauseous. A taxi was jackknifed onto the pavement in front of the apartment. Inside it was the body of a man but the body stopped at a ragged neck wound and the man's head was on the road beside the driver's door.

That was Monday and they did not move again from the apartment. Just sat and ate the remnants of food left in the cupboards and the fridge. There was still no phone signal or internet but the power came back and when they turned on the television they saw a curfew had been announced. Later the Uyghur girl quietly thanked them and slipped off. Saira had not even asked her name.

Neither Saira or her housemates wanted to be alone and the three of them slept in the living room again that night. When at last they walked out into the street, all the bodies were gone but the glass fragments crunched under their feet and there were ugly marks every now and then that the hoses had missed.

Saira soon found out that the violence in Urumqi was begotten by the violence that unfolded on the muggy night of June 25 more than two thousand miles south in the town of Shaoguan in Guangdong Province. There was a toy factory there where a group of migrant Uyghurs from Kashgar lived in close-packed dorms and worked a rotation of day and night shifts. A former employee of the factory had been spreading rumors, telling people that some of the Uyghurs had gang-raped two Han women. The factory's Han workers had found that easy to believe and armed themselves with bats, steel poles, cudgels and axes, then rushed into the Uyghur dorms as the day shift slept. They moved from room to room pulling men from their beds and pouring blows down upon them.

It became a mass brawl. Two of the Uyghurs were killed by the time it was over and more than a hundred were injured. That was according to state media. Others said the real death toll had been much higher and was being covered up. Those accounts spread slowly to Xinjiang along with video said to be from that night. Grainy footage from outside the dorms that showed wreckage thrown out of windows and every now and then a prone body. It was shared on instant messaging apps and posted on websites at a volume that overwhelmed government censors.

So Uyghurs had gathered furious in the alleyways around Urumqi's Grand Bazaar by the jade dealers and food markets and souvenir stalls. They had demanded that the incident be properly investigated and demanded too that they be treated as their Han neighbors were. The police soon dispersed the protesters but some among them turned their rage against anything Chinese and threw stones and overturned cars. The situation soon escalated into unchecked violence. Along with the attacks on businesses, they had dragged Han passengers from buses and beaten them and they had fought running battles with security forces. That was when the army and the paramilitaries had arrived and the shooting begun.

Mobs of Han men with their own cleavers and sticks and shovels had gathered to seek vengeance afterwards. They called for the death of Uyghurs and attacked any they found. This time the smashed-up businesses were the ones with Uyghur signs. The police tear-gassed some of the new mobs and let others move relatively unhindered. As they did, squads of officers were rushing into homes and hauling out hundreds of Uyghur men and boys, stripping them to their underwear and carrying them away even though their families swore they'd had nothing to do with any of it.

The official figures said at least 184 people were dead and that three quarters of them were Han. On television the same images looped over. Black smoke pouring from burning vehicles. Two scared and battered Han women holding each other. A bloodied man struggling to raise himself from the pavement. Graphic pictures of dead

Han were distributed to foreign media who had been flown in during the curfew. That must have been why the Uyghur bodies were being removed first, Saira thought.

State media quickly said the protest and the violence were premeditated and directed from outside the country. Xinjiang's heavyset, broad-jawed governor Nur Bekri blamed the Three Forces Abroad, meaning terrorism, separatism and religious extremism. The official news agency Xinhua said the whole thing was masterminded by Rebiya Kadeer but that was what they always said. Kadeer was Uyghur and had been a businesswoman and a prominent Party member until she was expelled and jailed for five years for passing internal communiqués to her husband in the US. She fled to join him when she was released in 2005 and had apparently been responsible for nearly everything that the government did not like in Xinjiang since then.

Urumqi mayor Jierla Yishamudin spoke at a press conference and said they were in a battle of life-and-death to defend the unification of their motherland and to maintain the consolidation of all ethnic groups. A battle, he said, that was fierce and of blood and fire. Then security affairs chief Zhou Yongkang said a proverbial steel wall had to be built to ensure regional stability and safeguard the interests of the people. He urged the government, Party offices, and security forces to stay on high alert and to nip all hidden dangers in the bud.

Saira started to hear rumors from Uyghurs and from Kazakhs too. They thought the protests might have been started by government agitators as a pretext to finally destroy the Uyghurs. They said that the official figures of Uyghur dead were a fabrication and that there were unmarked mass graves on the edge of town full of Uyghur bodies. She could not tell what of it was true. Then the Han began talking about

Uyghurs attacking people with hypodermic syringes deliberately infected with HIV. She did not know if she could believe that either.

The stories, the fear, spread through the streets and at the central bus station Uyghurs pushed onto sweaty sold-out routes to their hometowns to flee the revenge attacks and roundups already underway and those worse that were surely to come. The city's segregation intensified so that whole sections were considered places Han would never go and others just as unsafe for Uyghurs.

Authorities announced plans to demolish buildings belonging to Kadeer's company. The Akida Trade Center, which was full of Uyghur shops and where her family had lived. They did the same with the Akida company building and the Tuanjie Theater too. Then the *People's Daily*, the Party newspaper, announced the inevitable start of a new "strike hard" campaign. "Strike hard and punish" they called it this time and they promised to further consolidate the fruits of maintained stability, to eliminate security dangers, to root out places where criminals bred and change the face of the public security situation.

The campaign proceeded much like the others. One person would be accused of taking part in the protests and the people around them would be dragged into it too. Because of a son, a father would be taken away. Because of a husband, a wife, and so on with the people who had talked to the accused on the phone before the protests or who had drunk tea with them or been seen visiting their home. If you were taking a flight to inner China and the person in front of you was arrested, then perhaps you would be too. Or at least you would if you were Uyghur.

7

Police across the country have started a massive seven-month crackdown to curb rising crimes and ease escalating social conflicts.

Known in Chinese as yanda, or "strike hard," the campaign is targeting extreme violent crime, gun and gang crime, telecom fraud, human trafficking, robbery, prostitution, gambling and drugs, the Ministry of Public Security announced on Sunday.

Police nationwide were also told to watch high-risk places such as suburbs, and to nip violence in the bud by being more vigilant to social conflicts and helping resolve problems.

"China, during a process of social and economic transformation, is facing emerging social conflicts and new problems in social security," Zhang Xinfeng, vice-minister of public security, told a national meeting on Sunday.

"Police at all levels must fully realize the complexity of the problem."

This is the fourth such round of yanda in China since 1983. During the campaign, police usually take tough measures against crimes and judicial authorities hand down swifter and harsher penalties.

—*China Daily*, June 15, 2010

Seven months in Kazakhstan turned out to be enough for Tursunay. She and Halmirza had arrived in 2011 not long after her passport came through and decided to see how they liked life there. He had found work soon enough, doctors always could. She struggled but Halmirza earned better money than he had in China and it was enough for them both. They had rented a house and they had driven into Almaty but when the gray blocks and mirrored high-rises appeared, gathered, and engulfed them, she had seen no beauty in the traffic clogging its roads and the buildings crowded in on top of each other.

She searched every day for her father's relatives. She made calls, she looked online and wrote letters but she had so little information about them that it had only been during that seventh month that she had found them. There was an aunt and an uncle, elderly now, and there were children and grandchildren too. They lived about eighty-five miles east of Almaty in a town named Shelek.

Shelek was small and ordinary. It was built around grid streets with a few cafes, restaurants and guesthouses. There was a park in the center with brick-paved paths under avenues of trees where children played and men did calisthenics on parallel bars. Fields surrounded it and then mountains that were not as beautiful as the ones at home but beautiful all the same. Even for Tursunay, who was born under an up-turned horse cart and had grown up shooing cows off to graze on her way to school, it had seemed like wild country. Bare and dusty with winds that tore down from the ridgeline to envelop her so completely that sometimes all she could hear was the howl in her ears.

It was soon after Tursunay first visited her aunt and uncle there that her younger brother started calling her. The time had come for him to get married, he said, and with their parents dead he needed her to vouch for his suitableness as a match to the families of prospective brides. She relented. For him and because it already felt like she had been away so long. Halmirza's idea of life in Kazakhstan had sounded tempting but it was the first time that she had travelled much beyond home and the pangs of separation were starting to creep in on her. She longed to be around people that were truly her people and near the places that she knew how to navigate without a moment's thought. And now that she had found her relatives, keeping in touch with them would be simple and she could return to visit them whenever she liked. She told Halmirza what she had decided and he said that he would join her there as soon as he could.

She took the early bus towards the border crossing at Khorgos, joining the highway that ran from Almaty then two hundred mostly empty miles into the scrub-studded plains. It passed the cafes and motels of Zharkent and the ornate Chinese-Islamic minaret of the mosque there and a couple of smaller settlements to its east. After that were the lines of trucks with their once-white trailers waiting to make the crossing, tailing back along the side of the road or lined up in parking areas while their drivers crowded listlessly around whatever spots of rest and refreshment were to be found. Then the border revealed itself, delineated by razor wire and stretches of no-man's-land stretching up into the mountains to the north and with small towns clustered each side of the crossing.

There were big plans for the place. The governments on both sides of the razor wire said it was to be the gateway to Eurasia. Kazakhstan had that year established the Khorgos Eastern Gate Special Economic Zone and announced that one day soon it would encompass manufacturing areas, a dry port and a free trade area where tourists could shop in shiny malls unburdened by taxation. They dreamt more improbable dreams too. A new Dubai of massive luxury hotels and business centers with an ethnographic park, casinos, art galleries, theaters, a sports stadium and an airport. The towns on each side were to be developed too and all of that was to be connected to Almaty by a new four-lane highway and a rail link. So far there was not much more than an enormous customs building and lines of wind-bowed shrubs on the Kazakh side but warehouses were going up and earthmovers were scratching away at the foundations of more.

Leaving Kazakhstan was easy. Just a scan of her luggage and a brief opening and closing of her passport by the teal-hatted border guards. Then the signs were Chinese, the uniforms that familiar dark blue and it was jarringly clear that she had become a person of suspicion. The line moved through passport and customs controls and the criteria that guards used to choose who received extra scrutiny was plain. The Han passed simply enough but the Uyghurs and sometimes the ethnic Kazakhs were taken aside. They put Tursunay in a white-walled room and tore apart her luggage. They checked her clothes down to her socks and the lining of her jacket, looking for something that could only have been tiny. A memory card perhaps or some hidden USB drive. They went through her phone too, scrolling pictures and messages until they eventually lost interest. They let her go hours later and she knew that things had shifted. Everything was different, tenser and it must have been because of the "strike hard" campaign and the continued aftermath of the incident in Urumqi.

Development was further ahead on the Chinese side of the crossing. There were new commercial complexes and hotels connected by smooth tarmac marked with fresh white lines and lit by gold-painted street lights. She boarded a bus there and they headed east on the wide new highway. Most of the other passengers were Han, including a man who got on at one stop and sat down next to her but she noticed a doppa among the otherwise bare heads and was glad.

They hit the first checkpoint soon after leaving. Police who stopped the bus and looked in at them and looked at the luggage compartment.

There had not been checkpoints there before but that was the first of several that were much the same. One not far from home looked bigger and more permanent. The bus driver stopped and police climbed aboard to announce that they would be checking everyone's identification documents. The passengers scrabbled in their pockets and bags and the police moved down the bus aisle. The Han man who had sat down next to Tursunay apologized when they got to him. "I don't have my ID card with me," he told them. "I forgot it." The police did not seem to mind much but they looked at Tursunay's and told her to get off the bus. They told the man wearing the doppa to get off too and then they asked which luggage was theirs. They rifled through the luggage nearly as thoroughly as the customs officers had done, while Tursunay and the man in the doppa waited silently on the verge.

She at last got back to their place and the ache to be there was quickly replaced by the far worse suspicion that she should never have come at all. Those checks were not just on the roads but everywhere else too. Walks, shopping trips or visits to see family and friends all came with demands for ID or that she open her bag or tell them where she was going. The sense of it closed in around her until she understood that the only place she truly knew had become somewhere different in her absence and the things that had happened there had taken the life from it. There was no question of staying.

She had not much loved Kazakhstan. It had been good to find her family and her uncle had been especially kind to her but it was not with them like it was with her relatives in Xinjiang and she had felt apart from them. Yet she had not been asked for documents every time she went out because of the way she looked or had her belongings raked through because of her name and that now felt like freedom.

So she reasoned it through and decided that a Kazakh passport was the thing. If she were Kazakh rather than Chinese then she would be able to travel to China without any of the questioning and hassle. She would live where she wanted, she would leave when she wanted and she would not be treated as second class in the land that was hers. She called Halmirza, and she was sure, firm with him. "Let's do it," she said, "let's become Kazakh residents, then citizens."

"It will not be quick," Halmirza warned. "We'll have to stay five years at least." Tursunay did not know how she would manage that but she said yes anyway. No amount of homesickness would keep her from it.

8

The Urumqi riots of July 2009—the most deadly episode of ethnic unrest in recent Chinese history—continued to cast a shadow over developments in the Xinjiang Uighur Autonomous Region. The government has not accounted for hundreds of persons detained after the riots, nor investigated the serious allegations of torture and ill-treatment of detainees that have surfaced in testimonies of refugees and relatives living outside China. The few publicized trials of suspected rioters were marred by restrictions on legal representation, overt politicization of the judiciary, and failure to publish notification of the trials and to hold genuinely open trials as mandated by law.

Several violent incidents occurred in the region in 2011, though culpability remains unclear. On July 18 the government said it had killed 14 Uighur attackers who had overrun a police station in Hetian and were holding several hostages. On July 30 and 31 a series of knife and bomb attacks took place in Kashgar. In both cases the government blamed Islamist extremists. In mid-August it launched a two-month "strike hard" campaign aimed at "destroying a number of violent terrorist groups and ensuring the region's stability."

Under the guise of counterterrorism and anti-separatism efforts, the government also maintains a pervasive system of ethnic discrimination against Uighurs and other ethnic minorities, along with sharp curbs on religious and cultural expression and politically motivated arrests.

—**Human Rights Watch World Report 2012: China**

I t did not take long for Adiljan to decide that he lacked the strength of his friends in Ghulja. The arrests continued and a judge gave one of the men who had been picked up with him a two-year sentence then police took the man's wife too. It kept happening. Years in jail on vague charges of illegal religious practices usually but some men just disappeared. Adiljan was himself briefly detained twice more and that was enough. In 2004 he shaved off his beard and left for Hotan in the southeast of Xinjiang. The city did not impress him. It was hot and dusty and to him undeveloped without much opportunity for work. Out in the arid fields, corn and rice and cotton grew but he did not wish to become a laborer. Up in the Kunlun Mountains, men and women hefted pickaxes into the dolomitic deposits in search of jade while others picked through the shallows of the Yurungkash River below for smaller fragments. He did not wish to do that either but he watched the traders who bought the jade from market stalls and blankets spread by the roadside. There he saw opportunity and after a couple of years he knew the business well enough that he moved to Urumqi and began selling there.

There had been much to learn. The color of the stuff was determined by iron and chromium oxide content and ranged from dark olive green through to a yellowish cream known as mutton fat. It was the mutton fat jade that the Han liked most and Adiljan's customers were mostly Han. For thousands of years jade had been coveted in China for the status it indicated and the idea that it promoted a beneficial flow of energy and held healing properties. Some people said it would detoxify your body, ward off negative thoughts, aid fertility, ease childbirth, boost happiness and resistance to disease or even provide a link to the spirit world. It had been sought after for so long that deposits that had once existed inland were long exhausted but now that more people had a bit of money, everyone wanted some hanging around their necks or decorating their houses as figurines. The finest mutton fat was eventually worth more than gold.

Jade meant nothing to Adiljan or to most Uyghurs but he sold it on to Shanghai and Beijing and Guangzhou and started making good money. He set himself up in Urumqi's Grand Bazaar, prayed only at a government-sanctioned mosque and kept well away from anything political so he could focus on work. In 2007 he fell into chance conversation at a train station with a Uyghur woman named Mihribangul who was calm, devout and a few years younger than him. They were soon married. *Mihribanim*, he called her. My merciful one. *Wapadarim*, she called him. My loyal one. Before long she was pregnant with a daughter they named Bumaryam and soon afterwards a son, Muhammed.

The quiet life he wanted was complicated by the violence of 2009. Adiljan saw the beginnings of the protests while on his way to mosque and hurried away but ended up trapped at a friend's place unable to reach or even contact Mihribangul for two agonizing days. He emerged to see a mob of Han men looking for Uyghurs and beating a disabled shoe shiner in the side streets near the bazaar. The city was different after that. More police, new surveillance cameras. The "strike hard" campaign was unsparing, and death sentences and executions followed the mass arrests. It was a year before restrictions on internet access, messaging and international phone calls completely reverted to normal. More violence followed. Bomb and knife attacks blamed on Uyghurs. Riots. A failed attempt to hijack an airliner flying from Hotan to Urumqi.

Adiljan stayed careful and business kept getting better. When he was a child he had always envied the people who took trains to inland China. Now if he went, he flew, but his success and his wallet still did not shield him from the humiliation of being turned away from hotels there that clearly had vacancies once they saw his face and his ID. Or from the extra police checks, searches and harassment.

He moved his family to a roomy new house in a suburban gated community. They would all go out together when he was not working. To one of the newer fast food restaurants that had opened and he thought more upmarket than traditional Uyghur places. Or to the mall. Or to a fair with rides and bumper cars and shooting galleries of lined up balloons. Twice a year they all went to Aksu to visit her relatives and to Ghulja to visit his. To be that kind of success, to live in luxury and to have money like he did. Those were things he had never imagined but they did not altogether smother who he was and had been.

In the spring of 2012, he heard that Turkish Prime Minister Recep Tayyip Erdoğan would be making a four-day state visit at the beginning of April. No Turkish prime minister had done that for twenty-seven years but the real wonder was that he would be arriving not in Beijing but Urumqi. No Turkish leader had ever done that. It could only be because he believed the linguistic and cultural bonds between Turks and Uyghurs made them kin. At least that was what Adiljan and his friends said to each other when they talked of it over tea or after prayer and they knew in their chests that they were right.

Adiljan had felt that way for a while. No one he knew in Urumqi ever watched Chinese television or films. It was always either XJTV or the many Turkish serials that you could buy on pirated VCDs laid out on market stalls in contravention of laws that authorities rarely bothered to enforce. Adiljan liked the serials. Each usually had at least thirty two-hour-long episodes a season so he'd had plenty of them to watch. There was *Acı Hayat* (*Bitter Life*), about a working-class couple scrabbling to get by who are split apart by an evil playboy. There was *Kurtlar Vadisi* (*Valley of the Wolves*), which followed an undercover intelligence operative infiltrating the mafia. He liked that one most. It was all shiny suits with shirts open at the neck, brooding stare-downs and shootouts with pistols gripped in each hand.

The audio was often not translated so Adiljan did not perfectly understand what the actors were saying but Turkish was similar enough to Uyghur that he got most of it. When he laughed at the jokes and when his eyes welled up at the sad scenes, it seemed that Uyghurs and Turks were truly of the same people.

Turkey had been on their side in 2009. Erdoğan had described the Chinese government response as savagery and told it to stop trying to assimilate Uyghurs. There had been protests outside the Chinese embassy in Ankara where Uyghurs and Turks had stood together. None of that news was covered by Chinese media but it made it all around Urumqi's cafes.

Turkish exports became so popular afterwards that Istanbul fashions supplanted the Korean, Chinese and Japanese designs that had once set trends. Women's clothing mostly but men's suits too like the ones in *Valley of the Wolves*. Adiljan had bought himself some and wore them when he could.

Relations between the two countries had improved since then and trade volumes had grown because money and progress still came before anything else. Adiljan knew that was likely part of the reason for the state visit but it still made he and his friends feel there was a government out there that cared about them. Even if it was not their own.

So when he discovered that Erdoğan would be visiting the Grand

Bazaar and the mosque there, he decided that he had to see him. If it was only from a distance or just his passing car then that was better than to not see him at all. It would be a Sunday and he and several other men he knew from the bazaar planned to gather early.

News footage showed Erdoğan touching down in darkness, his Turkish Airlines–liveried plane illuminated by landing lights and camera flash as dignitaries and journalists waited in the shadows below. He stepped slowly out onto red-carpeted stairs in a long coat buttoned up against the chill with his wife Emine a step behind him. More dark-suited figures and then his daughter Sümeyye, who had her father's nose and wore a cream trenchcoat. On the apron there were formal greetings in spotlight glare and handshakes held far beyond propriety so that everyone got their pictures. The Tall Man, some of his people called Erdoğan, and he walked a head higher than the crowds. A girl in traditional red dress with a matching doppa presented him with a massive bouquet that he passed straight to an assistant. Erdoğan stood a moment in his habitual stoop then he was climbing into the back of a black Mercedes limousine parked at the end of the red carpet with a Turkish flag on the front right of the hood. The Mercedes took its place in a convoy and was off along highways blocked for his passage alone.

Adiljan waited at the square by the bazaar and it had already been hours. There was a crowd of them ten or twelve deep all with their backs to the Carrefour and the KFC and the minarets of the mosque. In front was a line of police who had delineated permitted space with traffic cones. At last came the Mercedes with a security detail hustled up around it so that Adiljan and the others saw nearly nothing. Governor Bekri was there to welcome the prime minister. Taller still than Erdoğan, he directed his guest deferentially around under the bazaar's glaring white lights as a throng of security, press and entourage schooled behind them. Erdoğan reached out to shake hands with vendors. "How are you?" he asked, shaking another hand. "How are you, how are you?" He stopped at some mounds of dried fruit sold by a mop-haired man who came to only a little over his shoulder. The man offered Erdoğan a sample. Then he took off his doppa and placed it on Erdoğan's head but the doppa was far too small so only perched there while the prime minister stared solemnly ahead for the cameras and chewed on his morsel of fruit.

Members of Erdoğan's cabinet had travelled with him. One of them was Transport Minister Binali Yildirim and he was happily wandering around the bazaar too. His hair was combed back, his suit jacket was unbuttoned and a navy tie lay on top of his belly so the end dangled as he chatted and chewed on dried fruit of his own. The police were still holding the line outside and Adiljan waited still. He had pressed close to the front but could not see much. Some men from the Turkish delegation approached the crowd. "Do you want to see Prime Minister Erdoğan?" they asked. "Maybe to meet him?" The crowd all called back quickly and loudly that yes, they would. And there he was facing them across the limousine and the square was so full now that the crowds stretched all the way to the back walls. The media had taken the best spots and were holding their television cameras above their heads, while the rest of them stood on anything they could for a better view with phones aloft to attempt pictures of their own. Erdoğan waved and held his right hand to his chest. His security detail pushed forward towards the cones and the prime minister was right in front of them. He reached in momentarily to shake hands as a rush of emotion took the crowd. Yildirim was there doing the same and one of the hands he shook was Adiljan's. Then Erdoğan was back in the car and it was pulling away with his security detail sprinting after it. Adiljan looked around and saw in the shining expressions of the youths and the men what it had meant to them. Next to him was a girl and her face was damp with tears. He felt it too. He was a Uyghur, he was Turkic, he was a Muslim and he was one of them.

Those things stayed with him and lent weight to something else that he had been thinking seriously on. He wanted to see Mecca. It was obligatory for Muslims who were able but the way people talked it was also what successful Uyghur men like him did. Let me go, he thought, and I'll see what kind of place it is.

It was necessary then to apply for a passport in your home province and in Ghulja he was able to secure his with the help of 15,000 yuan. Mihribangul tried in Aksu for herself and the children but they were refused. Adiljan decided that he would go anyway and he flew to Beijing and handed his paperwork and another 10,000 yuan to a man who told him two months later that he could not get a Saudi visa. A friend suggested that it was better to apply in a Muslim country. "Do it there," he told Adiljan, "and it will only be a matter of days." Adiljan thought first of Turkey but a travel agent outside the consulate said it could take months more. He settled on Egypt as he knew some Uyghurs studied at Al-Azhar University because it was a center of Islamic scholarship.

The visa was issued quickly this time and he boarded a flight to Cairo one day towards the end of June 2013 planning to return soon to Mihribangul. She was pregnant again with a boy they had already decided to call Omer and close enough to her due date that his mother had come to Urumqi to help look after her.

A half day in the air and he was passing dazed through the artificial cool of Cairo's arrivals hall. Passport control, the laden luggage carousel, customs, then out into a blast of dry heat and a roiling crowd of wolfish taxi drivers. He was sweating in the back of a cab negotiating traffic-clogged overpasses between sepia tower blocks. He eyed the dust and the litter through the taxi window and found the city surprisingly shabby. He had always assumed that other countries must be far more modern than Xinjiang but Cairo felt just like Hotan. The driver dropped him at a downtown hotel. He checked in, slept and called home.

Mihribangul answered. The baby had come early, she told him, but the news came stilted and apprehension stifled his joy. Adiljan's mother was there with her and Mihribangul passed over the phone.

His mother's voice was heavy with concealed emotion. She told him that his friends had been looking for him, slightly stressing the word. Looking for him in Urumqi, she said, but they had gone all the way to Ghulja to visit their family and had been asking a lot of questions. Adiljan knew well that by friends she meant police of some sort. Perhaps officers from the Ministry of State Security to be doing something like that.

His mother did not hand the phone back to Mihribangul.

"You have always been a good son and you have my blessings," she said to him. "Take good care of yourself and never come back here." Then she hung up and Adiljan was alone with the sick feeling tight in his stomach. He got a hold of himself enough to think it through and he saw it was serious. Some combination of his travel plans and his background must have triggered a security alert. Made them decide he was an extremist or a separatist. And if they were going to that kinds of effort to find him then they could only intend arrest. He could not go home right away. They might snatch him before he had even left the airport and he would end up like all the disappeared men he had once known in Ghulja. He needed to handle it the right way but he was adrift from everything he knew, and he had no idea how.

9

Heart disease requires heart medicine. For Xinjiang, this "heart medicine" is a correct view of the motherland and nation, Chinese culture, the core value system of socialism and the core values of socialism. It is necessary to use this medicine to support the correct, remove evil, strengthen the body, and strengthen the heart. We must adopt effective measures to strengthen the recognition . . .

Regarding those who violate the law, those who should be seized should be seized, and those who should be sentenced should be sentenced, there must be no one above the law. The national level must expedite the process of [enacting] counterterrorism legislation, and Xinjiang should also draft relevant local regulations to promote the normalization of counterterrorism and stability maintenance work.

—Xi Jinping's speech at the Second Central Xinjiang Work Forum in
Beijing, May 28, 2014, via the Xinjiang papers

Five years and Saira was used to the village again. Towards the end of 2010 a classmate who she had not spoken to in years had called her unexpectedly. They exchanged quick pleasantries and she got to the point. "Saira," she said, "we know you're living a beautiful life in Urumqi and we're all so proud that you're doing so well and meeting all of these important people. But don't you need your mother? You have to take care of her too."

"What do you mean?" Saira asked. "I send her money every month. We built a whole new house. She's well taken care of."

"But do you know how she spends her days?" Saira did not.

"Every morning," her friend said, "your mother walks to the cemetery, to the grave of your brother and she sits there crying, crying, and she does not come home until late in the afternoon and then she just sits in the house instead. She's all alone and she's having such problems. She needs company, someone to talk to.

Saira was appalled. She had gone to Urumqi for herself but for her mother too, and what was the point of making all that money if her mother was so unhappy? Both of her sisters were married and they could not move back in so it was for her to do something about it. She bought tickets home and left a city that had close to doubled in size since she stepped off that bus almost a decade earlier. Back she went to the village and to the house that Urumqi had bought. Seven rooms, a yard and a wall around it taller than she was. She embraced her mother and said she was sorry for not being there. They talked and ate together and her mother seemed much comforted.

It was nice at first. Feeling the clean, cool air in her lungs. Seeing the familiar icy peaks and the green slopes. Her mother still rose long before dawn and woke Saira up as she always had done. "Wake up, my daughter," she would call, her voice still strong. "The early bird catches the worm and it's afternoon already." Saira would groan and check the time and rarely find it after six. "Why are you shouting so loudly?" Saira would call back. "I want to sleep more." Then she would smell the baursak and the tea and stir herself.

She met up with her old friends and soon saw the gulf that had opened unnoticed between them. "My crops were bad this year," one would say. "I planted as usual, I did everything right but nothing grew."

"My animals are sick," another would add. "They always are this time of year." Then one of them would offer some home remedy that she swore would help and another would offer one that she was just as sure of. It was the provincial talk of pastoral folk. A world that was no longer Saira's. She said her goodbyes and she went home and cried at all she had left behind.

Her mother smiled when she explained why she was upset. "Ok, my daughter, ok," she said. "You can go back to Urumqi, and I won't stop you. But if you stay, I promise that after three days you will be talking the same way as them."

Saira knew she would not and she knew too that she could not leave, especially after she discovered that her mother had developed heart problems. Life had brought her back so she could only make the best of it. She sold her apartment in Urumqi and wrapped up the business concerns that she could not handle remotely. Then she shipped back her belongings and set herself up with a new concern in the village. It was an export business again and sent the kind of handmade and embroidered Kazakh clothing that she and her mother had once made to Almaty and Astana along with fabric, furniture and homeware. She opened a store too that sold and leased the clothes to dancers, musicians, tourists and traders.

She knew what she was doing this time and soon had more than thirty people in the area working for her. A team of women produced the clothing from home as she once had but for fairer wages. Then accountants, receptionists and an office manager handled the things she had no time for. Local authorities lauded her in a series of ceremonies. They gave her certificates for expertise in the design, production and management of ethnic embroidery and an award for excellence. They invited her to speak at an entrepreneurship forum in front of a grand stage hung with red curtains and to participate in an expo promoting the many benefits of doing business in Altay.

Those were years of growth and reform. Things were as open as

they ever had been, passports relatively easy to obtain. A few Chinese
Kazakhs that Saira knew took their chance to travel to Kazakhstan
and apply for citizenship.

One afternoon Saira sat in a cafe talking with a friend and the subject came up. "You know," he said to her, "the border will not always
be open like this. If you ever want to move, you should do it and take
your whole family. Otherwise you might not be able to see each other."

That was around March 2013, when Xi Jinping was named president of China at the 1st Session of the 12th National People's Congress.
Parliamentary delegates voted 2,952 for him with one against and
three abstentions. That officially endorsed a shift in power already
inevitable because Xi had been chairman of the Central Military
Commission and general secretary of the Party since the previous year.
There were always changes and policy shifts with a new president but
there was about Xi the idea that he was the man to take on corruption,
to further reform the economy and to help clean the air and the land
with it. He talked of the China Dream and the great rejuvenation of
the Chinese nation and of building a moderately prosperous society
in all respects. Businesspeople saw opportunities and Saira thought it
would be prudent to stay while things were going well. Anyway her
mother and sisters had no desire to leave. She would not be forever
split apart from them as her grandfather had been from his brother.

An opportunity came to her. The same regional trade-relations
organization that had organized the expo on doing business in Altay
was putting together a delegation to tour events much like that one in
Mongolia, Russia and Kazakhstan. They wanted Saira to be part of it.
Authorities processed a passport for her in three days and handled her
visas and her tickets and hotel bookings. The trip was dizzying and

regimented. She wore her best clothes with a lanyard slung on top and moved around with the expo people shaking hands, making conversation and talking up the opportunities of home. In Kazakhstan she thought of her great-uncle but there was time only for work and the authorities now had such a high opinion of her that there would surely be another chance to travel there.

She kept writing. For local and regional papers and magazines and on a book of her own. The book was a novel following the lives and varied fortunes of several young women who travelled to Urumqi in search of work and opportunity. Some parlayed sweat and chance to success like she had and some were the versions of her who got close to the wrong people and were dragged down into the mire of the city. Some got pregnant, some married and of those some settled happily and some met bitter divorce. It was good work, she was sure of that, but it was not always easy to find time to make it as good as she knew it could be and often when she set aside an hour or two and sat down with intent, she could not write. Inspiration came instead at some forlorn hour of the night so she would stir herself and scrawl or type whatever had come to mind.

She started on another book too. One quite different but a direct result of the kind of thoughts that came to her in the darkness. It was philosophical and argued against the idea often repeated around her that when a baby was born its destiny was already written by God and stretched out before them unchangeable. Saira believed a person could shape their own path.

Together the manuscripts at last came to around six hundred pages but they never quite felt finished and she kept going over them. Refining, rewording, catching previously elusive typos.

Her social circle broadened from childhood friends to entrepreneurs, poets and artists. The kind of people that reminded her of her Urumqi life. New business acquaintances were just as keen to meet her as they had been in the city. Kazakh and Han, local and from far away. They presented her with gifts and money and they sat her down for the best meals and insisted that it was on them. She had suitors once more but still she turned them down. Sometimes one of her friends would lean towards her, concerned when she told them about the latest of them. "Saira, you need to get married," they would say, "you need to have children, a new generation to leave behind. You're already in your thirties, and if you wait much longer it will be too late." Saira gave no thought to any of it. "What do I need with a new generation," she would ask, "with a husband and children to look after? I could have ten children and each one be useless. If I write a book that becomes a bestseller, I would mark my place in history that way."

They talked, and Xi shaped the country anew. There were financial reforms. Committees that spoke of increased roles for market forces and of carefully opening up state enterprises to competition. Of more private sector involvement in the economy and perhaps even foreign businesses. There was always something new then and some of those things crept in unexpected. Like when Saira noticed the fencing going up around the apartment blocks towards the end of 2015. Sections of tight-spaced steel adding, joining and extending until they were one unbroken perimeter twice as high as she was and topped with spirals of razor wire. The only ways in or out were through wrought-iron sections with barred turnstile gates and there were new security guards too. If you wanted to see a friend living in one of the blocks then you had to show your national ID card and tell the guards who you were visiting. It was for prevention of security incidents, authorities said.

That made sense because there had been an increase in theft and vandalism but no thief could have broken through that.

That must also have been why they installed new cameras by busy roads and residential areas, Saira thought, and why state and public security officers became visible in a way they had not been. She would see them around. Han who had moved to the area and local Kazakhs with them. The Kazakhs who joined were usually a particular sort. Ambitious men obedient to the Party in and outside work. They would do whatever their supervisors told them and they would marry and start a family before they were thirty and stay in that marriage if it was unhappy because that was what was expected.

It was not until 2016 that Saira's friends started to talk guardedly about people they knew being arrested. "Oh, did you hear?" someone would ask and mention a name. "They were taken the other day." The reasons her friends gave for the arrests were so peculiar that Saira did not always believe them. Things like having a Quran at home or messaging someone abroad too often or habitually wearing traditional clothing. "Be careful," Saira's friends would say to her, "don't spend too much time around the mosque, they might take you too." She scoffed at them. What would the government do to her just for walking by the mosque as she always had? They were not that stupid.

Saira knew exactly how things worked. Follow the rules that were written and those that were not, work hard and you would be left alone. That was what she had always done and it was known that she was not a troublemaker and certainly not some sort of extremist. The opposite. Authorities so respected her for her accomplishments that they sent her abroad to represent them. It would make no sense for them to throw away their investment.

10

Chinese President Xi Jinping has called for "nets spread from the earth to the sky" to defend against terrorist acts in Xinjiang, stressing long-term stability as the main goal for the region.

Xi made the remarks at the second central work conference on northwest China's Xinjiang Uygur Autonomous Region, a two-day meeting which closed on Thursday.

While urging strengthened precautions and international anti-terrorism cooperation, Xi called for "walls made of copper and steel" and "nets spread from the earth to the sky" to capture terrorists.

The meeting was held in the wake of a series of bloody terrorist attacks in the region, including one in an open air market in Urumqi, the region's capital, which left 39 people dead and 94 injured on May 20.

Calling for "meticulous" religious work, Xi stressed that there should be a focus on helping religion adapt to a socialist society and ensuring the role of religious figures and believers in boosting economic and social development . . .

The president urged all ethnic groups in Xinjiang to "show mutual understanding, respect, tolerance and appreciation among themselves, and learn and help each other," so that they could be united together "like seeds of a pomegranate."

"The more separatists attempt to sabotage our ethnic unity, the more we should try to reinforce it," the president said, adding that unity is the "lifeline" for people of all ethnic backgrounds.

He stressed the importance of Xinjiang residents, no matter their ethnicity, identifying themselves with China, its culture and socialism with Chinese characteristics.

—Ministry of Foreign Affairs of the People's
Republic of China, May 29, 2014

A diljan decided he should wait out whatever trouble had come for him back home. And if it did not pass, then perhaps Mihribangul and the children could travel to join him. The heat and clamor of Cairo seemed no place to do that so he gave up on Mecca and thought again of Turkey, where there was a bigger Uyghur diaspora than anywhere but Kazakhstan. He made his way to the Turkish embassy in Bab al-Louq among the hotels and government offices studded with air-conditioning units and he found a visa section behind a chain-link fence, then submitted an application. It was granted in two hours.

That was where he heard of Zeytinburnu district in Istanbul. Many Uyghurs lived there, people told him. All he needed to do was go and he would have no problem finding them. So he stepped off a flight at Ataturk Airport in early July and took an orange cab to streets of concrete high-rises and pastel-shaded housing blocks with shops and cafes below.

The first broken conversations he had with Turks returned the affinity for the country and for its people he had formed during those hours watching VCDs of Ottoman courts or Istanbul mansions. They already knew about Uyghurs and what they had suffered under the Chinese government. "You come from the land of our ancestors," they would say when he told them about Xinjiang. "You are a true Turk, you are our brother." It moved him keenly to hear it and he felt there might be a kind of home in the city that he had never experienced.

Zeytinburnu was just as he had been told. He quickly found other Uyghurs and introduced himself. They helped him navigate estate agents and notaries to find an apartment and directed him to the chaotic government offices where his visa could be turned to temporary residency. They also advised him to take an alias and use only it whenever he was in the company of Uyghurs. Everyone did, they told him when he asked why, and they did it because there were spies among them. The city was full of them in truth, they said. All reporting back to Chinese authorities. And if a spy found out your name then authorities might try and convince you to go back by threatening your family. It was hard to believe so far from home but Adiljan did as they suggested and chose for himself the name Lokman.

He had a plan of sorts. First he would find a way to make money and work at it as he had done in Urumqi until he was again a success. Then Mihribangul and the children could come and live this new life with him once she had secured passports. He took those warnings of spies seriously and he made sure to avoid any kind of gathering that could be considered political. As a Uyghur that meant nearly everything.

He thought it would not be too dramatic a move for his family. There were passing moments when Zeytinburnu felt like being back in Urumqi. Traffic choked the streets and people the pavements. The shop fronts overflowed with tracksuits, sneakers and knockoff designer bags draped from battered mannequins. On market days vendors hauled awnings tight from anchored ropes and hawked piles of fruit and vegetables to throngs of shoppers till their calls grew hoarse. There was a mosque where the Uyghurs and other central Asians tended to go too. The men gathered to chat outside afterwards and often went to drink tea. Uyghur restaurants served *laghman*, hand-pulled noodles with meat and vegetables, as well as polo rice and spiced lamb kebabs. He even met people that he had known before. One was an old friend from Ghulja he had long lost touch with.

Another he found when he walked into one of those restaurants and was greeted by a man who had run a place in Urumqi he sometimes ate at.

He discovered shops opened by Uyghurs that stocked brilliantly patterned Etles silk, ornate cushions, doppas and patterned and embroidered shirts of the kind that had been sold near his place in the bazaar. They stocked goods too that would have been forbidden in Xinjiang. The East Turkestan flag and its image on clocks, plates, crests and calendars.

It was the same with the outlawed literature sold in Uyghur bookshops. One of those shops was not far from the train station in a unit shared with a mobile phone repair store. Uyghur ran across its faded signage and the spines crowding its gauntlet of shelves. There were translations of Sartre, of Orwell, of Kissinger and of so many others. Works by Uyghur authors too and beyond the censors' reach, the faces of writers and poets jailed, exiled or disappeared gazed out at customers. Young men and women busied themselves digitizing, translating and editing in an office at the back with cluttered desks and torn leather sofas. Preserving abroad the fragments of a culture lost at home.

Adiljan's first business venture was a butcher's shop. Turkish butchers sliced everything into separate, filleted cuts, he noticed, whereas much of Uyghur cooking was bone-in. There he saw opportunity. He rented and outfitted a little space and hired Uyghurs who knew what they were doing to staff it. Things went well enough but it was nothing like jade and there was not much left over after paying wages and bills.

Then a man he knew told him about the trade supplying Turkish clothes to the shops and stalls of Urumqi. There was good money to be made in it and nearly no overheads, the man said. All you needed to do was find a customer and take their order to the local whole-sale markets and have the bales of clothing packed up and shipped. Simple enough.

It was. Adiljan tried it a couple of times and gave up the butcher's shop. He was soon doing much better. He bought himself new suits because appearances were important if you wanted to be taken seri-ously in business but he still lived frugally and saved most of his earn-ings for when Mihribangul and the children arrived. It felt good to plan but he missed them terribly. He called Mihribangul whenever he could. Sometimes she would put the children on but they were con-fused and too young to understand why he was not there. He would call his mother too and his uncle and his brothers. They had to be careful in case authorities were listening in so mostly it was him de-scribing the mundane details of his new life.

He worked as often as he could and passed the rest of his time in his apartment scrolling social media for news of home, at prayer in the mosque or in cafes having guarded conversations about nothing much with other lonely Uyghur men whose real name he never knew. It sounded as if most of them had family they cared about stuck in Xinjiang as well but that was not the kind of thing that was talked about with acquaintances. Some of those men, Adiljan discovered, were educators and intellectuals working to preserve their language and national identity. It was important, but they were surely being watched, so he had nothing to do with any of it.

He was especially careful to avoid the travellers he saw or heard of sometimes who were passing through Turkey on their way to Syria.

Hard-faced men who had grown their beards long and given up on any hope of a peaceful life. Most would join a Uyghur militant group with links to al-Qaeda that was fighting there alongside the opposition to Bashar al-Assad's government.

Chinese authorities launched another "strike hard" campaign in May 2014. Against violent terrorism in Xinjiang this time. They said they did it because of attacks that had been the work of Uyghurs and they ordered migrants in Urumqi and other cities to obtain a new kind of ID called a People's Convenience Card from their hometowns. The card functioned like an internal passport and had to be displayed at checkpoints and hotels and on long-distance trains and buses. Han got them easily and sometimes remotely. Uyghurs often had to travel back to apply and sometimes found the applications were denied when they got there. Like that they were forced to remain in places they had found short enough of opportunity to have once abandoned them.

Adiljan called Mihribangul one day and she said sparely that she and the children were back in Aksu with her mother and Adiljan thought of her mother's house with the cracked concrete yard and cinder block walls. Her urged her again to apply for passports. She told him she could not. He knew that meant she would not because of what had happened to him. He hated it and he understood it. There would be no one left for the children if they took her too.

That was around the same time that calls to his male relatives started to ring out or would not connect at all. It happened too often to be chance and he asked Mihribangul about it. She told him that some of them had been summoned by the police after speaking with him and were now too afraid to pick up. Soon she told him to stop calling her too because the police had phoned and questioned her for three or four hours. It would be best, she said quietly, if he never used her number again.

He wanted so badly to listen to even the few words she could say to him, to hear the children in the background and the sounds of home but he agreed because even in Turkey, he had become a danger to them.

11

Q: The US State Department released the 2014 Report on International Religious Freedom on October 14, criticizing China's performance in terms of freedom of religious belief. The report said that the Chinese government increasingly cited concerns over the "three evils" of "separatism, religious extremism and terrorism" as grounds to enact and enforce repressive restrictions on religious practices of ethnic groups. What is your comment on that?

A: The Chinese government protects citizens' freedom of religious belief and all kinds of normal religious activities in accordance with the law. The American side releases such kind of report year after year in disregard of the facts and makes unfounded accusations against other countries' performance in terms of freedom of religious belief. It will only draw aversion and dissatisfaction from the Chinese and people of all the other countries. We urge the American side to discard political prejudice, respect the facts, stop issuing such kind of report and desist from interfering in China's domestic affairs under the pretext of religion.

I would like to underline that the Chinese government fully respects and protects in accordance with the law freedom and rights of religious belief to which people of all ethnic groups are entitled. Separatism, extremism and terrorism pose threat to national security and social stability of all countries as well as safety of people's life and property. The Chinese government cracks down on the "three evil forces" because it is what needs to be done to uphold national sovereignty, security and social stability, as well as regional peace and stability.

—Foreign Ministry Spokesperson Hua Chunying's
Regular Press Conference, October 15, 2015

Shelek was not home but Tursunay wanted to be close to her family and she made it as much one as she was able. She and Halmirza bought buildings and land left over from the Soviet administration on a dusty hillside outside town. They converted one of the buildings into a house and another into a clinic where Halmirza set himself up as a GP serving the townspeople and the farmers that lived outside it. He diagnosed flu and fever and skin complaints, set broken arms and legs and performed any other minor procedure that could be done under a local anesthetic. Tursunay worked alongsuide him.

On that hillside, she tried to recreate her heavenly patch of Künes countryside. She wanted it to be a Uyghur home and she remembered her mother's flowers. The lilies, cyclamen and peonies. The potted figs and clambering vines. She dug beds in the front yard and planted them, splitting bricks and arranging them into triangles along the edges as she and her brothers and sisters had done. She added something new as well that she had seen the townspeople around Shelek do. She took car tires worn flat and discarded and she placed them on their sides filled with earth and planted more flowers in them.

Things had not always been happy there. Work was fine but she also had to cook and clean and every so often Halmirza's relatives descended on them and she would have to cater for them all. She would spend a whole day and more cooking up huge spreads then clearing up after they left everything in disorder and they never helped even set a table or pick up a dirty plate. It exhausted her and she would say to Halmirza that she did not wish to do it again. There would be no kind words from him to that. Instead he would tell her that she should do what he asked of her because it was her duty as his wife. His sister and his brother told her the same sometimes. "It's because of Halmirza that you are able to live in Kazakhstan," they said if they thought she was being stubborn. "You should show some gratitude." Halmirza's young nephew was different. A bright, kind boy who Tursunay watched grow up and soon loved dearly. If she had ever had a son, that was how she imagined he would have been.

It was true that Halmirza had made her life there possible. While he was working through the process allowing ethnic Kazakhs to become citizens, Tursunay was still on only a visitor's visa. She had not been able to get even a residence permit.

Her family there were not much comfort. Her uncle had loved and supported her but then he had died and the way the rest of her relatives treated her changed. She knew she was not one of them either.

Eventually her marriage was not enough to shield her from Kazakh authorities, and in November 2016 they told her that because her passport would expire soon, she could stay no longer unless she returned home to apply for a new one and a Kazakh visa with it. If she did not leave within fourteen days, they said, they would deport her and ban her from coming back. Five years had earned her nothing. So she called her family to tell them she would be back and she was excited to see them. She had not spoken much to them lately. Calls and messages but fewer of them and less said too. They had not even mentioned the new Party Secretary who had been in charge of Xinjiang since August. Chen Quanguo was his name and he had been transferred from the Tibet Autonomous Region.

Halmirza travelled with her this time. They took the bus along the highway into the desert with the mountains in the distance. They passed through Zharkent and passed by the trucks and their dusty roadside stops. Then came Khorgos and it was far bigger than last time Tursunay had seen it. The new train lines stretched up to the beginnings of the dry port and the ground was levelled where the highway and new buildings would be.

"Ah," said the Chinese border guard when he looked at her passport. "You lived five years in Kazakhstan." Tursunay took it as an expression of sympathy. An acknowledgement of how she must have yearned for home. That was not how he meant it and he ordered her away from Halmirza to an interrogation room. Two hours they questioned her. They wanted to know why she had been so long in Kazakhstan and what she had done there. She told them that Halmirza was Kazakh and about the clinic but that just meant more questions. "What kinds of people visited the clinic? Did the women who went there wear the hijab? Did they pray?"

One of her sisters and two of her brothers were waiting when she at last got out and their reunion was joyful. Halmirza was with them and had already met with relatives of his own. They asked if she was hungry. She was and she put her luggage in her brother's car and they took her to a restaurant right near the border crossing. It was strange, the restaurant. There was a security check at the door and guards went through her and her sister's handbags and patted down the men before they were allowed in. None of the others acted as if it was unusual.

Her brother took the Ghulja road. The checkpoints that had made her decide to make a home in Kazakhstan were still there and some had grown to the size of small police stations with demarcated lanes and barriers and cabins. They stopped at each one and officers told them to get out and directed them into one of the cabins. More officers with sticks and shields were waiting inside and others scanned their luggage and directed them through a body scanner.

There was a smaller room off from the main cabin in the first one and the door was half open. The room was itself a good size and Tursunay saw a chair positioned in the middle of it. The chair was not like any kind she had seen before. Its frame and seat were metal, there was a hinged apparatus at the front that looked something like a lunch tray and there were metal fastenings on the tray and on the legs. Perhaps it was only for off duty police to sit in but she could not understand what the pieces could all be for. At the next checkpoint there was a room with a chair just the same and another at the one after that.

They slept at her sister's place in Ghulja and police arrived at eight the next morning demanding to see her and Halmirza's passports. Tursunay asked what they were doing barging into the house like that. The police only glared and her family tried to hush her. "Please," her sister said, and she looked scared. "Don't talk like that, just stay quiet." Tursunay eyed her surprised because she had always been so bold and there had never been reason to really fear the police unless you had broken the law. The rest of them were just as fearful, just as subdued. Different from how she had known them.

Authorities in Künes rang the day after that and said that she and Halmirza would have to go and register themselves there because that was where they had last lived. The officers at the police station there were nice enough that by the time she was back in Ghulja, Tursunay was letting herself enjoy being home. She and Halmirza sat down with a succession of family and friends that they had not seen for years and ate and talked and laughed. She walked the streets and she took in the familiar sights and sounds and voices. Familiar and not because things were not all as they had been. There were new cameras. Cables and boxes and dark-sheened lenses of every kind gazing out impassive over roads and walkways, shopfronts and doorways. More security checks too and they were everywhere. Body and bag scanners at the entrances to nearly every building of any size. If you took a taxi then the driver would check your bags first. She mentioned it to family but they only avoided the subject.

Once she went with her sister to a mall. The scanners were not working so they went in without being searched and walked together between shops. They were still walking when Tursunay reached into her handbag and sharp metal bit into her finger. She jerked her hand out and examined a bead of blood. In her bag was a knife she had used to peel an apple before they went out and somehow taken with her. Just a little one, just for fruit. Tursunay's sister was ashen and panicked when she saw. "If they find it," she said. "We're done. You'll be sentenced for many years." The panic was infectious. "Let's throw it into a trash can," Tursunay said. "Just get rid of it."

"Look up," her sister said, and Tursunay did and saw a camera. "If you throw it in there and someone finds it then the police will be waiting for us by the time we get home." They did not dare take a taxi and walked back as fast they could without looking conspicuous.

The scare focused Tursunay once more on Kazakhstan. Her passport renewal would take time and the visa application required travelling to Urumqi so Halmirza said he had better go back to check on things while she dealt with it. Ten days after he left the Ghulja police asked her to come back in. An officer asked for her passport again and she gave it to him. No examination or questions this time. He glanced briefly at it then slipped it into his pocket with utter casualness. "This passport," he said, "it should stay with me."

"I need it, Tursunay said. "Please give it back." He told her to leave.

She rang Halmirza in tears and he promised that he would come back and that together they would fix it. "If I go to police station and request your passport, I'm sure I'll be able to get it," he said. A couple of days later Tursunay waited outside as he marched into the station all confidence. He returned robbed of it, all confusion and disquiet. "You know what," he told her. "They took my passport too."

Halmirza was properly worried after that and he spoke to Tursunay of things he remembered growing up during the Cultural Revolution. "These kinds of situations have a cycle," he said. "And one is happening now. We should get our passports and we should leave no matter what." Every day he rang the police and lodged polite, official requests to have them returned. Officers told him that it would not be possible so often that they rented an apartment. Small and up on the fourth floor of a large block. They settled in with the little they had brought with them and bought what they did not. Whatever was happening or was going to happen, it would happen to them too.

12

Although a certain number of people who have been indoctrinated with extremist ideology have not committed any crimes, they are already infected by the disease. There is always a risk that the illness will manifest itself at any moment, which would cause serious harm to the public. That is why they must be admitted to a re-education hospital in time to treat and cleanse the virus from their brain and restore their normal mind.

—Xinjiang Uyghur Autonomous Region Party Youth League recording: "What Kind of Place is the Educational Transformation Center." October 11, 2017 via Radio Free Asia

Adiljan woke with nothing much to do on the last Monday of March 2016 and lingered late in bed. That was how it was most days because there had been no orders from the Urumqi importers for some time and he had found no other work. Prolonged inactivity was draining the remaining purpose from his life but he was still the kind of man ready to meet opportunities wherever they appeared so he trimmed his neat goatee before he showered and picked out his black suit, a dark shirt and loafers.

A while after eleven he walked out into scattered spring sunshine and multi-storied concrete. He made the familiar way to a broad pedestrian boulevard with restaurants and tea houses and the mosque he went to. The week was beginning slowly there too and there was no one he knew around so he sat down on a wooden bench and let time and the city move past him.

He took out his phone. He had still heard nothing from his family but he checked Uyghur Facebook groups and news sites constantly to glean some idea of what was happening.

"Lokman," a voice called his alias, "Lokman." He started up and saw Abdullah. "As-salamu alaykum, brother," Abdullah said. "How are you?"

A mutual acquaintance had introduced him to Abdullah the previous December and told him Abdullah had been part of the wave of Uyghur immigrants who reached Turkey in the 1980s and so had a Turkish passport. Perhaps, the friend had suggested, he might be able to help Adiljan do the same for himself. Adiljan had taken in a crumpled figure of at least fifty wearing a zip-up sweater and thought Abdullah as normal a man as you could imagine. He did not look a success in any way Adiljan recognized but it turned out that he worked in textiles too and had a factory producing women's underwear and bikinis, among other things, and that he often travelled back to China for work. That made him useful to know and Adiljan hoped to learn more about doing business in Istanbul from him.

Abdullah lived in Uskudar, on the Asian side of the city but drove over to Zeytinburnu nearly every day to have a meal or a coffee or to see friends. Adiljan had run into him a few times since that first meeting and Abdullah had seemed glad to see him and invited him sit down for a while in restaurant a cafe. Once Adiljan had dared ask if Abdullah would loan him money to expand his business. Abdullah had refused but when Adiljan had a large order of clothing to pick up near the Grand Bazaar, Abdullah had given him and a friend a ride and waited while they carried the tight-bound bales back to the car.

So Adiljan had decided he was nice enough. Even if he had sometimes asked the kind of personal questions that exiles generally knew
not to ask each other. Questions about his wife, his children and his
background. Or about whether he had ever considered going to Syria
to fight or knew anyone who had. That had unnerved Adiljan but
perhaps it was just that Abdullah had been in Turkey so long that he
no longer shared the same concerns as the rest of them.

Abdullah had also asked if Adiljan planned to bring his family to
Turkey or if he ever visited them. Adiljan said vaguely that he would
only go if he was sure that he would have no issues doing it. Abdullah
said that because he had a Turkish passport and travelled back and
forth for business sometimes, maybe he could take a message to
Adiljan's family. He knew a man too, he said, who could check to see
if it was possible for Adiljan to return safely.

"If you really want to go," Abdullah had said, "I will find some
way to help you do it," and he asked for a copy of Adiljan's passport
to give to the man. Adiljan put off doing that because he wanted to
believe Abdullah but was not ready to give over his identity.

That morning Abdullah seemed cheerful. "What are you doing,
Lokman?" he asked. "Let's drink something you and I." Adiljan was
glad of the company and they walked together to a nearby teahouse. It
was one he liked. A quiet place at the corner of a park with a fenced-
off children's play area out in front where families flocked on the
weekend. There were old photographs on its varnished pine walls and
purple cloths stretched over the tables where men met to nurse their
tea glasses and play endless games of okey. Adiljan and Abdullah sat
down on adjacent sides of a table towards the back and soon began
to run out of pleasantries. A waiter came over and Adiljan ordered

a Nescafé with milk. He was still not used to the coarse, bitter coffee Turks drank. Abdullah opened his phone so Adiljan did the same and again scrolled through his news sites and his Facebook groups. He was still absorbed when the drinks came but a noise cut through the chatter, footsteps and clinking glassware that made him glance sharply up. The abrupt click of a camera shutter.

Abdullah had his own phone in his hand and a new, guilty expression on his face. Adiljan looked at him a moment. "Brother," he asked, smiling a nervous smile and slightly unsure, "did you just take my picture?"

"No brother," Abdullah said. "Of course not."

Adiljan asked if he could look at Abdullah's phone, and Abdullah held the handset out. It was surely a bluff but Adiljan snatched it and opened the image gallery. A jolt of anxiety when he saw it. A picture of him hunched over the table with his head bowed but his face still clearly enough in view.

"Come on, Lokman, it's nothing," Abdullah said, trying a smile. "Just a joke." Adiljan thought of Mihrimbangul and the children and anger gathered in him.

"I'm living here and my family is in East Turkestan," he hissed at Abdullah. "If you take my picture and send it to the government, it'll be dangerous for me and for them."

Abdullah tried to placate him and suggested he delete the picture and hand back the phone. Adiljan did not want to risk it being retrievable. "This is evidence," he said to Abdullah and he dropped the phone into his pocket and promised to return it the next day after checking for any other mention of himself. Abdullah protested. There was personal information on there, he said, and pictures of his wife.

He grew desperate and offered to loan Adiljan the money he had refused before. Adiljan knew then that he was hiding something.

They left the teahouse with drinks untouched. "My car is nearby,
let's talk there," Abdullah said. Adiljan thought a beat then started
down the street at a sprint. He was not used to exercise and was almost immediately out of breath but he quickly outpaced the pursuing
yells and when he looked back saw Abdullah had stumbled over after
only a few steps.

Adiljan went to the apartment of a friend named Mustafa who
lived nearby. He explained to Mustafa what had happened and asked
him to witness what he found when he looked through the phone.
Mustafa agreed and Adiljan took the phone from his pocket and saw
it was locked. Of course it was. They conferred and went back out
to the tea house where Abdullah was still standing forlorn. Adiljan
said he would hand back the phone if only he could delete the picture
himself and Mustafa said he would guarantee it. Abdullah protested
again but relented and traced the Z-shaped gesture that unlocked
the keypad in the grime of a car parked next to them. Adiljan looked
long enough to be sure he had it then ran again and hid himself in
an alley.

Back in Mustafa's apartment and Adiljan began going through
Abdullah's WeChat messages. A few stood out right away. Conversations
that consisted mostly of voice notes with men who had unidentifiable
profile pictures and who Abdullah had saved only as nicknames.

One of the men was a Uyghur-speaker that Abdullah called Abbas
and who seemed to work on the Chinese side of the Khorgos crossing.
Abdullah appeared to have recently met Abbas while travelling from
Xinjiang to catch a flight from Almaty back to Istanbul and messaged

him again a few days afterwards offering to make himself useful. "If you have anything you want me to do," Abdullah said, "I'm ready to serve you."

There was another man that Abdullah listed only as Watcher who spoke Uyghur with a light Chinese accent. And there was another still Abdullah referred to as Mukhtar. All three of them had instructions for Abdullah.

Abbas asked for information on the bombing that had killed more than one hundred people outside the central train station in Ankara the previous October and wondered whether a Uyghur might have been involved. He wanted details of events organized by Uyghur foundations in Istanbul and a list of attendees for a meeting of the organization that called itself the East Turkistan Government in Exile. Abdullah provided names but stressed that he would not be there himself. "I don't go to these things because I'm not a member of any association," he said. "I'm not with them, you need to make this clear."

Watcher sent passport-style headshots of different men and asked Abdullah to find them in Istanbul and take further pictures once he did. He asked for information on Uyghur restaurants too, including one in Zeytinburnu that Adiljan knew well. Who worked there, he wanted to know, and did they fly the East Turkestan flag? Abdullah did as he was asked whatever the order and supplied photographs of several men with details of their employment and a picture of the restaurant facade taken from his car.

Then there were the messages referring to Adiljan. After a call that must have mentioned him, Abdullah told Abbas that he had taken a picture of this Lokman but that you could not see his face in it so he would try to get another later that day. He then sent a picture of

Adiljan standing at a restaurant counter in his cream slacks with his body turned away from the camera. It was from a lunch a few weeks earlier that Abdullah had insisted on.

Abdullah offered Adiljan up to the men as a useful source of information with numerous friends and connections in Istanbul. "He has a very large circle and that circle is very important," Abdullah said in one message. "So let me take a picture of him and of his passport to clarify his identity."

Everything the two of them had done together he reported in detail. Often as they did it. "I couldn't reply to you before," one voice message went, "because Lokman and another guy were in the car with me." He was speaking of the friend of Adiljan's who had helped him carry his bales of clothing. "The two of them are doing business and have things to buy in the bazaar so they were with me."

In another message Abdullah said he had spent many days trying to follow Adiljan but had not got much information out of him. He went on to say that he was trying to set up a meeting between Adiljan and a Chinese contact in Istanbul. That must have been the man who Abdullah had said could arrange for Adiljan to return safely to Xinjiang. A trap that would have ended in his disappearance.

"Now look," Adiljan told Mustafa and put down the phone. "This man is 100 percent a spy."

It was not shocking to see when it was all laid out in front of him but he was angry. Angry for himself, for his family and for all Uyghurs trapped in Xinjiang. At least Abdullah's handlers had only a picture of his back and a pseudonym. They could not know his real identity. Adiljan did not delete the teahouse picture from the phone yet. He wanted proof of what Abdullah had done.

Abdullah called Adiljan the next day from his usual number. He must have reported his phone stolen and got a new SIM card. "You're a spy," Adiljan told him, nearly yelling, "a traitor."

"If you don't return the phone," Abdullah said, "I'll tell the police that you and Mustafa are members of the Islamic State, and they will arrest and deport you."

"Do what you want," Adiljan told him, and hung up. As a precaution he took a video on his own phone of the WeChat conversations, playing the voice notes out loud and opening the pictures. Then he went to the chairman of a Uyghur association in Istanbul who also owned one of the restaurants mentioned in Abdullah's messages. He explained the situation and handed over a copy of the videos. "Don't worry," the chairman said, "if anything happens, I'll send you a lawyer."

Later in the week Adiljan met up with Mustafa again and the two of them wandered Zeytinburnu together. It was not long before men in civilian clothes and short haircuts approached from each side of them and showed their guns and badges. "You're under arrest," one of the officers said, "on suspicion of Islamic State membership and for threatening a Turkish citizen."

Abdullah must have made good on that threat and probably pointed them out because there had been no questions about their identity. The officers cuffed them and put them in the back of a Ford van with blacked-out windows. Then they drove the short distance to Zeytinburnu police station, processed Adiljan and Mustafa and took them to holding cells in the basement.

Turkish police officers were nothing like the ones who had arrested him back in Ghulja. There were no insults or violence and he was able to call the association chairman, who said a lawyer would be with them soon.

The police still started their questioning angry. "How did you dare to threaten a Turkish citizen?" they asked. Adiljan told them that he had not threatened anyone but that Abdullah had taken his picture to send to the Chinese police and so put his family in danger. What else could he do, he asked.

Their manner softened. They knew about Uyghurs and about Xinjiang.

"You were betrayed by one of your own countrymen," one of the officers said. "That is unforgivable, but stealing a phone is still illegal and our responsibility is to protect our citizens." They asked Adiljan which phone was Abdullah's and they would not let him turn it on to erase the picture before he gave it back.

The chairman's lawyer soon arrived at the station and Adiljan and Mustafa were released into a world subtly shifted. If Abdullah had his phone then he would be in touch with his handlers again. Chinese authorities must know exactly who Adiljan was.

13

Break their lineage, break their roots, break their connections, and break their origins. Completely shovel up the roots of "two-faced people," dig them out, and vow to fight these two-faced people until the end.

—Chinese religious affairs official Maisumujiang Maimuer, August 10, 2017

One day in April of 2017 they took a trip to Künes to see Halmirza's sister there. Four cramped hours and Tursunay stepped off the bus ravenous. Her phone rang before they had a chance to move any further. The police and momentary excitement that their passports were to be returned but the officer asked only where she was and told her to stay there because they had something to talk to her about. A siren approached and officers told her but not Halmirza to get in the car and go with them.

Tursunay asked them where and they replied she needed to attend a meeting. "I'm very hungry," she said. "I want to eat something first." They told her to forget about that because there would be food there and that it would not take long. The officers took an arm each and steered her towards the car. She shook them off. "Don't," she said, "I'll get in myself" and she sat in the back of the car. Halmirza stood there as the doors closed and watched still and silent as they drove her away.

They stopped first at the office that issued identification cards. They took her fingerprints and a blood sample. They scanned her

retina and her face from every angle and they made her read from a
sheet of paper to map her vocal patterns. Then they were back in the
car and this time drove to a school of some kind. The building was
quite beautiful, Tursunay thought, with well-maintained grounds and
a fence around it. They went in through the front gate and then on
to an assembly hall on the left-hand side of the complex that was full
of Uyghurs and Kazakhs with some Hui among them. Hundreds of
women and men altogether and some that looked still children. Police
were stationed at the doors and at one side were officials who seemed
to be in charge. Tursunay moved closer to the officials and heard them
complaining to each other. Asking what they were to do with so many
people and how they were supposed to look after them.

The others there stood or sat in cowed groups. Tursunay saw the
fearful, questioning looks on their faces and thought them like herds
of sheep. She would stand up to it all even if they would not. She
raised her voice until she was shouting, screaming almost, and she
demanded to know why she had been brought there. "Why don't you
release us," she asked them. "What am I guilty of?" A police officer
came over to her. "You should shut up," he said. "If you don't we
have orders to shoot you." He took his pistol out of its holster and the
hall spun when Tursunay saw the dull, heavy metal of it. It was spin-
ning still when one of the officials began to address them in Uyghur.
Something about them having to learn to resist extremist ideologies
and illegal religious activities. Before they were allowed back to their
homes, he said, they would all have to be educated.

Guards took them to the school's dormitories. There must have
been students in them not long before because there were beds and
bedding already there. Tursunay and a few other women were directed

to one of the dorms and a guard closed the door behind them but did not lock it because there was no lock. He told them to stay there until someone came to take them to the canteen for food and Tursunay messaged Halmirza to tell him that she would not make it back that night.

The other women were mostly older than her. They fretted and cried and asked each other why they had been brought there and what would become of them. They kept at it as the sky darkened outside and none of them had slept much by morning.

Things did not seem so bad after breakfast. The food must have been what the students had been getting and it was pretty good. Boredom encroached on their anxiety in the dorm and they mostly lay on their beds and talked about when they were going to be released. It would surely be soon. Mealtimes came around and the ones who did not feel like eating just stayed where they were. On the third day a guard told them that would no longer be allowed. "You all must listen, you all must follow the rules," he said. "When it is mealtime you come, you line up and you wait for your food." They did and the men did the same on the other side of the canteen. There were soon more men than there had been in the hall that first day and some of the women saw their husbands among them.

A week and the place felt like no kind of school. The good food was gone and every meal was a bowl of soup with a small steamed bun. The soup was ladled dark from a large pot and said to be vegetable but was not any Tursunay recognized. The guards told them then they would no longer be allowed simply to stay there for free. It would be necessary to study, they said, and lessons would begin soon.

The lessons took place in the school classrooms. One was led by a man who guards said was from the courthouse and who told them about the Chinese legal system and the importance of rule of law. One was about the two-child family planning policy and the punishments awaiting those who violated it. The guards introduced another teacher as an imam from a nearby mosque. He was solemn and turbaned like an imam but he did not talk like one. He said instead that they need no longer pray nor wear a headscarf nor even necessarily hold their faith because they should above all believe in the Party. That was too much for Tursunay and she could not imagine why a man would go against everything he had committed his life to. It was shocking and it was wrong and it was absurd. Everything the opposite of how it was supposed to be.

There were more new rules. No speaking Uyghur or Kazakh or anything else but Chinese. Those who could not speak Chinese should say nothing. During breaks the guards would take them to the school yard and make them sing red songs like "East is Red" or "Without the Communist Party, There Would Be No New China."

> *Without the Communist Party, there would be no*
>   *new China*
> *Without the Communist Party, there would be no*
>   *new China*
> *The Communist Party toiled for the nation*
> *The Communist Party of one mind saved China*
> *It pointed to the road of liberation for the people*
> *It led China towards the light*
> *It supported the War of Resistance for more than*
>   *eight years*
> *it improved the people's lives*

> *it built bases behind enemy lines*
> *it practised democracy, bringing many benefits*
> *Without the Communist Party, there would be no*
> *new China*
> *Without the Communist Party, there would be no*
> *new China*

One of the older women did not know enough Chinese to sing along properly and so she was punished. Tursunay saw it all. The guards made her stand a whole day out in the courtyard. It was hot with no clouds for solace and the old woman stood with her eyes down and her hands by her sides and she began to tremble. She trembled so much that she fell to her knees but the guards only made her stand again and Tursunay cried because they could do nothing to stop it.

That blackened soup got her sick enough that she threw up every time she ate and grew quickly weaker. Classes continued. Laws, government, history, the dangers of religion. The teachers talked of the need for improvements in their mental hygiene and of the dangers of the ways they had been living. Then one day the classroom dissolved in front of Tursunay and she passed out. She came to in a clinic and called Halmirza from her bed. She called him the days after that too and sent him pictures of her medical charts and begged him to help get her out. Because he was a doctor they even let him in to see her. It would be ok, he said. He would speak to someone, he would make sure of it.

He soon messaged to say he had taken reports of her condition to the camp chief who was Kazakh and seemed reasonable so would undoubtably help. A week in hospital made it mid-June and guards returned Tursunay to the school. She found it changed again. The windows were barred and there were locks on doors that had not had locks before. She did not have time to see much more because guards soon called her from the dorm and told her she would be allowed to go back home. Halmirza's visits had secured an order for her release.

She felt only glad to be out but Halmirza was worried still. He went back to the police station to ask about their passports and he pleaded with them until they agreed to return only his. Tursunay would have to stay as a guarantor so that if he caused any problems or talked negatively about China and the Party then the repercussions would be visited upon her.

Halmirza tried to argue but Tursunay insisted he go. He was the Kazakh and it was his citizenship being processed. Once that was done it would be easier for them both. So he left and she remained alone in the Ghulja apartment. He called when he had made it home. "It will be ok," he said once more. "Just wait for me to contact you."

14

Uyghur students enrolled in schools outside China are being ordered by Chinese authorities to return to their hometowns by May 20, with family members in some cases held hostage to force their return, sources in Xinjiang and in Egypt say.

Launched at the end of January by authorities across the Xinjiang region, the campaign has frightened targeted students, some of whom have disappeared or been jailed after coming back, a Uyghur studying at Egypt's Al-Azhar University told RFA's Uyghur Service.

"It seems that everyone who went home from Egypt has simply vanished," RFA's source said, speaking on condition of anonymity. "We haven't been able to contact any of them."

—Radio Free Asia, May 9, 2017

A Saturday at the beginning of June and the morning sun poured into the kitchen as Saira sat down with her mother for an unhurried breakfast. Around ten her phone rang. It was Kayrat from the local public security branch. Kayrat was Kazakh and Saira knew him well enough to say hello in the street when she saw him and she did often enough. She knew his family too. He was a few years younger than her. Good-looking but with something cold about him that made her sure he was the kind of man who would do whatever was asked of him and not think a moment about it afterwards.

He told her they needed her passport. The police were collecting everyone's for safekeeping, he said, but no need to worry. She would be able to get it back if she had to travel.

Saira was irritated but not particularly worried. The same thing had been happening elsewhere and she was not well enough connected to be an exception to any new rule. By eleven she was outside the security office and the day was warm and gleaming with a brightness almost oppressive. Kayrat was waiting inside with others she recognized. Kazakhs too, Kazakhs like him.

She greeted them. "I think we've met before," she said to one of them. "Do you know me?"

"All of the village knows you," he said, and he did not smile.

She gave them her passport. Then they demanded her phone and the jewelry she was wearing.

She asked why they needed them and said she had done what they asked but she took out her phone and unhooked her earrings and bracelets anyway. They told her to put her hands out in front of her and the recognition of something badly wrong twisted in her as the cuffs closed cold around her wrists. Saira shivered in her chair and recited silent prayers that it would soon be over.

Some Han officers joined too. They wanted her phone's pin code. She gave them it and they looked through her phone but apparently did not find whatever they were looking for because they put it down and started asking questions.

Was she a member of a religious group, they wanted to know, or a political one.

"No," she said, "I'm a businessperson. I'm not into politics."

What about Serikzhan Bilash? Was she in contact with him? "No," she said, "of course not."

She had heard of Bilash in an indefinite way but no more than that. He was a Chinese Kazakh who had emigrated to Kazakhstan then started businesses there and blogged sometimes about his international travels and about Kazakh issues and identity. They did not seem to believe her because they pressed her about him as if he was a person of some concern but she had nothing else to tell them.

They asked it all again. About politics, about religion, about Bilash. It became so drawn out and so frightening that she could not keep track of how long they had been at it.

"Don't you know about the new policy?" one of the officers asked after a while. "Anyone who reads banned books, who prays at the mosque, and who has WhatsApp or any of the other banned apps is in trouble. Give us the names of the people you know who do that and who have them."

It must be a ruse of some sort. She did not use apps like WhatsApp or Facebook that were not permitted by the government and she would have heard about a policy that arrested people for praying.

She told them she had no names for them. That she was not political, that she was not a criminal and that she knew no criminals either. They said that they would hold her for a while somewhere where she would receive training.

Saira did not understand. She asked what kind of training and they said she would learn how to speak and to write Chinese. She said she was a Chinese-Kazakh translator and had been for years.

"Well then," they said, "you will learn how to do business."

"I already run businesses here in the village," she said. "You know I do." They told her not to talk back to them and one of the officers noted something about her in a notebook.

"You have travelled too much and been exposed to foreign influence," they said. "That is why you need extra training."

"I did not travel alone," Saira told them, "the government took me to represent them in Mongolia and Russia and Kazakhstan. They issued me a passport and secured the visas."

They ignored her.

"What terrorist groups have you met in other countries?" they asked. "How do you know Serikzhan Bilash?"

"None, of course none."

"Well," they said, "we have a list of countries that support terrorism and extremism. The first one is America, the next is Turkey and the third is Kazakhstan."

They told her that they were going to search her house and took her to a car with an officer gripping each arm. Then they put her in the middle back seat and kept holding on to her like she might be crazy enough to leap out while they were moving. More of them got into two other cars, and they turned on the sirens and drove wailing and flashing blue through the streets.

The noise filled her ears so completely that she asked if for the sake of her mother's heart they might at least turn off the sirens when they got closer to her home. They did and she asked them if they might also park around the back of the house and enter through the yard so as not to worry their neighbors. The officers looked at each other and spoke of the irrigation canal running a way behind the house. One of them suggested that perhaps she might get free of them and throw herself into it to escape. The idea was absurd, it all was. Saira could think only of what mistake could have been made for her to be taken like this because there was nothing she had done that could possibly be connected with the Three Forces. She had known so many Kazakhs in China. Writers, shepherds, entrepreneurs. Not one had ever suggested that Xinjiang was their land alone and should be taken from the Chinese. It had not even occurred to her. They would soon realize that and it all would be resolved.

There were ten officers altogether. Six Kazakh and four Han. Saira's mother looked scared when she came to see who was hammering on the gate but said nothing and gave Saira a look that demanded obedience. The officers walked Saira through the house and stopped first at her library. The books there interested them greatly. She had well over a thousand. Novels, poetry, theory and along with them the printed manuscripts of the two she had written. The Han could not understand the titles but the Kazakhs cast over them and yanked several from the shelves.

They found a Quran first and asked what she was doing with that. She explained that it was not for religious purposes but a resource for the book she was writing on the violable nature of destiny. They did not listen and brandished a collection of poetry by a nephew of the great Abai named Shakarim Qudayberdiuli. They showed each other the monochrome cover portrait of Shakarim with his long beard and black skullcap. They pointed at his beard and asked why she was reading a book written by a terrorist.

"He died a hundred years ago," she told them. "At that time everyone had beards and terrorism did not even exist. And he is the nephew of Abai, a famous writer."

For that a notepad was produced and something written that she could half read about not cooperating with them.

In another book an officer found a passage about fasting. "And this? Why are you reading this Wahhabi?" he said, speaking of the strict Islamic movement.

"It's a description," Saira said. "The author's not a Wahhabi. He actually used to drink a lot." The one with the notepad wrote something again. Then the Kazakh and Chinese officers talked to each other and one of them fetched some large white sacks of the kind seed or fertilizer come in. They started collecting her books and putting them into the sacks. It took ten sacks altogether. Packed so full that it took two or three of the officers to lift each one. They carried the sacks out behind the yard and dumped them in the half-dug holes of an abandoned construction project and then brought Saira out with them.

Officers flanked her while another appeared with a jerrycan of gasoline and she felt a nauseating awareness of what was to come. She glanced around. Her mother was watching from a distance and gave her the same look as before and Saira knew she was scared that she might start crying and anger the officers or make some wild, impossible attempt to stop them.

The books did not burn easily. First the officer with the jerrycan glugged some gasoline into the hole and held a lighter to it. Flames darted quickly over the sacks and subsided again. More gasoline went in before it caught properly but then it was really going and it was awful to see.

Saira held back the tears that smarted her eyes and squeezed tight the sob rising in her throat while the officers chatted with each other, indifferent. They stood out there past an hour. Two or three perhaps. The sun weighed on her and the heat from the flames radiated out into the still air so she felt it on her hands and her face. She was sweating but the shivering came again and she could not stop.

The officers took her back inside and carried on searching the house. Each room, each cupboard. Under beds, under mattresses. They got tired of it every so often and took breaks to smoke cigarettes but their collection grew to include flash drives with Saira's company documents, her laptop with her work files as well as the electronic copies of her books, her camera and her spare phone. When there was nowhere left to look they took Saira back to the yard. It was starting to get dark and the books were still burning weakly. They poured the rest of the gasoline on and when the flames died down again asked Saira's mother for a shovel and started piling dirt on top of the ashes and charred spines.

The officers took her back out through the house. Saira's mother saw that they were leaving and she tried to delay them. "Wait," she said. "Please sit down, I will make us all tea if you just wait a moment." The officers told her no and Saira looked blankly behind her as they put her again in the back of the car and turned on the sirens and lights.

They drove the short distance towards the local prison and stopped outside a tattered two-story place around the corner that had once been a cafe with a motel above it. The authorities must have taken control of it but the ground floor still looked pretty much like it always had, only the tables and chairs were stacked and shoved to one side. Upstairs their feet met motel carpet. The doors in the corridor were all closed and the ones on the left of the corridor had been fitted with locks on the outside.

A man appeared from one of the right hand doors. The boss of the place from the way the officers acted around him. He looked at them and at Saira and asked if she had been given a medical checkup. The officers said no and the man looked worried. "I cannot accept her today," he said. "If she has some disease, she could infect the other trainees."

Back in the car and they drove around to the prison. In the gloom she saw a whole new building had gone up next to the old one. Her cuffs were removed inside and guards led her down a corridor and stopped at a metal door. They opened it and she saw a room with a series of narrow beds. Hands shoved her down onto one of them and tossed a grubby blanket in after her.

She looked around and saw she was not alone. Lying on one of the beds was a woman who looked Kazakh and who avoided Saira's gaze. Sitting up on another was a Han woman of around fifty who was looking on impassive and eating sunflower seeds from a bag.

"Well," asked the Han woman, "why are you here?"

She carried on ferrying one seed then another to her mouth, cracking them expertly between her teeth and spitting out the cloven hulls, then swallowing the kernels. There was a pile of the hulls by her bed.

Saira said she did not know why she had been taken. "In that case," the Chinese woman said unhurriedly, "you'll probably be in here for something like ten years. Maybe twenty."

Saira's head spun. "But why?" she asked. "I'm not a criminal. I've done nothing wrong to anyone."

"Exactly, you're a political criminal," the woman said. "Your kind of cases are much more serious than the others."

"What about you then, why are you here?"

The woman was a sex worker, she said, and she had agreed to sleep with a customer who paid for it as usual. Afterwards he insisted that they do it again but said he would not give her any more money. So she had refused and they had argued and he stomped off with his wounded pride and called the police to denounce her.

"They will let me out in a couple of days' time," she said. "I'll be fine."

Quick anger at the injustice of that and of everything else rose in Saira.

"You actually are a criminal, you broke laws," she said, raising her voice. "You could give a man a disease which could infect his wife, ruin his family. I didn't do anything at all."

The woman did not seem much bothered by that.

"Listen," she said, pausing briefly to crack, hull and swallow another seed. "There are many people like you around here. When I said you would be here for ten or twenty years, I was just trying to make you feel better. You'll probably be in here for the rest of your life."

The tears that Saira had stifled earlier rushed back and overwhelmed her so completely that she could only lie there gasping at the air with her head sunk into the blanket. She must have fainted then slept deeply because the next thing she was aware of was the spoonful of vinegar that someone was pouring into her mouth. She coughed back to consciousness with the sour, sharp taste on her tongue and the awful remembrance of the previous day. Guards surrounded her and from outside the room she could hear a man's voice telling someone that she should not be there, was not his responsibility and would have to be transferred back to their department instead. A while later that same man came into the cell. He was middle-aged and Chinese and he told Saira to stand up and then kicked her in the back of the legs so her knees buckled.

"Look at her," he said. "She's worse than a dog."

More guards came, including one of the men from the day before. Youngish, with a mole over his left eyebrow.

They cuffed her again and took her to a local medical clinic where nurses took blood and ran tests and after a while said that Saira was perfectly healthy. Then it was back to the old motel above the cafe.

Guards gave her a uniform to change into that was blue with four pockets and a number on the back. They gave her a blanket and it was the cheap, thin kind that cost only 10 yuan at the store. They gave her a toothbrush as well and it was not like any she had seen before. It was really just the head and the bristles were attached to a piece of plastic the size and shape of a thimble.

Then they pushed her through one of the doors into the stuffy warmth of caged bodies. It was recognizably still a motel room but the sharp edges were covered and the window was barred. Eight beds were wedged inside and all but one were occupied. Saira collapsed onto the free bed and realized how empty her stomach was. She had eaten nothing since the previous morning.

15

The fourth point is that we must continue to fight the "three battles and one war." The first battle is our "Strike Hard" campaign. We must continue to maintain our posture of striking hard and keeping up the pressure. This is among the General Secretary's series of strategies for governing Xinjiang—especially the spirit of his important speech delivered when he participated in the discussion with the Xinjiang delegation, in which he called for a full-fledged "Strike Hard" campaign to "root out existing terrorists, reduce their numbers, and clear the soil that allows them to grow," and to crack down on them by delivering heavy punches, by destroying the weeds and digging up the roots, and by exterminating evil once and for all.

Three critical tasks. First, we must round up all of the key individuals involved in violence and in endangering the safety of the people, and we must arrest all those who ought to be arrested. After rounding them up, we must severely punish those who are unpardonably wicked according to the law, and hand down harsh sentences for them. For those who deserve less than five years of imprisonment, we can release them, but "release" means to put them in training camps to learn both languages, technical skills, and the law. We will release them into employment whenever they are transformed, whether it takes one year, or two years, or three years.

—Secretary Chen Quanguo's Speech During a Video Management Meeting of the Autonomous Region Stability Maintenance Headquarters, May 28, 2017, via the Xinjiang Police Files

Serikzhan knew it was bad when he heard Chen Quanguo was to be the new Party secretary of Xinjiang. He opened some of the WhatsApp groups that Chinese Kazakhs used to forward and share news and he began recording voice notes with anxious urgency. "A storm is coming, Chen Quanguo is coming," he said.

"He made a genocide in Tibet and now he will make a genocide in Xinjiang. Only one thing can be done. Run, just run and run now because if you delay by even a second it might be too late and you will find yourself trapped."

During Chen's time in Tibet he had enacted a brutal and insidious extension of the state apparatus aimed at stomping out any signs of separatist thought. Surveillance, oppression, control. Thousands of Han were transferred to the region. The government said it was to boost economic development but the well-paid jobs and new positions all went to them. It sounded familiar to Serikzhan.

Newly arrived police deployed to the smallest villages and staffed the precinct buildings being set up every city block or two. The authorities called them convenience police stations and justified the name by saying they stocked first-aid kits and phone chargers. All they really did was watch unceasing over their section of security grid. To ensure nowhere went unseen, neighbors were instructed to keep an eye on one another and inform the police about any irregularities they witnessed. Families were told to do the same.

Stability Maintenance, Chen's policies were called, and his stability required arrests. Anything could be considered a provocation to Party rule. Police went after those who called for independence as they always had. They went after Buddhist nuns and monks too, demolishing their homes and taking them off to camps and re-education centers. They went after the self-immolators, beating them if they survived and harassing their families whether they did or did not. They went after the people who prayed and carried pictures of the Dalai Lama. They gave years in prison for things that had previously been allowed like having religious or historical texts on a phone. They took social and cultural leaders, writers and artists. They took children.

There were protests and police responses so unsparing that they provoked more in areas that had previously been quiet. Those were crushed too. People talked of the many disappeared, the unexplained dead.

It was all hidden from the rest of China by censors and firewalls. The mostly pro-government Kazakh media did not much mention it either. Serikzhan spoke good English and he read the reports by international papers and human rights organizations. He watched videos online. He saw everything wrought by Chen Quanguo and knew it would come to Xinjiang.

So he expected a bigger reaction to his messages. Urgent replies, outright alarm. They met mostly silence and the suggestion he was exaggerating. He kept on going anyway. Recording voice notes, typing out Facebook posts or setting up his phone for a YouTube video. "Go," he would say, "just go. Chen Quanguo is coming, and he is a killer."

That was not how Serikzhan usually spent his time. Business took up much of it. His concerns included an import operation, four residential buildings around Almaty, and herds of cows and horses managed by members of his extended family. He was a success by any measure but he did not flaunt it with a blacked-out Mercedes or villa slung with chandeliers like some of Almaty's rich and influential. He lived with his wife Laila and their son in a three-room apartment and he drove a Nissan Almera. What he did do with his money was travel anywhere he felt like going at any time he felt like it. If a city occurred to him then he would simply call a travel agent and fly out the next day. He had a good circle of relatives, friends, classmates and colleagues too. Every weekend there was a celebration of some sort. A wedding, a birthday party. Sometimes three or four. It was a good life and it satisfied him greatly.

He periodically wrote about his trips abroad for a modest online following and sometimes added his thoughts on the Kazakh people, homeland and history. There had been a time when he thought himself destined to be a writer and dreamed of taking his place among the great voices of Kazakh literature. That was back in the late 1990s when he was not long past twenty and still living in Xinjiang's Bortala Prefecture about a hundred miles northeast of Khorgos. He had written several long pieces on Kazakh life in China for local magazines and people had liked them. It had felt like a calling. His father had founded a high school for the children of nomadic Kazakh families and growing up there Serikzhan had never thought of himself as being Chinese and had not seen many similarities between themselves and the Uyghurs either. He was a Kazakh and he lived on the land where the grandfathers of his grandfathers were buried.

Because that was still land ruled by China, he moved to Kazakhstan and sought out the opportunities of Almaty. He had loved its avenues and its tower blocks and the mountains enclosing it and decided to make it his home. There were several writers there that he admired and he met with some of them but economic necessity pushed literature aside for more tangible returns. He got residency and a while later citizenship so he gave up his Chinese passport. A brother joined him. Eventually he met Laila.

The realities that he left behind sometimes impinged uneasily upon his life. His parents moved to Urumqi and he went to visit them in the summer of 2009. He saw the beginnings of the horrors of July 5. Student protesters it looked like. Some of them carrying Chinese flags to show they bore the government no hostility. Police had already surrounded them when he passed and were filming their faces with a kind of handheld camera he had not seen before.

Evening came and the electricity went out. Mobile signal and internet too. His sister-in-law's parents in Kazakhstan must have known something was wrong because they called the landline to ask if things were ok. Then the landline went out too and the gunfire began. Morning and they found the outside walls of houses on the street pocked all over with bullet holes that no one ever came to patch up.

Serikzhan boarded the long-haul bus for Almaty at the central terminal a month later. The mass arrests were well underway and police on the roads towards Khorgos must have stopped them twenty times to check IDs. He was a Kazakh resident with a passport and visas so he was safe but he saw the Uyghurs separated out and ordered off the bus to have their documents examined and their luggage scoured. And he saw some of them taken away while the bus continued onwards.

Xi Jinping's appointment as general secretary of the Communist Party at the end of 2012 and president in March the following year had filled Serikzhan with vague dread. It reminded him of the things he had read about Germany in 1936. He began to write more on Facebook and WhatsApp whenever time and inspiration coincided and he called on Chinese Kazakhs to reunite with their people in Kazakhstan. "Come here," he would say. "I know that Ili, Altay and Tacheng are our historic motherlands but it may no longer be safe for you." He talked about history. Of the Kazakh military leader Osman Batur, who fought the Chinese communists and was hanged for it. Of

Qazhyghumar Shabdanuly, who had been jailed for his words alone. He talked about the various Jewish communities that had existed in China and been subsumed into the rest of the population with little trace. In Europe, he said, even after the centuries of persecution that lead to the Holocaust, there were still Jews who maintained their identity. "It is impossible for you to coexist in China and keep your culture and religion," he said. "China will devour everything, assimilate everything and history will repeat itself."

The Chinese government did not view its Kazakh population with quite as much suspicion as it did Uyghurs but it could be difficult for them to get passports too and Serikzhan had suggested ways to do it. A bribe could be effective. Like taking the right police officer out to dinner or for a night of drinking. Or just handing over cash. Another way was to travel to Hong Kong with the help of an excuse that involved commerce. And another was to buy one of the vacation packages advertised everywhere. Five days in North Korea and Japan or a week in Singapore, Malaysia and Thailand with tickets, hotels and a guide all included. The tour companies, he explained, were often able to smooth passport applications out with the police for the sake of their own bottom lines.

He told new arrivals what they should do when they reached Kazakhstan. How to find work, how to find an apartment. "It is not so difficult," he would say. "You already speak the language and Almaty is only 180 miles from Khorgos. Once you're here, you'll find many Chinese Kazakhs and they can show you how to get residence papers and green cards and eventually citizenship."

Serikzhan's parents and his sister came too and he was glad of it because Xi's rule was already hardening. In 2014 he heard things about certain imams being arrested along with other religious figures. In that there were echoes of the Cultural Revolution.

Chen, though, Chen meant worse was to come. So Serikzhan carried on with his posts and his voice notes. "A disaster is coming," he told them. "You must leave any way you can. And you must do it now.

He could not have said more, implored more urgency but few followed up with him and it was as if he was pouring his warnings into an abyss of indifference.

16

Reasons for Detention

The Qaraqash Document is a list of people in the "re-education" system [of Qaraqash county, Hotan province] who have relatives overseas, suggesting that overseas relatives are a major reason for suspicion by the government. However, only a small number of entries in the document list overseas relatives as a reason for internment. The numerous other reasons listed in the "reasons" column provide evidence of why the government is sending people to internment.

Reason	Number
Birth policy violations	115
Unsafe post 80s, 90s, or 00s person	91
Ex-convict or other past law violation	40
Wore veil/wife wore veil/had beard	33
Applied for passport (and didn't leave the country)	25
Reason related to religious practice	23
International travel	20
Religious extremist thought infection	19
Related to prisoner	12
Movements within China	8
Possessed or watched illegal media	5
Two-faced official	5
Related to someone outside of the country	4
Did not obey shequ personnel	4
Fraudulent marriage certificate	3
Overseas communication	2

—Uyghur Human Rights Project, "IDEOLOGICAL TRANSFORMATION": RECORDS OF MASS DETENTION FROM QARAQASH, HOTAN

T hings in Ghulja slipped further still from the way Tursunay re-membered them. Not just the cameras and the scanners but the checkpoints every 350 feet or so and the police more often than that. So few women wore headscarves and the men were all clean-shaven. No one talked of much of anything in public and at home people would hide their phones when they had even the simplest of conversations. They made calls only with the greatest care and were sure to never say things like Bismillah or inshallah, God willing, or As-salamu alaykum.

It all put her on edge and she did not go far from the apartment unless she had to. Once that meant the hospital where a doctor wrote her a letter to say that she was sick and would be receiving treatment that she sent to the camp boss in Künes. Often it meant the police station after they invited her in to talk. They wanted to know where Halmirza had gone exactly. What he was doing and when he would return. She told them what she could. He was a doctor, he would be tending to his clinic and he would return in time.

There were training centers in Ghulja as well. Several of them. One was at the old flax factory. One was in what had been a hospital and another was in what had been a Party building. They were well guarded and the guards were not just outside but on the approach roads behind metal barriers and rolls of wire. So none of Tursunay's neighbors knew much about them but that they were sure they did not want to see inside.

Tursunay did not believe that she would be taken again. She had been reeducated. Whatever the Party was doing there was no reason to do it twice. She was not as sure when she would be allowed back to Kazakhstan. And she could not just sit at home while she waited so she decided to look for a job. She applied for a few but even the ones that at first sounded receptive turned out to be no longer looking once they had run her identity documents. Eventually she stopped trying.

Fear had set in all about the city by the middle of 2017. Police patrols made continual rounds of the streets during the day. Glance out any time at all and it would not be long until you saw one. Body armour and helmets on. Sticks and shields ready. They reminded her of soldiers ready to fight some ancient war.

At night they came to take people away. Up at her fourth-floor window she saw and she heard all of it. The sirens closed in first then then came the engines and the brakes and the blue lights shining behind the blinds. There would be slamming doors and shouted orders and groups of police fanning out to doorways. Often enough it was her building. Heavy boots echoed in the hallway and she counted the flights of stairs as they came. Sometimes they stopped short of her door. Sometimes they carried on right past so close she could hear their breathing and she shrank back despite her certainty it would not be her. Then they would be at a quickly opened door and Tursunay would try and work out which apartment it was and who they were there for.

Daylight revealed the missing. One half of a familiar couple walking bowed and silent. A grandparent failing to calm young children. A front door gathering dust. There were shops on Tursunay's block. Convenience stores, bakers, butchers. The kind where the owners knew their customers and if one did not have enough money for their milk or their flour or their bread one day then the owner would tell them to take it anyway and pay the rest tomorrow. When Tursunay walked out some mornings she would see the shutters still pulled down on a shop that usually opened early and they would remain down the next day and the days afterwards. There was a store near her. An old couple ran it and were always sitting side by side behind the register chatting to customers and each other. One day Tursunay walked in to pick something up and the place was silent. The husband's seat was empty, his wife silent. It pained Tursunay but she looked ahead and said nothing because the missing were not to be acknowledged. When she talked with friends and neighbours and asked after someone she had not seen recently they would make sure their treasonous phone microphones were hidden well away and simply whisper "taken, taken" then talk of something else.

In those same conversations Tursunay gathered snatches of the ways they had been living. They listened to the raids too but without her assurance that the knock would not be at their door. No one slept anymore, they said, and when they expected their time was soon they would lie in bed fully dressed. They did not wish to be dragged from their home in their underwear and if they were to be held until winter then they wanted to make sure they had warm clothes with them.

17

Writing in the official Xinjiang Daily, the region's deputy foreign publicity direc-
tor, Ailiti Saliyev, said Xinjiang was stable, harmonious, prosperous, open and
modern.

Visitors see this for themselves when they visit, subverting the impression
created in Western media of the opposite, he added.

"Many people say from the bottom of their heart: 'The happiest Muslims in the
world live in Xinjiang'," he wrote.

—**China official says Xinjiang's Muslims are "happiest in world",**
Reuters, August 25, 2017

They were woken by "March of the Volunteers" blaring tinnily outside.

> *Arise, ye who refuse to be slaves!*
> *With our flesh and blood, let us build a new Great*
>   *Wall!*
> *As China faces her greatest peril,*
> *From each one the urgent call to action comes forth.*
> *Arise! Arise! Arise!*
> *Millions of but one heart*
> *Braving the enemies' fire! March on!*
> *Braving the enemies' fire! March on!*
> *March on! March, march on!*

Then came footsteps and shouted orders to get moving. It felt early.
The guards soon opened the door and told them that they would be on

cleaning detail. Down to the prison yard and she saw men were held there too. Most of the others were Kazakhs but there were Uyghurs and a few Hui. She recognized some of the women. A dancer who would come to the shop with her friends to rent clothing for their performances, an older woman from a few streets over. She examined them with quick glances and decided that they must also not be regular criminals but the political kind.

The construction work next to the prison had finished but the place was still a mess. "Whoever does the best job cleaning it all up, whoever works the hardest," the guards said, "they will be able to leave first." All of them believed it so when the guards split them up into groups and handed out tools, they began sweeping and scraping their way through the new building as quickly as they could. Saira twisted her finger so badly she thought she might have broken it but she carried on while the guards kept a lazy eye on them and chatted.

The guards talked as they herded them around and told them prosaically that the government had plans for them. The new building was to be a training center where Saira and the others would soon be but a factory would be built next to it and they might work there as well.

So in the end, the guards said, they might all be kept there indefinitely.

Some of the younger people tried to bargain with them. "Ok," they said, "if you want to keep us here, we can't do anything about it but at least you could give us our phones back." The guards laughed and told them to be quiet. Saira said nothing because the guards must only be trying to scare them and the things they were saying could not be true. She was sure to be released after a month or so and certainly no more than three. There was no law she had broken and it was like the proverb went, there are no waves without wind. Only criminals ended up in prison.

For fifteen days they worked and then they were moved into the new building and placed in one of many metal-doored cells opposite a wall with a long list of rules on it. The cell was around two hundred square feet and there were only five of them in there but it was much worse than the motel because the floors were concrete and there were no real beds. The only other things in there were a toilet in one corner and a security camera hanging from the ceiling next to a loudspeaker. Saira suddenly missed the motel window and the fragments of the world she had glimpsed from between its bars. In the new cell, they never saw the sun at all.

Days had a new rhythm there. The speakers woke them at six and they would raise their aching bodies to attention until the last crescendo had died away. Then they had five minutes to fold their bedding as neat and straight as a soldier in a barracks. That was not easy when the threads were soon coming loose from their flimsy blankets but if it was not done right then the guards would snatch it up and tell them to do it again.

They were allowed to use the toilet in the cell after that. Each would take their turn and for Saira, for all of them, the humiliation was absolute. Everyone could hear everything, smell everything. The guards would come again and take them one cell at a time to a row of sinks along the corridor where they would each be allowed another five minutes to wash their hands and to use their thimble-small toothbrushes.

Back in the cell the guards brought them breakfast. It was a soup of sorts like all their other meals. Carrots, potatoes and cabbage boiled together and served in a plastic cup. The vegetables were obviously never properly washed because Saira could feel the grains of grit and soil in her mouth. There was around twenty minutes for that and they mostly sat silently after they finished because there were strict rules about the ways they could talk. Only short exchanges were permitted and they were never to say anything that might be considered religious.

Eight and the guards put on their body armor and their helmets, picked up their shock batons and opened all the cell doors to herd the trainees to their lessons. The classrooms were lines of desks and small plastic chairs facing an area with a whiteboard where the teachers stood that was separated from the rest of the room by metal bars. Around fifty women and men were taught in each one, all crunched in three to each desk. The guards distributed exercise books and stayed in the room the whole time. Sometimes they moved people around to make sure the young people were sat apart even though the trainees were only permitted to look silently ahead.

The teacher would arrive and the class would begin. First was usually Chinese language. Speaking, alphabet, writing. Continuing implacably through the course no matter that some of the trainees could not follow it.

Then Chinese history. There was Confucius, the Han dynasty, the Century of Humiliation and the atrocities inflicted on China by the Japanese. Mostly they were taught of the glorious heroism and sacrifice of the revolutionary days. That meant the Long March and Mao Zedong's rise to lead the People's Republic of China all the way through to the country's rejuvenation through Xi Jinping Thought on Socialism with Chinese Characteristics for a New Era. The way they talked about Xi was like Saira's grandmother's stories of Mao. It was him they were being taught to thank for their good fortune, their employment and their bread.

There would be a break of twenty minutes and during the break, they would stand up and sing red songs.

Videos after that shown on a television that was also behind bars. Some videos were on history or how China's military had grown more powerful even than America's or how the One Belt One Road international infrastructure project was creating a Chinese world order. There were educational films explaining correct modes of thought and the dangers that extremist beliefs posed to the trainees and to the country. There were others on the conflict in Syria and the Muslim terrorists fighting against the government there. "Without us," the guards would tell the trainees afterwards, "you would be just like them."

Lunch was back in the cells and they would sit with their gritty cups in enforced silence before classes started again. The afternoon lessons would be on Chinese society and the legal system. The rules they were supposed to follow on marriage and terrorism and work. Those were often taught not by their usual teachers but by worried-looking people working for relevant government departments. Sometimes they were neighbors or old classmates of Saira's. They said nothing but they must have recognized her and she felt ashamed to be seen like that. Two hours and some more red songs and they would be taken for their daily exercises.

Those were military-style. Calisthenics, marching on the spot. Some of the older trainees could not do all the things ordered of them and the guards would grow irritated at their struggles and yell or stroll over and kick at them.

Six and there was thirty minutes for soup. Afterwards they would wedge themselves into their chairs for more videos. That was usually time for Xi Jinping Thought and an overview of his latest accomplishments. They would have to memorize his words and principles. A new one every day.

> The youth must refine their professional skills. Study is the ladder of progress and practice is the way to improve capability. Quality and capability of the youth is directly linked to the course of realizing the Chinese Dream.

One might go, or

> The whole society should vigorously promote the spirit of hard work, encouraging people to realize their dreams and change their fate through honest work, while opposing negative thoughts such as profiting from other people's work, opportunism and indulging in pleasure and comfort.

There was a woman in Saira's cell who was hunched and gray and could never remember them properly. The guards shouted at her for it and she would always cry. It got so that she would start crying just at the sight of Xi for fear of the berating to come but that only made the guards shout at her more.

Then the day would be over and there was nothing left to do but lie down on the concrete draped in that flimsy blanket. There were rules for how they did that too. They were never to pull the blanket any higher than their chests and they were not to lie face down so that their heads would always be in view of the cameras.

Saira started keeping a calendar on scraps of exercise book paper she slipped from class. Tiny grids of digits that she crossed off with each day that passed them by. It helped her remember there was still a world outside. It was strange, she did not think much about her business or the money she was losing. Or her phone, her laptop or even her family. What she longed for most was to be out in the countryside. To feel the sun and the wind on her face and to sit under a tree and read as she had as a child. To breathe in deeply and freely of the land that was hers.

Interrogations interrupted their routine every few days. Someone from the security apparatus would do them. A Chinese man with pockmarked skin and his hair cropped tight to the sides of his head often led Saira's. He always asked his questions gently but persistently and the way he did she knew he'd been trained for it.

"Tell us," he would say, "who did you pray with? Who among the Kazakhs that you know were political? Give us a name and you will leave this place sooner." Sometimes the interrogator was the man with the mole over his left eyebrow who had been there when she was arrested. He knew what he was doing too. Occasionally it was a woman. Kazakh and young with neat hair and perfect eyebrows. She was always nice to Saira and interspersed her questions with excuses and supplications. "Don't worry," she would say, "I won't hurt you. I am obliged to be here and I have no choice so please don't hate me." Perhaps that niceness was all just part of her training.

Once a week they had to write essays against harmful ideologies or influences or people. The subject was often religion and they would regurgitate the words of their teachers. All faiths had been created to govern the people and the workers and were a disease to correct modes of thinking.

Other assignments involved attacking the ideas behind Kazakh statehood or denouncing Chinese Kazakhs like Serikzhan Bilash or Osman Batur or the welterweight boxer Kanat Islam. Islam had won an Olympic medal for China but left to live in Kazakhstan and renounced his Chinese citizenship. The guards seemed to particularly hate him for that. "He is a traitor," they would say. "He was born and raised in China but left and started making propaganda against us."

People in surgical masks, lab coats, hairnets and gloves would come every Friday to empty a large syringe into their upper arms. It was to protect them against getting the flu, the guards told them. It scared Saira and it scared her cellmates and between them they wondered quietly what might be in the syringe and what effects it might be having on them. Friday was also visiting day and sometimes Saira's mother or her sister were able to come. The visits were in an empty room and both the trainees and their visitors would be escorted by guards. They could not embrace and Saira would have time only to shake her mother's or her sister's hand and ask how they were.

On Saturday or Sunday they were allowed into the shower block, where it never dried out and the water was always cold. They usually had three minutes each to take off their clothes, wash and get dressed again but sometimes the guards hurried them out in less and they would have to step out of the shower with soap still in their hair. They began making the most of their time by taking off their clothes in the queue and standing shivering with their uniforms clasped to them.

They were able to wash their uniforms afterwards. That had to be done in one big communal tub of water as cold as the stuff they showered in. They kneaded away up to their elbows in it and quickly started to lose the feeling in their hands and their forearms. It was rough work and Saira and the other women felt bad for the young girls and for the older ones among them. Often they would tell them to pass their uniforms forward and would wash them for them even though it was forbidden.

It was a wash day the afternoon that the guards mustered them in the yard and the loudspeaker told them to sing one of the red songs they had learned. The trainees sang and kept on singing and as they did the guards started taking them away in groups. They came to Saira and took her and a few others to a room where there were two guards already. A Chinese woman and a Kazakh man Saira recognized. The Chinese woman was holding scissors and the man said that there were orders to cut their hair. For hygiene reasons, he said, and so that none of them would be able to hang themselves with it. Saira's hair was long and satin. She often wore it in one thick braid that reached nearly to her waist and she had always been proud of it.

"Why would you do this?" Saira asked him in Kazakh. "You know hair is the beauty, the dignity of a Kazakh woman." The Chinese guard asked what she was saying, so the man translated. "A lot of Chinese women have their hair short," the guard said, and she was angry. "You have no right to ask why you were taken here, why you are kept here, and why you do this or do that. So shut up."

The students stood and waited and cried when the woman came to them. She would grab a fistful of hair and hack her way crudely through it right up to the base of their necks. Saira cried too. There was no mirror but she could see the bony faces and big eyes of the others looking out from their ragged crops. Without their makeup and their clothes, they already felt bad. Losing their hair was much worse.

They filed into class the next morning, and the male trainees flashed shocked glances their way. Saira watched them back and she could see their white knuckles and the veins popping from their temples and their necks. She could nearly hear the flexed tendons, the rushing blood. The men could no longer hold their fury and they stood up. A few, then all of them. "We are not criminals," one said, "or you would have given us sentences. But tell us how many years you want to keep the women and how many years you want to keep the men and give us the years for the women. We will stay here for them because they are the mothers of our children and our future generations. You have no right to humiliate them like this."

The guards did not know what to do and Saira saw fear in them, real fear, and it was a while before they had control of the room again.

She wrote a couple of lines of poetry in her head afterwards.

I may not have my long hair
But I still have the pride it once gave me.

18

Instructions for how to answer questions asked by the children of concentrated education and training school students when returning home.

1. Where are my family members?

They're in a training school set up by the government to undergo collective systematic training, study and instruction. They have very good conditions for studying and living there, and you have nothing to worry about. Tuition for their period of study is free and so are food and living costs, and the standards are quite high. The provision for food is 21 yuan or more a day — that's even better than the living standards that some students have back home. Our officials accompany them at study every day, offering counseling and assistance, and they eat the same food and live in the same dormitories, so you have absolutely no need to worry about how they're doing.

2. Why do my family members have to take part in studying?

Your family member has been sent to study because they have come under a degree of harmful influence in religious extremism and violent terrorist thoughts. If at some point the "Three Forces" (terrorism, separatism and religious extremism) or people with ulterior motives incited or bewitched them, the consequences would be severe. If they came under the sway of extremist ideas and did something that they shouldn't do, they would injure not just innocent members of society, but also themselves and other family members, relatives and friends, including you. I don't think that's something you would ever want to see happen. So for everyone's security, for the happiness of your family, and so that you can focus on your studies, we had to send them to a school at the first opportunity to undergo concentrated education and study.

—Issued as part of the Xinjiang Party Committee's Announcement
Concerning Doing a Good Job of Ideological Education
and Management Service Work for Middle School, High School,
University and Technical School Students Returning Home
on Summer Break Period and Whose Family Members Are Being
Punished, 2017, via The New York Times.

Adiljan never saw Abdullah again. He was gone from his usual haunts around Zeytinburnu and people said he had not been seen at his factory or his office either. So Adiljan returned to his life of worry and lonely quiet.

Summer settled over Istanbul and the heat stifled his days then radiated from the concrete after dark. At the end of August he read about Chen Quanguo's appointment as Xinjiang Party head and it all became unendurable. He had to speak to his family, to know what was happening at home. No phone calls. He would not risk their well-being by checking on it. He opened a WeChat account, then found a friend of Mihribangul's on there and messaged asking if she could get Mihribangul to open an account of her own. Mihribangul did and his joy and relief was infinite.

There could be no expectation of privacy from the state so their conversations were intermittent and mundane. Just a few words a week usually but he still called her *Mihribanim*. My merciful one. And she called him *Wapadarim*. My loyal one. She sent pictures sometimes. A few were selfies but most were of the children. Smiling happily at home, playing outside, bundled in comical layers when the weather was colder. Bumaryam and Muhammed were so much older than he remembered. Omer, the son he had never met, was already a round-cheeked toddler up on his feet.

He would open his phone and flick through those pictures in his many spare moments. There was one of Mihribangul that he particularly liked. It showed her gazing levelly at the camera in neat makeup and a cream headscarf patterned with lilac flowers. He set it as his phone background and looked and looked at it. She had always been so devoted, so good to him. He had performed the duties of a husband

and father well but he had not always felt that same devotion to her. Only now that they were apart had he realized that no one would love him as she had or understand him as she had and it hurt unbearably that he had not appreciated her as he should have.

Adiljan used WeChat just for Mihribangul but it had become one of the only ways to speak to people back home so his Istanbul friends had accounts with long contact lists and busy newsfeeds. Around that time they started to tell him the app was behaving strangely. They would be exchanging messages just as usual and then the recipient would be simply gone. Removed from their inbox and unsearchable. Parents, children, friends, neighbors, old classmates. All gradually disappeared until those contact lists were empty and newsfeeds blank. Uyghurs in Istanbul had all heard Xinjiang residents were being detained for receiving international calls so perhaps they were just blocking anyone they knew abroad for their own safety. Adiljan hoped that was all it was.

Then he started to hear of the surprise calls friends had been getting from some of those same relatives. Often people they had not contacted in a while for fear of endangering. The calls consisted mostly of instructions. Shave your beard and cut your hair short, some were told. Stop wearing a headscarf. Take down Facebook posts mentioning Uyghur history or Instagram photographs with Turkish flags in the background. Visit the Chinese consulate and affirm you are still a Chinese citizen. Strange requests in a manner strange enough that it was clear they came from the government.

He heard too about the go-betweens. Strangers who used WeChat or messaged on WhatsApp from Hong Kong or Russian or even Turkish numbers unbothered by the Chinese ban on it. They usually

said they were in an exile's home town and introduced themselves po-
litely as Party cadres or members of the local security apparatus. The
go-betweens would make it clear that family contact was to be only
through them from there on and they might mention the possibility of
a video call. In exchange for this kindness there would be questions
about the exile's life in Turkey. What was their address? Where did
they work or study? When would they be coming back to China? Had
they had children abroad and if they had, what were their names?
Could they send pictures of them?

Answer those questions satisfactorily and the news from home during
that promised call was always good. Everyone's relatives had new jobs
and had become rich. They were all so happy because things were better
than they had ever been right across the district. None of them ever said
As-salamu alaykum when they first spoke or God bless you when they
waved goodbye and darting eyes and out-of-place shadows or muttered
words of instruction betrayed the presence of others in the room.

News of what Chen was doing in Xinjiang began to make it to
Istanbul. In cafes people talked of messages the Party's local neighborhood committees had sent to Urumqi resident networks informing
people of new security policies. Residents should volunteer to have
their phones scanned for harmful content, one said, and so should
report promptly to the neighborhood committee building with their
handset and a charging cable. Those who did not volunteer would
be subject to further police checks and the committee would not be
responsible for what happened then.

Authorities summoned people to gather biometric information for
a third generation of identity cards. The second generation Adiljan
had already contained a digitized photograph and a microchip holding

personal information within its laminate construction. These new ones would include blood and DNA, fingerprints and retina scans.

Adiljan read of the new flag-raising ceremonies at each housing block like the ones they had in schools and government offices. Uyghur residents had to present themselves in the main courtyard every Monday morning at eight then form into neat rows and sing the national anthem good and loud with no talking, wandering or headscarves permitted. There was something else called the Join Up and Become Family Scheme that filled him with awful dread. It sent Party cadres to live with Uyghur families and share their food, their homes and even their beds while compiling detailed accounts of their behavior and watching over their ideological hygiene.

Adiljan could ask Mihribangul about none of it, only continue their mundane and spare messaging. Others in the city whose relatives had disappeared from WeChat tried desperately and repeatdly phoning any number they had that still connected. Sometimes someone would answer after weeks or months with wild and uncharacteristic excuses. Everything was fine, they would say. They had only taken a trip away for a while and forgotten their phone. Or they might say they had been in the hospital and unable to reply but had now recovered.

There was no way to tell for certain but when things like that happened, the suspicion was that they had been taken to the camps. Vocational training centers, the government called them, but they were said to be heavily guarded and apparently tens of thousands of people were held in them already. Even in Istanbul there were euphemistic ways to talk about them. When people spoke of the big school they meant prison. When they spoke of the small school that meant a camp. Adiljan could not stop thinking about it.

He had nothing to do but think because his clients in Urumqi all went completely quiet. He talked to others in the export business and they said it had happened to them too. Word eventually sifted through that the police had closed all the Uyghur-run import offices dealing with Turkish goods and arrested everyone involved.

April 2017 and Mihribangul messaged for the first time in months. She told Adiljan abruptly that they would have to cut contact completely and she would have to delete him from WeChat. She was going to work in an Aksu fabric factory, she said. Adiljan panicked and tried to persuade her not to. She was not a seamstress, he said, that was not her job, and the children needed their mother. "We need to go," she replied. "It's the order of the government and they'll take us there."

There was another thing, she said. The government had told her she needed to have sterilization surgery, and it would be performed before she left. She said goodbye, and she disappeared from his contact list.

In the awful weeks that followed, Adiljan fixated on that conversation. He replayed it constantly in his head and tried out things he could have said that might have persuaded her not to go. He wondered what it was like there in the factory and imagined her sat at a production line of sewing machines.

Then in July, a message appeared in his WeChat inbox. It was one of Mihribangul's friends and there was something she had to tell him. Adiljan's father had been taken to the big school, she said. There was more and it was the thing Adiljan had not allowed himself to think. Mihribangul had been taken to the small school and the children were with her mother.

19

Q: Our fellow-Kazakhs are asking us for help. Ten of them have recently been convicted, allegedly for praising Kazakhstan and staying in contact with fellow Kazakhs there, but also for talking about their wish to move to their historic homeland. Young men get convicted for just going into a mosque to pray. We can't allow this to continue. If bridges are broken, how can we have friendship between peoples? There are no terrorists among our people.

A: We know about the problems in Xinjiang. They have terrorism and extremism there, but I've never heard about Kazakhs being persecuted.

—President Nursultan Nazarbayev at the World Kurultai of Kazakhs, a global gathering of Kazakh diasporas in Astana, 2017

T he first of the women started coming to Serikzhan in the summer of 2016. They would call or message asking for help and he would invite them to an Almaty cafe or serve them tea at his family's apartment. That was not particularly unusual. Individual charitable appeals circulated continually on Kazakh social media. Funds being collected for widows who could not make rent or for parents struggling to care for sick children. For families whose homes had burnt down. For orphans and the elderly. Serikzhan always donated what he could and did it often enough that people sometimes just contacted him directly.

These women were struggling to get by too but they explained that it was because their husbands were gone. One of them was named Sagira and called Serikzhan in tears to tell him what had happened.

She and her husband were Chinese Kazakhs who had recently emigrated to Kazakhstan with their young children and applied for citizenship. Her husband's passport had neared expiration as they waited for their applications to be processed and Kazakh authorities had told him that it must be renewed if he wished to stay. He had gone to the Chinese consulate on the eastern outskirts of Almaty. Passports were swiftly renewed there for Han workers and just as swiftly replaced for Han tourists who had lost theirs but Sagira's husband had been told he must go back to China. So he had and then he had disappeared. No word since shortly after he crossed the border, Sagira said, and calls to his phone did not connect.

More women. Five, six, seven, ten. More missing husbands. Chinese Kazakhs as well, the women told Serikzhan, but who had long before moved to Kazakhstan and settled there, started families and in some cases become citizens. They had returned to China for different reasons. Answering summons from hometown authorities demanding some piece of paperwork, visiting family, working a cross-border job. A few had called their wives and said that police had confiscated their passports so they could not return. Others had been arrested according to their families back home but they did not know why.

Still others were, like Sagira's husband, just gone. The women wept as they told Serikzhan that without their husbands, they had nothing to care for themselves or their children. Serikzhan was easily moved to tears and he would cry too and promise to help. He paid electricity and gas bills and gave them money for food but he assumed that these were isolated problems. That the men were victims of bureaucratic errors or had broken the law and kept it from their wives. Perhaps he should have seen it sooner but he was not a prophet, he told himself afterwards. It was not so easy in the moment.

Then there were still more women and stories that added concerning new details. Some of their husbands had received calls from their family in China saying that the police had visited and made it clear that if the men did not go back there would be problems for them. A few of the men who were still in touch with their wives had said that they were staying in China to attend a government training course on Chinese language and politics. That made no sense. Why would a man in his forties or fifties with a job and a wife and several children in Kazakhstan suddenly decide to study Chinese? The pattern revealed itself with each case and Serikzhan realized that the things he had warned of were coming to pass. Chen Quanguo's work had begun.

By 2017 it was not just wives who sought his help but mothers and elderly fathers too until there were fifty or so of them and it was too much for him alone. He began to call sympathetic friends, mostly businessmen who were well off or truly rich. They divided out the women and parents between them depending on their resources. "You take care of these five," Serikzhan would say, "for you these ten," and soon they were a makeshift network meeting the needs of those left alone.

Word of what they were doing was passed around and the requests grew to include help of a different kind. Would it be possible, wondered the husband of a missing wife who had worked across the border at Khorgos, to trace what had happened to her? Might Serikzhan know, asked the mother of a son who had gone on a work trip to purchase fabric and never returned, if there was a way to rescue him? Serikzhan always tried to console them. "Don't worry," he would say, "We are all brothers and sisters and we will try our best to get them back for you." And though he said those words in the moment, he had no idea whether there was anything they could do.

Conversations with members of his new network always came around to Xinjiang because it was becoming clear that things were happening on a scale even Serikzhan had not imagined. Not only to Kazakhs but to Uyghurs too and other mostly Muslim minorities. The Hui, the Kyrgyz, the Uzbeks and the Tajiks. A darkness was gathering there and when they searched for information there was little of it to be found. The border seemed to be closed to all but Han and a few privileged others. Calls and texts and WeChat messages were going unanswered.

They wrote letters to the Kazakh foreign affairs ministry and heard nothing. They wrote more that fared no better. Serikzhan organized his best-connected friends then he flew to Astana. He took a taxi towards the gleaming surreality of the capital's skyline, the two-hundred-foot Pyramid of Peace and Accord and the twin golden towers everyone called beer cans, and he met with deputies and told them what he knew. He had been confident in his mission. Sure that the Kazakh government would solve whatever was going on. Because were not Kazakhstan and China both original members of the Shanghai Five and the Shanghai Cooperation Organisation who jointly abided by the Treaty of Good-Neighborliness and Friendly Cooperation?

And was not President Nursultan Nazarbayev *Elbasy*, (Leader of the Nation), who had made supporting the Kazakh diaspora one of his foreign-policy goals?

Once Nazarbayev found out what was happening, Serikzhan reasoned, it would take only a phone call to Xi Jinping and the Kazakhs held in China would be released.

He soon realized the extent of his naivety. The officials he spoke with at the Ministry of Foreign Affairs and the others too said that it was not their place to interfere in internal Chinese issues. "These people are not foreigners," Serikzhan would say. "Some of them are Kazakh citizens, and the rest are married into Kazakh families. How is that a Chinese issue?" The politicians never explained but some of them mentioned with detached generality that the Kazakhs living in China had once run from Kazakhstan and the implication was that they were less Kazakh than the ones who had stayed to suffer violence and famine.

It had obviously been decided high up that there must not be a fuss. Part of it was surely the economy. There were billions of dollars of trade with China and more every year. Chinese influence was growing to match. Kazakhstan was a crucial point of the One Belt One Road global infrastructure campaign and China owned and ran nearly everything in the Khorgos zone. There were Chinese interest groups, Confucius Institutes, trade and business and educational ties. There were statements expressing satisfaction with the significant achievements of bilateral cooperation in various fields. There were vows to strengthen political mutual trust and mutually beneficial cooperation and make continuous contribution to safeguarding regional and world peace and sustainable development.

Kazakhstan was not closed off like China. You could download apps and watch mostly what you wanted but Nazarbayev had controlled the country since before 1990, before it was even independent. Elections were not free or fair and protests and dissidents were punished swiftly. If Nazarbayev wanted relations with China that way, that was how they would be.

Serikzhan and his network saw that they must do what the government would not. In the spring of 2017 around twenty of them formalized their activities into an organization and called it *Atazhurt* (homeland) for the common roots that Kazakhs shared. More brothers, sisters, wives, husbands, parents and children kept coming to them and they themselves would travel from village to village, home to home. They soon needed a space to work from and for people to gather so they rented a small office. Serikzhan shifted his attention further from his various business ventures until he was dedicated to Atazhurt nearly full time. He made the journey to Astana again. He invited deputies and foreign ministry officials to the finest restaurants and paid influential acquaintances to set up meetings with the kind of people who would not otherwise have seen him. It made for only months of nothing.

He tried something new. Politicians might have decided to shut their eyes to what was happening but if more people knew then it might force them to act. Atazhurt organized a conference in Almaty in the fall of 2017 with families of the missing. They invited all the journalists they could think of and many of them came. Serikzhan stood with the families in front of arrayed microphones as they spoke about their loved ones and cried. The journalists crowded in to capture their tears and reported eagerly on it. People paid attention. Activists, writers, poets, celebrities.

Atazhurt kept going and organized a second conference at the year's end. Nearly none of those journalists who had reported so enthusiastically appeared when it came time. That seemed odd until Serikzhan heard that intelligence officers from the National Security Committee had been visiting different newspapers and channels and telling them to drop the subject.

NSC involvement was a problem because most of the press was either controlled by the government or supported it and the outlets that did not found themselves the subject of threats, harassment and ugly lawsuits. The only way forward, Serikzhan thought, was to involve the foreign media, the Western media. He was the only Atazhurt member who spoke much English, so it fell to him.

First he needed information. He started a WhatsApp group and added friends originally from Altay and Tacheng and Urumqi. From Changji and Barkol and from Mori too. He shared voice notes explaining that he wanted to speak with people who had information on what was happening in Xinjiang and asking that his call be spread as widely as possible. It was not long before people began messaging or asking to meet and telling him about the detentions and new restrictions that they had heard of or seen themselves. Serikzhan made notes and recorded what he could.

More kept coming. There were Uyghurs among them, ethnic Kyrgyz, even Tatars. With each, Serikzhan asked if he could publish what they had told him. They were mostly too afraid to but a few gave their permission. He translated it and Laila helped. "Look," he told journalists when he messaged them, "this is what is happening in China, in Xinjiang. It is a genocide."

Reporters from American and European newspapers, channels and websites contacted him with questions. The recordings he had made turned out not to be enough and Serikzhan started sending out phone pictures of the families of the missing. Then one of the journalists he was speaking with asked if he could send higher-quality pictures and possibly some video too. Atazhurt hired a camera operator named Galym. The videos they made were simple testimonies. The facts of a case given by a family member in Kazakhstan speaking directly to the camera. It was Galym's idea to upload them to Facebook and to YouTube. Whenever someone came to interview Serikzhan about Atazhurt's activities, he made sure that Galym videoed and posted that as well and he enjoyed being at the center of it all.

He bought more phones just to keep track of the people contacting him. There was one for journalists, one for politicians, one for researchers. There was another for Atazhurt members and another still with a number that he gave out to anyone who wanted it and that lit up at all hours with calls for help finding a relative or paying bills. He ignored his businesses except sometimes to sell livestock to finance Atazhurt but he still never found time to sleep much. Four or five hours, he would say, that was enough for him.

With the attention came problems. The threats began at the end of the year. The NSC first. Then letters from court officials and prosecutors saying that he was organizing illegal meetings and conferences and inevitably that he was violating Article 174 of the Kazakh criminal code.

Article 174 was supposed to protect against incitement to hatred against ethnic, religious, national or tribal groups but it was broad and vaguely worded and authorities used it as a pretext to arrest activists, political opponents and journalists. Serikzhan tried to register Atazhurt as an NGO so that at least their operations would be legally recognized but his application was refused.

Another letter arrived and NSC officers visited Serikzhan asking that he sign a document saying he had accepted a warning about his activities. He signed it but he knew that the security services were operating on China's behalf and that China did not want anyone knowing what they were doing.

So when a young man he did not know invited Serikzhan rather formally to dinner at one of Almaty's most expensive restaurants, he first thought that the man might be working for the government in Beijing. "We don't know each other," Serikzhan said. "Why would you invite me for dinner?"

"We just want to say thank you in as special a way as we can."

"But why?" Serikzhan asked again.

"There are a group of us," the young man said, "nearly twenty. A year ago, you said run, and we ran. We are living, we are still breathing, we have freedom because of you."

20

Mr. Hu Lianhe (China) said that citizens of the Xinjiang Uighur Autonomous Region, including the Uighurs, enjoyed equal freedom and dignity, economic and social rights and civil and political rights . . . There were no re-education centres or counter-extremism training centres. To secure the lives and property of all ethnic groups, the Xinjiang Uighur Autonomous Region had undertaken special campaigns against violent terrorist activities in accordance with the law . . . It was completely untrue that 1 million Uighurs were being detained in re-education centres.

—Communist Party Official Hu Lianhe's remarks to the U.N. Committee on the Elimination of Racial Discrimination, August 13, 2018

Every week or so the guards would bring a new trainee to the cell as scared and confused as Saira had been. She and the others would try vainly to look reassuring and explain what should and should not be done in as few words as they could. October made five months since her arrest and she thought there must be seven or eight hundred in the camp. More of them she knew. A singer, a writer, a waitress, a friend of that first dancer. Occasionally people were taken away too. Names called from the corridor, women ordered from the cell and the door closed behind them. Saira once dared a look through the door's peephole to see what happened afterwards and made out a fish-eyed glimpse of cuffs being placed around wrists and black hoods over heads. The only one she heard of who ever came back from that was a man named Nurlan and news of his return passed fast from the male cells to the women's block.

Nurlan had been perfectly fine before he left. Bright and healthy, talkative as much as was possible there. He returned with nothing behind his eyes. He could not move properly, the other men said, he could not speak and he needed their help to eat his food and to use the bathroom. They could not tell what had been done to him but it did not look like he was ever going to get better.

There were twenty women in Saira's cell. The youngest was only a girl and the oldest was well into her seventies. There were mothers among them whose husbands had been taken too so their children were left alone at home. And there were daughters who had cared for an elderly parent or been the only member of a family able to work. So many more of them there meant everything took longer, even just the morning wait to use the toilet. A minute or two each and almost an hour had passed by the time they had all gone. She got used to the smell of the room but it must have been bad because the guards put on surgical masks every time they opened the door.

Saira still believed that it would not be long until she was released. Her original estimate of three months had been wrong but it could not exceed six. Those hopes had been sustained by a couple of heady days preceded by rumors that some sort of fact-finding commission would be visiting from Kazakhstan. Or possibly a group of foreign journalists or an inspector from Beijing. The guards had hurried around giving them back the clothes that they had been arrested in and shouting that they should change into them and return their uniforms. Then had come detailed instructions of what they were to say if anyone asked. That they arrived every morning for training and left when evening came to pass the nights at home with their families. That they were well taken care of and had learnt so much from their instruction. The food had been so much better those days. Rice, bread and a wan steamed bun that was more delicious than anything Saira had ever eaten.

No one ever came and winter settled in, bringing with it a slightly thicker uniform and a wakeup time at five. The uniform did little for them. They could see their breath as they lay there in the room and when the snow and wind got bad, flakes found their way through a gap at the far side of the cell and gently thawed on whoever was lying there. Family visits became less frequent and the guards forbade them any physical contact at all when they did come. Hope seeped away from Saira as the new year began and her six-month mark passed noted only by her. She abandoned her scribbled calendar.

Saira knew everything about the camp and a good bit about the other trainees by then. The guards could not stop them talking completely and they whispered their stories to each other at night in the cells or among the crowded arms and sloshing water of the laundry tub. The dancers she knew from before had been taken for showing signs of extremism. Both were a bit younger than Saira. They had always been glamorous when they visited her shop and she had known they were not religious from their stories of nights in bars and their latest boyfriends. That had not saved them because of an evening in 2013 when they visited the home of a dombra player they knew to cook and talk and make music. The night had also been Laylat al-Qadr, when Muslims believed that God sent the Quran down to the world. Four years later the police called them in and said they were on security camera footage celebrating an Islamic festival. One of them had married since and was two months pregnant when she was arrested. The police told her that if she did not have an abortion then her training would last longer and her husband would be taken too. They drove her to a clinic for it and she signed a piece of paper saying that it had been her decision.

Others had stories more like Saira's. The girl in her cell, the young one. She had been studying in Almaty because her parents had thought that would be better for her. Then her father had fallen ill so she rushed back through Khorgos and the police arrested her right there. One of the older women had been a faithful Party member all her life and her husband had been too. She had invited suspicion on herself twice over. By sending their children to study in Kazakhstan and by visiting them and extending her visa for a few days before returning to China.

Saira knew the guards too. Their names and faces and footsteps. Who was harsh, who was lazy, who might go easy on them. The worst were the ones who wanted to be there. They were paid well and were focused on their own advancement so enforced every rule and more. There were Han and there were Kazakhs too and it was difficult for Saira to understand those of her people who had chosen that. Their positions meant that they would have known at least something of what was to happen and could have warned others or at least left themselves. They had not and some of them enjoyed their power. Nurzat was like that. She was young, careful with her appearance and enthusiastically cruel with the trainees. Saira and her cellmates had to ask the guards for a sanitary pad when they were starting their periods. If Nurzat was on duty, she would always refuse until she saw that the blood had stained their uniform trousers. There were others like her. Dariga, impassive and round-faced behind her glasses, Zhanar, who had a Han grandparent but was raised Kazakh.

Sometimes they would pass by the cells to taunt the trainees. "Idiots," they would say. "You used to pray five times a day so that you would go to heaven, but why is your God not saving you? Your God is Xi Jinping now and if you do what he says then you actually will be in heaven. Don't you know, every single word written in the Quran supports men but not women? That is why you all need the Communist Party."

They spoke often of the list of terrorist countries. The US and Turkey may have been first and second but it was Kazakhstan that they seemed to hate most. "You all talk about going to your mother-land," they would say, "but do you think they'll open their hearts and celebrate you arriving? The government there can't support you. It's been thirty years since they got their independence, and they still buy everything from us. They can't even make toothpicks. It's because in Kazakhstan men are lazy and irresponsible, and because most Kazakh women are prostitutes and have five or six children with different men. There's no future for a society like that."

"You know," they said another time, "we already caught and arrested Serikzhan Bilash. In five or ten years China will govern Kazakhstan, and we will build camps there and educate the rest of the Kazakhs." It sounded believable to Saira, inevitable, and she went to sleep that night hoping not to wake up again. Better to die than live to see that.

The trainees cried in their cells sometimes and if the guards saw then they were sure to tell them how lucky they were. "There are other camps in Ghulja and in Urumqi," they said, "and trust us, the people there are having a much worse time than you are."

Not all the guards were like that. Some were new and really

did seem not to have much of a choice but to be there. There were signs around the place directed at them that said SPEAK IN A GOVERNMENT LANGUAGE. That meant Chinese. Saira heard that if any of the guards were caught talking to each other in Kazakh they would be fined 50 yuan by their supervisor and if they were caught again then it would rise to 100. There was one guard who she had known before from when she too was a singer and a dancer. In the camp she was usually responsible for monitoring the trainees via CCTV cameras and if one of Saira's cellmates had a fever or flu and had been denied medicine by the other guards, sometimes the woman would sneak a tablet into the cell. There was another Kazakh man who was usually nice enough to them as well. Saira saw him walk by with his thoughts elsewhere and bump his shoulder into a doorframe. Automatically, accidentally, he said Bismillah to himself. And the same moment he looked up and around to see if anyone had heard with a look of such fear on his face that Saira could only feel sorry for him.

There were assigned punishments for the trainees too. For something small the guards would make them stand facing the wall with the rules painted on it with their hands by their sides and their noses just a few inches away so they could not see anything. There were seventy-five numbered rules and the guards would call out a number every so often. "What is the thirty-seventh rule?" they might ask. "What is the twelfth, tell me that." If the trainees got it wrong, they would have to stay there longer. When it happened to Saira, it was because she had been caught washing some of the older women's uniforms. It happened again after she asked to see a doctor and grew faint and fell backwards so her head smacked off the concrete. Long after it healed she could still feel a bump when she ran her fingers across the back of her skull.

Then there was the black room. Everyone knew about it and they kept people there for days sometimes. Saira saw it only on cleaning duty. Its walls were pitch and there were no windows or lights . It scared her just to see it and she imagined sitting there alone in the unbroken dark. Trainees were sent to the black room for more serious offences. Things like talking too much to each other, insisting too loudly on their innocence or trying to get a note or message to their family through one of the more sympathetic guards. That went for the Kazakhs at least. Uyghurs seemed to be sent there for anything at all.

There was another still worse room that Saira had never seen. Inside that one was a tiger chair. A woman from her cell was taken once. Satina was her name and she was sweet and friendly with everyone. It was because during class she had leaned over and said a few words to her boyfriend, a handsome young man who had been arrested at the same time as her. Seventy-two hours the guards had her in the chair, she told Saira once she could talk properly again. An overhead light blazing in her face the entire time.

The days groaned by and when anything did change, it was not by much. Saira got sick enough once that they took her to the infirmary and they cuffed her left arm and her right leg to the bed there so she could not even turn herself over. Sometimes different people did the interrogations but the questions were always the same and she continued to hold her silence. She never knew if any of the other trainees gave anyone up but she preferred to think not. Perhaps she was only there because someone had said something about her. Perhaps that was the only reason any of them were there. She would not inflict the pain she was living through on someone else for a vain promise of reprieve. And the place was full. They did not want more women jammed into their cell.

Nights were the only time she could think. She would lie on the cold ground with breaths and bodies around her and remonstrate with herself for not making connections with useful people in the local government. She had thought she had no need of them but she should have played along and taken them for meals or brought them presents. That was how things were done. Then they might have helped her. Even without them, she should have taken the signs of the danger enveloping them seriously and followed the advice she had been given about leaving. She wouldn't have been able to take her businesses to Kazakhstan but she could have emptied her bank account and it would have been enough to set herself up again.

Sleep came and she dreamt of home. She smelt the baursak puffing in bubbling oil and the fragrant tea brewing in the pot. She heard her mother's voice calling to say that it was high time that she was awake but she was warm in bed and never wanted to wake up. She would wrap herself up tighter, tighter and then it would all fall away with the opening bars of "March of the Volunteers," and there would be nothing but humiliation and concrete and dirty soup.

The sun and the birds and the trees. She thought always of them and missed them terribly. Sometimes as they were moved around the camp she saw the tops of the boughs outside and she would look at them as long as she could. There must have been sparrows there, singing and fluttering about as they pleased but she never heard them.

What else equals freedom?
Even if you have a short walk
For people locked in a small room
Happy is the bird sitting on the branch

Lines like that came often to her and she would hold them in her head, appraising and reshaping them as she had done long before. It made her feel better, lighter, but often she would arrive on something pleasing only for it to pass from her again. So while they were issued with paper and pencils for their essays denouncing Kanat Islam or Serikzhan Bilash, she began writing them down in a tiny hand on torn corners. She would gaze at the confined letters until she had fixed them in her memory and flush them away when she was permitted to use the bathroom.

She did the same with well-known Kazakh poems for her cellmates and they would pass around those snatches of verse to read and to memorize. It helped them, they told Saira, to remember who they were and that they lived still. The ones among them who were poets began composing too and they would also share their work in paper scrap or whisper form.

Saira thought often of Qazhyghumar Shabdanuly. She had read that he was once asked why he named his book *Qylmys (Crime)*, and he had said that it was because the day he was born in China to a Kazakh family, his existence had been a crime. So it was with her and the other trainees. Because whatever the reasons given for their arrest, what connected them all was that they were were Kazakhs or Uyghurs or Hui.

21

"The training has only one purpose: to learn laws and regulations . . . to eradicate from the mind thoughts about religious extremism and violent terrorism, and to cure ideological diseases. If the education is not going well, we will continue to provide free education, until the students achieve satisfactory results and graduate smoothly."

— Speech by Chinese Communist Youth League
Xinjiang Branch, March 2017

The Künes police called Tursunay early in March of 2018 and said they needed to speak to her again. She asked if they were going to take her for more education and they said only that she should report to the station within 48 hours. So be it if they were. She could endure that if it meant they would consider her once more graduated and return her passport. She swept and tidied the Ghulja apartment and the next day she went to them by taxi.

It was as she had thought. Two officers drove her and she recognized the road to the same facility but when they approached she saw it transformed. Massive metal gates. Fences topped with spiralled razor wire. High walls and watchtowers. A roadblock stopped anyone from getting within a hundred meters of it and even the police had to pass through two checkpoints. Closer still and she saw the guns the guards were holding and the buses parked up in front. The buses were disgorging hundreds of women and men and children of every age. Police were lining them up and separating the children from the rest and putting them onto another bus. Their mothers and fathers howled and cried out and clung on but could do nothing to stop them.

The car stopped and the officers passed Tursunay to guards who took her through a metal door that was also new. It closed behind her and there was a line of other women and guards all around them. The guards were moving the new arrivals fast through a body scanner and confiscating scarves, jewelry, phones and clothes down to the underwear. More of them stood idly by watching and they had guns and shock batons.

Tursunay stood in that shuffling queue and felt fear like she never had. An old woman was next to her. Thin and stooped in a long dress. The guards ordered Tursunay to strip and take out her earrings. Tursunay began undressing but the guards went for her earrings before she was able and yanked them out hard. She cried out and clutched at her lobes and saw blood on her fingers. The pain was shocking but she forgot it when the guards turned to the old woman. They grabbed the woman's headscarf and her hair was white underneath. They tore off her dress and she stood in only a loose undershirt. She held her arms across her chest to cover herself but the guard told her to stand straight with her hands by her side. The woman did and she was shaking at the shame and terror of it.

The guard gave them uniforms to change into. Blue trousers and a blue top. Then those guards handed Tursunay and a group of others to new guards and the new guards led them through rooms and corridors with more metal doors and gates that all closed behind them. Tursunay asked one of the guards why everything had changed so much, what was going on. "You haven't seen the real changes yet," he told her. "Now shut your mouth."

Into a building different from the last dormitory. Up flights of stairs and along a corridor lined with cells. The guards paused by one and ordered them in. There were about 20 trainees inside but only a couple of beds and a small plastic stool each. Instead of a toilet there was a bucket without anything to cover it. There was no ventilation either but on one side was a window with a crack of view outside. Above them was an array of cameras. One that moved constantly and two more in the corners. A television hung out in the corridor.

It was not possible to live like that. Tursunay had to get out. She had been released the last time because she was sick so perhaps that could happen again. She decided that the fastest way to be hospital-ized would be to not to eat. Their meals still consisted only of the black soup so were easy to refuse.

There were no classes like before at first and the guards just gave them booklets with the words to red songs in them. They sat on their stools facing the television for hours with their backs straight and their hands on their laps watching videos about Xi Jinping Thought. The videos stopped and they sang from their booklets and recited loyalty oaths. It was occasionally interrupted by the horrible wail of an emergency siren. That signalled a drill that Tursunay never knew the point of. The moment the siren started the trainees had to kneel on the floor fast and interlink their fingers behind their heads. Not doing it fast enough meant punishment. Sometimes they had to stay like that for an hour or more until their knees ached unbearably but moving meant punishment too.

During the day they were at least permitted to use a bathroom in the hallway but only for three minutes each. She and the other new arrivals could not bear to use the bucket except sometimes to urinate. Otherwise they would hold it until morning came.

From the cell she made out glimpses of what the camp had become. Through that crack of window she saw buses bringing new trainees to be lined up and hustled in as she had been. From her stool she heard the things that were going on elsewhere in the building. Screams, wails, sobs. In the cell across the hallway the voices of two or three women called out that they were citizens of Kazakhstan, that they were not supposed to be there and demanded to know why they had been arrested. The guards told them to be quiet or they would send them somewhere worse but the women were not quiet and after two or three days they were taken away.

Tursunay continued to refuse the soup and she grew frailer. Late on the fifth day she passed out in the corridor but there was no trip to the clinic this time and the guards only dragged her back to the cell. She started eating after that. Necessity had overcome shame by then and the bucket fouled the air.

She discovered other new things. The medicine. Injections every 10 days or so and white pills more often. The pills were difficult to get down and soon made you feel so thirsty that all you could think of was water. They fogged your head so that you barely knew where you were and could not hold onto a thought for long. After a while it felt as if something was crawling underneath your skin. Vitamins, the guards said.

The brutality. Once a woman took too long in the hallway bathroom and one of the guards screamed at her to finish. The woman said her stomach felt bad and the guard went in there and he beat her with his shock baton while the rest of the trainees waited mute and terrified.

The raw fear. All of them felt it. Women and girls would be taken away every night and brought back silent or not at all. Tursunay heard that once when the siren sounded a young woman in a cell with bunk beds jumped to the floor in terrified haste and broke her leg. A woman in a cell on the other side of the corridor lost her mind completely. She kept pulling her hair and slapping herself in the face until at last the guards came and gave her a sedative. She started doing it again when she woke up so they took her away too.

The interrogations. When it was Tursunay's turn, they wanted to know about her foreign contacts. They asked absurd questions about whether she knew Uyghurs living in the US and about something called the World Uyghur Congress that she had never heard of. They asked over and over and told her to tell them the truth but they did not believe the truth when they heard it. They tied her down to the chair and wanted to know why she had been in Kazakhstan and what she had done when she was there and whether she had worn a hijab.

Tursunay grew sick even though she was eating again. They all did. Feverish and weak. She thought it was the vitamins. The vitamins were probably also why most of them in the cell stopped getting their periods and perhaps why some bled far too much. Guards made some of the women get sterilization procedures anyway and others have IUDs inserted.

In May guards told Tursunay she was to be moved and took her down a long corridor to a new building that smelled of recently poured cement. Every cell she passed looked full. Tursunay's was too but there was nearly nothing else in it. No bedding, no mattresses, no heat. She shivered at it. Classes began again and they were like the ones before. Law, Chinese, Xi Jinping Thought. Teachers told them they should be thankful to the Party for feeding them and educating them and helping them free themselves from extremist influences.

The cold and the damp got to her badly enough that the guards cuffed and shackled her for a journey to the clinic and only took them off when they arrived. She saw other women there in red uniforms and in yellow but the ones in red still had the shackles and cuffs on in their beds. She came to understand that those uniform colors tallied with the seriousness of the offences the trainees had committed and that those committed by the ones in red were the most serious of all. Religious crimes. Like praying five times a day or fasting for Ramadan.

Women were taken from her new cell too. For interrogations it seemed but one was away three days and when they brought her back she collapsed onto the floor. The guards let her lie like that for an hour or more. No one was ever allowed to do that so Tursunay found a moment the following day to ask the woman what had happened to her. The woman just clung to Tursunay and cried and could say nothing that meant anything. They must have beaten her badly, Tursunay thought. Then when it came to shower time she saw the marks across the woman's body. Bruises and scratches all over her back and her thighs. It looked like she had been mauled by animals.

The guards fed them even less and the hunger was a ceaseless ache in her stomach. There was a teacher who was Uyghur and who seemed to like Tursunay in particular. One evening she slipped her a piece of bread. Tursunay looked at it and saw it was dry and had started to go moldy but she went to eat it as soon as she was able.

Another woman saw when she did and Tursunay noticed her watching with an unendurable look. Tursunay tore the bread in two and they ate their pieces silently together and they cried.

One of the women who had been bleeding too much passed out one day after being brought back from an interrogation. Tursunay and the others checked her and could feel no breath and find no pulse. They called the guards and a crew all in white with medical masks arrived with a guerney to carry the woman off and never brought her back. The woman could only have died, Tursunay thought and the illusions that had sustained her split apart. She had held to herself the idea that the kind of misery they were living could only be temporary and that she would be released the following week or the following month. She saw the cold, still body wheeled away and understood the lies she had told herself.

The guards took Tursunay for another interrogation and it was not like the others. The room was dark and had no cameras. It was the only one in the whole complex she had seen like that and she knew it would be bad. The interrogation began with the usual questions about Uyghurs outside the country she did not know and demands she confess to things she had not done. Then the guards grew violent with her. They yanked her hair and they hit her every so often and the passing time eluded her in the darkness so it felt she had been there forever. One of the guards brought her food. Tursunay said she did not want it and she started to lose control of herself. She shouted at him. She did not know about any of these things, she said, how could she even have found out about them. She grabbed frantically at him and another guard ran in and kicked at her hard enough that she hit the ground. He kept at it and he swore at her as he did. Heavy-toed boots to her head then her stomach and the blows kept landing so it felt like she was splitting apart.

She must have lost consciousness because she woke up back in the cell. All of her hurt and her stomach was so bad that she thought she was going to die. Some of her cellmates helped her to the bathroom and she found that she was bleeding and that it would not stop. The other women told the guards but they did not care a bit.

They came for her again one night soon after that. Guards called her and another woman by name from the cell and alongside the guards was a man in a suit with a surgical mask on his face. The other woman was in her twenties and she looked as scared as Tursunay was. The guards took them along the corridors together and then to different rooms that were dark again and again had no cameras. The man in the suit and some of the guards went with the other woman and three stayed with Tursunay. They began to question her and the questions were still the same questions but after a while she heard the other woman screaming. It was an awful, pitiful sound, difficult to even listen to but it did not bother the guards.

The guards backed off and Tursunay heard them talking to each other about her and one of them saying there was something wrong with her and that she was bleeding because of it. That did not stop them. What those guards did to her then was worse than any beating. Worse than anything she could have imagined. They took turns at first and then it was all of them at once. They used something metal and they used shock batons and it felt like her insides were being pulled out.

When it was over and she collapsed back in the cell she knew her body must look like the body of the woman she saw in the shower. Like she too had been mauled by wild animals. She passed out again and when she dragged herself to unwelcome consciousness she saw the woman who had been taken with her and who she had heard screaming. The woman was catatonic. She would not talk or move or do nearly anything but sit hugging her knees to her chest.

If Tursunay had known what awaited her in the camp that time then she thought that instead of reporting to the police as she had been asked, she would have killed herself. It would have been far better than to live through what she had.

22

At present, Xinjiang has entered a critical period for laying a solid foundation for social stability and long-term peace. It has entered the decisive stage for winning the battle against poverty and building a moderately prosperous society in all respects. However, the situation is still difficult and complicated, and the tasks are still arduous. This requires that we focus on maintaining social stability as the key to work in Xinjiang.

First, we must deepen stability maintenance as well as the "strike hard" and rectification activities. We must further promote the special campaigns of rooting out terrorists, reducing their numbers, and clearing the soil that allows them to grow; maintain perseverance in cracking down on violent terrorists and violent terrorist groups with high pressure and overwhelming force; and carry out precise and devastating strikes in order to gain the time and initiative to fundamentally solve the deep-seated problems affecting Xinjiang's long-term stability and peace.

—**Chen Hong, Professor, Xinjiang Uyghur
Autonomous Region Party School, October 9, 2017, via
Center for Strategic and International Studies**

The Kazakh government seemed at last to have taken an interest in the arrest of its people in Xinjiang but it involved itself only delicately. Some detainees had apparently been released through diplomatic channels yet the details were kept quiet and officials continued not to acknowledge what was happening. Serikzhan and Atazhurt kept on as they had. They moved into a larger Almaty office on the seventh floor of a tower block, then opened another office in Astana.

People came in the thousands. Sometimes work would not finish until one or two in the morning because there were still people waiting to record videos who had travelled from Zharkent or Shonzhy and who had no money for a hotel overnight. Serikzhan would not refuse them.

Chinese authorities were obviously watching because people whose relatives made videos with Atazhurt had been released and it happened often enough that Serikzhan saw a pattern to it. Someone describing themselves as being part of the Chinese security apparatus usually approached the family members in Kazakhstan via phone or message after the video had gone live. They would tell the family to be quiet and that they were putting their loved ones in danger. If the family ignored the warnings and persisted that could be enough that in the weeks afterwards they got word that a wife, husband or child would soon be crossing back into Kazakhstan.

Some Kazakh citizens travelling via Khorgos or who had flown into Beijing or Shanghai or Urumqi told Serikzhan that there had been questions about him at customs. Officers had wanted to know whether they listened to his voice note lectures or whether they knew him personally. Most of them had denied it and some even said they disliked him but the boldest said that of course they had heard of him and that everybody knew of him now.

He kept trying to register Atazhurt as an NGO but the authorities still refused him and Serikzhan knew that trouble might come for them or for him at any time at all. Whenever a journalist came to visit, especially from abroad, he carefully copied down their email addresses and phone numbers and shared them with other Atazhurt members. "One day something will happen to me," Serikzhan told them, "perhaps arrest or perhaps something worse. When that day arrives, you must write to those journalists and tell them. It's the only thing that might help."

National Security Committee officers visited him again and this time they took him to an Almaty police bureau and questioned him for nearly three hours before they let him go. Article 174 again. He did not publicize this brief detention because he was concerned that Chinese Kazakhs who had been born into a system that tolerated no disobedience would stop coming to him if they knew and would give up fighting for their loved ones. If he was not safe, they might think, then how could they be?

Then the NSC picked him up from his house. The interrogation was at their local headquarters and they recorded it with a video camera. An officer told him he was committing a crime and must stop any kind of activism whatsoever.

Serikzhan asked him what sort of crime and the officer said that he was publishing fake news and that China was a friend of Kazakhstan.

"If China is a friend," Serikzhan said, "please tell them not to arrest our brothers and sisters."

"That is an internal issue for China," the officer said, "it is not our concern. If these people are Kazakhs, it was their mistake to go to China."

The officer warned him again before they let him go. "Don't do something you regret," he said. "We will arrest you, and this will be our last warning."

Serikzhan saw several reasons that the government did not like what he was doing. There was the external. China wanted no light shed on Xinjiang so it was applying pressure. And there was the internal. Kazakh scholars, bloggers and columnists had begun to ask why the government held its silence when their brothers and sisters were in concentration camps. Why it gave no reaction at all when families cried for their loved ones on social media. Why its representatives met their Chinese counterparts and talked only of their neighborly relations, their business links and their oil and gas pipelines. They were questioning the authorities in a way they had not before and the authorities did not like to be questioned.

Then there was Serikzhan's own mounting profile. President Nazarbayev had his billions, his army, his secret police, his nearly twenty years in power and the parks, streets, airport and university that bore his name. He had built up Astana in towering glass and gold to mirror the image he wished to cultivate for himself and the country. He remained popular for it but still feared opposition and his unbound and undiluted rule meant criticism of any part of the government had become criticism of him that would not be tolerated.

So they went after Serikzhan and Atazhurt and they went after those who spoke to them as well. The woman Sagira who had been among the first to come to Serikzhan for help called him one day and said that the NSC had visited her. They told her not to publish any more provocative videos and risk destroying the friendship between the Chinese and Kazakh people, she said. There was more. A man had begun loitering outside her house until past midnight. Just standing, waiting. Serikzhan suspected it was an attempt to smear her and suggest she was having an affair while her husband was detained.

She called again some days later to say a new man had appeared in place of the other. This one would park outside after dark. He was there every time she looked and she was afraid to leave the house anymore. Serikzhan and a group of others went down there and crept up on the car. They dragged the man out and hustled his phone and ID card from his pocket. He was young and local. "Shame on you," they said to him. "This woman is alone, without her husband and with children to look after. She has nothing, and yet you make her life worse still. You are Kazakh too, why would you do a dirty thing like this?"

They took pictures of his ID. "If we see you again," Serikzhan said, "we will publish your name and your photograph everywhere we can." The man was abashed. He apologized and said he would not come back. He did not but Serikzhan saw that would not be the last of it.

23

China stated that the Xinjiang vocational skills education and training institutions, which had been established for counter-terrorism purposes in the Xinjiang Autonomous Region, were focused on the study of legal knowledge, vocational and language skills and on deradicalization, and that they were employment oriented. Through such education, those institutions helped the few people who had been exposed to and affected by extremism to shake off terrorist and extremist thoughts. Instead of cracking down upon those people after they became terrorists and a danger to others and to society, the institutions helped them reintegrate into society, rather than becoming hard-core terrorists or victims of terrorism. As part of the preventive antiterrorism measures, such institutions had been established in accordance with the law and had produced the expected results. They represented the efforts of Xinjiang to explore an effective counter-terrorism approach and another important contribution by China to the international counter-terrorism endeavour.

—**Summary of China's comments to the UN Human Rights Council's Working Group on the Universal Periodic Review, November 2018**

Adiljan spent a year mired in sorrow. A terrible gnawing, hollowing-out of himself like none he had ever known. And with that sorrow came guilt because of the punishment meted out to his family for actions that were only his. There had been stretches of nothing and times when he had done and thought things completely unlike himself. He had wandered the streets blindly for days and he had decided more than once that there was nothing left but to take his own life. All that had stayed his hand was the knowledge that in Islam that was a sin and the idea that he would once more be abandoning Mihribangul and the children.

It was the desire not to that finally dragged him from his despair. If the world knew how things were in Xinjiang and what was happening to his people then they might do something about it. He was not delusional. He knew he could not make a difference on his own but perhaps he would inspire enough others that they all would.

He wrote out a short script on a few sheets of paper, hung an East Turkestan flag on his apartment wall and put on his doppa and a traditional embroidered shirt. Then he propped up his phone, sat down and began to talk. A few false starts later and he had a take he was satisfied with.

The footage showed his head and the top of his shoulders below the flag. He spoke in Turkish first. "As-salamu alaykum, my Turkish brothers," he said. "The current situation in Xinjiang is very bad and urgent. Millions are imprisoned. They are brainwashed and sterilized. Chinese people are ordered to be in every Uyghur's house. Uyghurs are facing extinction silently. But you can't be silent, my brothers."

He talked about his father and Mihribangul and her father and brothers, who he had discovered had also been taken.

"Please don't be quiet," he said. "Support us, please."

Then he switched to Uyghur and urged other members of the diaspora to speak out for those who could not. "We need to act quickly to be the voice of the detained and tell the world of their situation," he said. "Let's try our best to reveal the true intention of the Chinese government. Let's speak about the inhuman treatment in our motherland through videos and on the internet and live broadcasts. This is what I expect of you."

He trimmed the video and then uploaded it to Facebook, set the privacy to public and clicked post. Some of his bolder friends in Istanbul liked and commented on it. The especially brave shared it. Those shares spread on beyond his network and then beyond the site. The video was copied and posted onto YouTube and forwarded through WhatsApp and Signal groups and Telegram channels. That was far more publicity than Adiljan had ever hoped and it began to make him nervous.

Ten days later he was sitting in his apartment and received a series of WhatsApp messages from a Turkish number he did not recognize. He opened the chat and tapped frantically through it appalled at what he saw. There were pictures showing his children sitting in the corner of a room on a low couch next to Mihribangul's mother. Bumaryam in a red-and-white tracksuit top with a colorful neckerchief, her hair short and her cheeks pink. Muhammed in a traditionally patterned shirt. Omer clutching a toy tractor to his chest.

There was a video too that was soundtracked by a flute- and string-scored ballad. It began with footage of the children and Mihribangul's mother in their backyard. The boys pushed the toy tractor between themselves on the dusty concrete. Bumaryam was on her feet, in and out of shot. Then it switched to the scene from the images as the ballad built to a chorus. "I forgot all the pain in my heart," the singer crooned, "when my child called me father for the first time."

Whoever had taken the video panned back and forward across their faces. Bumaryam laughed as the ballad continued and her lips moved wordless. Omer gazed up and he too looked happy. Only Muhammed seemed worried. He turned away and cast his eyes to the floor. Mihribangul's mother tried to encourage him but then the camera lingered on her and she too looked uncomfortable.

There was an audio message along with the images and video. A man with an Aksu accent addressing Adiljan both as Lokman and by his real name. "How are you? How are you doing in Turkey?" the man said, smooth and polite. "We haven't heard from you for a long time. Do you remember them? Perhaps you posted that video because you missed them too much."

Adiljan tried to hold his voice steady when he replied in a note of his own. "Of course I remember them. They are my children, she is my mother-in-law," he said. "Who are you? Where are you sending these messages from?"

"I'm a cadre appointed by the government," the man said. "We haven't spoken before but let's be friends and keep in contact."

"If you want to be friends," Adiljan said, trying for any advantage he could, "I need to know who you are and who you work for. Send me your name and a picture of your ID card please."

The man said his name was Izmet and that he had been ordered to Adiljan's family's case by the government. He was sorry but he could not send his ID card or disclose exactly who he was working for.

Adiljan switched to typing because he didn't want to have Izmet hear his voice any longer. Izmet did the same. "I'm dealing with the problems of your family," Izmet wrote, "I'm responsible for them now. You're a man who doesn't care about your family. You left them and are hiding in Turkey."

If Adiljan cooperated, Izmet continued, he would have a chance to see his children again. The Chinese government could even send them somewhere to visit him if he would prefer. Adiljan knew well that cooperation meant providing information on his life and on other Uyghurs. Becoming a spy like Abdullah, who must have had a conversation of his own much like that one.

Adiljan chose differently. He switched back to voice messages and this time he was nearly shouting.

"My family has nothing to do with my problems," he said. "Only I am responsible for the things I've done. But don't expect cooperation from me, I would never betray myself or my people."

Izmet replied right away, switching back to voice notes too. "Just be calm and take it easy," he said, still smooth, still polite. "We will speak again soon and perhaps you will reconsider."

Adiljan was beside himself. He told an elder in a Uyghur association about everything that had happened and asked for his advice. The man said he should delete his WhatsApp account and not to engage with any further contact. Adiljan did and his desperation emboldened him. He wondered what else he could do to help his family.

There was a protest planned in front of the Chinese consulate on July 5. The anniversary of the night in Urumqi when blood and gunfire in the streets had kept him from Mihribangul. He decided he would go. What else could they do to him by then? The fifth was a Thursday and it got sticky and hot early. Adiljan dressed carefully in the colors of the East Turkestan flag. Blue jeans, blue sneakers, a blue long-sleeved shirt he bought specially with a white star and crescent on the left breast. The organizers had arranged buses from Zeytinburnu to drive them up to the leafy calm and luxury of Sariyer district on the banks of the Bosphorus.

The bus stopped by the marina, a notch of an inlet sheltering motorboats and sailing yachts at rest in placid aquamarine. Adiljan spilled out with the others onto the broad sidewalk and it was hotter still with nothing but occasional trees for shade. There were hundreds of them there and more still arriving. Women, men and children in doppas and embroidered shirts carrying banners and placards with faces of the missing. Everywhere was the same flag as on his breast. It adorned the matching vests that some of the men wore over their t-shirts and the blue plastic masks concealing the faces of those who feared to show their identities. It formed headbands, hijabs and niqabs and above them it undulated continually from sticks and poles.

They turned their backs to the water and started up the hill towards the consulate. There were journalists ahead of them pointing long-lensed cameras their way. Some of the crowd stayed out of shot but Adiljan had no reason to anymore. A man passed him a flag and he pushed through towards the front. They passed an empty lot and a corrugated iron fence pasted with a palimpsest of promotional posters then climbed sharply towards whitewashed houses with louvre shutters and high garden walls containing overflowing green. They continued past the houses and they sweated so their necks glistened and their shirts clung to their backs. After a bit they curved left for the last stretch towards the consulate but waiting in front of them were riot police with transparent shields and white helmets. There was no way past and the procession halted hard with the rear still tailing back down to the main road. Some of the men in their matching vests formed a line at the front, linking arms and holding hands. Adiljan passed his flag backwards and joined the far end next to a thin man with a short goatee who was a little taller than him. He took the man's hand and they stood solemn.

The crowd was not done. Behind Adiljan they surged but the police pushed them back and there was stumbling, shouts and children crying in the confusion. They reconciled to the spot and a few of them set a Chinese flag alight. It went up in a whoosh of flame and they cheered and recoiled from the heat of it. The flag fell burning to where the grass pushed between the cobblestones and a man in a checked blazer held the others away from it. Then someone set down a portrait of Xi near the melted remnants of the flag and people cheered and stamped on it.

Afterwards Adiljan thought of the attention they had won from passers by and from journalists. Every time there was a protest from then on, he would go.

The others were not often so big but in them there was purpose. He designed two posters and had them printed off then glued them to pieces of cardboard. On one were images of Bumaryam, Omer and Muhammed taken from the video and from the ones Mihribangul had sent him on WeChat. To those he added an illustration he found online of a man in a helmet with a red armband dragging two screaming children away from a parent's outstretched arms.

WHERE ARE MY CHILDREN? he captioned it in Turkish.

The other placard used his favorite photo of Mihribangul in her white and floral lilac headscarf and perfect makeup. He added another illustration he had found of what he imagined she must be suffering. It showed a woman from behind sunk to her knees on the hard floor of a prison cell. Her hair running down her back and her hands pressed to the wall. Underneath he added her name and the words MY WIFE IS INNOCENT. RELEASE MY WIFE.

He carried them always to protests and, in his newfound fervor, to a solitary vigil he staged in Istanbul's historic Eminonu district. He wore all white and set himself up on a sunny afternoon not far from the Blue Mosque with chains hung between his wrists to symbolize the imprisonment of his people. Tourists and sightseers approached curious. He told them what had happened to him and many of them promised they would post on Facebook about Xinjiang. Some of them cried. Then the police saw him and took his chains and his signs away. It was illegal to stage a protest without permission, they told him, and they could arrest him for it. He said that he would stop and asked if he could have his things back but they would not give him them.

24

One, responsibilities for watchtower work

First, to conduct upper area surveillance and open area surveillance of the school's interior areas; second, to conduct upper area control and surveillance during trainees' extracurricular activities; third, to maintain well the handover log for firearms and ammunition, and for the guard handover registration, etc. 2. In case of an unusual circumstance or attack, first, promptly initiate early warning and report [the incident]; second, assist the Strike Group and the main gate through high-altitude fire support and direct suppressive fire towards the terrorists.

Two, workflow

1. Duty roster: 6 special police officers are on duty, implementing a "three shifts and two operations" model, with each shift lasting 6 hours.

2. On-duty weapons and equipment: On-duty staff must wear standardized uniforms with stab-proof vests, carry light machine guns and QBU-88 sniper rifles.

3. Scope of work: In watchtowers, mainly use light machine guns and QBU-88 sniper rifles. From the watchtowers/high-level patrol walkways, monitor and control the study areas with their security perimeters. Following leaders' instructions, the drill commander and incident response command leader surveil and use firepower and suppressive fire to control the designated areas.

—**Security operations and incident response plans**
for the Konasheher New Vocational Skills Education and
Training Center, via the Xinjiang Police Files

December 22, 2018. Guards ordered Saira out of the cell by name and told her to face the wall and listen carefully to them. "A commission has come from Beijing," they said, "and you must talk to them in Chinese and say what we tell you."

She asked what she was supposed to say.

"Tell them this," they said. "That before you came to the camp, you were unemployed with nowhere to live. That you did not know even one word of Chinese and that because of the Party, you were given a warm place to stay and learnt Chinese and about the laws of the state and that now you are even to be given a job. Say it, and you'll have a chance to leave."

They took her up to the third floor and to a room where around thirty official-looking people sat and watched her from behind a long table. The people questioned her and she replied just as she had been instructed. She had not spoken any Chinese before her training and she'd had no job and no home but thanks to the Communist Party, she had learnt the language and laws of the country. The commission members nodded as she talked then whispered between each other afterwards and Saira heard them say, "She passed, she passed." She hid long-suppressed hope within herself and stood still and patient.

They asked if she had a parent or guarantor. Her sisters were married, she said, so there was only her mother. They nodded and noted it down and the guard took her away. "Am I free?" she asked the guard on the way back downstairs. He did not reply to that but he warned her not to tell anyone about what had happened and that hope remained.

Her cellmates were all sitting looking at the television. They did not move when Saira came in but they whispered. "Sister, sister," they said, "tell us what happened." Saira tried to calm herself and whispered back. "Keep your eyes forward," she said. "But listen carefully to me. There is a government commission here and it seems that perhaps we are going to be released."

That afternoon the guards called women from her cell and from others too. After that they went around and asked who among the trainees had relatives in Kazakhstan. Some who did answered yes and the guards noted down their names and made them sign papers without time to look at what they said. Some who also did said nothing because they were scared that it might be a reason for punishment. A while after dusk all the lights in the corridor went off and the guards called the names of the people from their list and took them from the cells. Saira was sure then that she was right.

In the next day's rounds, the guards asked who had government connections or family working for the state. They took down the names and had some of them sign papers of their own but they only had them sign if they were Kazakh. The Uyghurs and Hui were ignored.

Saira and the other trainees usually exchanged words and glances as much as they could while they ate because they were together in their unhappiness and there was a fellowship in that. The knowledge of who among them would soon be free and who would not brought only silence and lowered eyes. Evening came and in the dark the ones who had signed the papers were taken.

They asked for businesspeople on the morning of the twenty-fifth and again it was only Kazakhs. Saira told them she ran several businesses and she signed papers of her own. There was that same hush during lunch and guilt at her own fortune pricked at her. She looked over the faces of the women who had formed her world and who she would be leaving behind. The Uyghurs and Hui who appeared to have no chance of escape. The Kazakhs who had no useful connections or who had been too cautious to admit to having family abroad. She wanted to acknowledge their parting but found no way to.

Later on, when things were quiet, she managed to write down a few phone numbers on behalf of cellmates who were not being released. They were of family members who they'd had no contact with since they had been taken and they thought might not know what had happened to them. Saira promised to call as soon as she was able.

The lights went off again and she sat until they called her then walked out into a pool of the guard's flashlight. Others were also being called on further down the corridor and ushered through the darkness. The guards told them the terms of their release. House arrest with permission required to go anywhere at all. They gave them clothes sent by their relatives to change into and made sure the trainees had nothing of the camp with them. Saira scrunched up the tissue with the numbers when they searched her and managed to keep it on her. Then she was in a minivan with four or five others driving out through a series of security gates and fences that had not been there when she first arrived. The gates opened into more darkness and she saw that the power was off everywhere.

Ten or fifteen minutes and the headlights played on the yard walls and metal gate of her house. The guards told her to get out and they knocked on the gate. Her mother would not usually have answered in the middle of the night without someone else in the house but she must have been told Saira was coming because she soon appeared with a flashlight in her hand to unlock it and nodded a repressed hello.

"We have brought your daughter," the guards said. "You know everything, right?"

Her mother said she did, the van door slammed and the two of them stepped inside the gate. Her mother locked it again and they stood like that until the sound of the engine disappeared and then they embraced.

The blackout meant that her mother had not been able to prepare any hot food so she handed Saira a mug of cool tea with milk and showed her to her newly made bed. Clean sheets. A warm blanket. Soft pillows. She lay down and nothing had ever felt better but her mind was still awhirl and she did not sleep until the night was fading.

The smell of baursak and of brewing tea and she heard her mother moving around in the kitchen preparing breakfast. She opened her eyes it all stayed where it was. No "March of the Volunteers" plucking her from her dream and no concrete at her back. She sat down with her mother in the kitchen and it was just as it had been eighteen months earlier before the phone call summoning her to the police station. They ate and Saira asked questions about her sisters, her relatives, her friends and the town itself but her mother seemed uncomfortable and chose her words carefully. She did pass on the instructions that had been given to her regarding Saira's release. They were not to speak to their neighbors about it or to celebrate Saira's arrival and if the neighbors did ask where she had been then they were to say that she had just returned from a business trip. After a while her mother bustled through and gathered up the clothes Saira had arrived in. Then she muttered a few words over them and threw them away so as take that time of misfortune with them.

Saira showered and it was a proper shower. The room was clean, the water gloriously warm. She meticulously scrubbed her face and her hair and her body, taking as long as she wished and thanking God for it all because nothing was better than home. She emerged clean and glad and found a pen and paper to write down some of the poems that she had composed inside the camp and the phone numbers from the tissue.

She dressed in her own familiar clothes and she thought of her earrings with the crescent moon and star that had saved her back in Urumqi. It would be nice to wear them again. She looked through the jewelry in her room but they were not there. Then she checked anywhere else she thought she might have left them or her mother might have put them. They were not there either.

"Where are my earrings?" she asked her mother. "My favorite ones." Her mother said quietly that the sign on them, the image, would have brought them bad luck, so she'd had to get rid of them. She meant that police would have taken them as a symbol of extremist thought.

Other things had changed around the house, strange things. There were photographs on the walls of her mother with Party cadres. Harsh light, cheap suits and joyless smiles. Then in one room was at least twenty kilograms in bags of flour. Rice and sunflower oil too, more than her mother could possibly need. "What is all this?" Saira asked, and her mother said that every week people from the mayor's office had been coming to visit her and that they often brought goods that they said were from the Party. They would tell her that they needed to take a picture all together and that she should print it out and hang it up. It was to show they were looking after minorities in Xinjiang.

Nearly all of the knives were gone from the kitchen drawers. Only three were left. One for bread, one for vegetables and meat, one of the kind used for slaughtering sheep. Each had an identification number engraved on the blade. Saira's mother explained that a limit had been introduced on the number of knives that each household could own and that they had to be registered at the nearest security office. That way if they were used in a crime then the authorities would know exactly who was responsible.

Local officials contacted Saira with more detailed guidance for her behavior. One of the most important things, they said, was that if ever a foreign journalist contacted her then she should say nothing to them but immediately report it to the authorities. And if she wanted to leave the house then she would have to apply for permission by contacting the mayor's office and explaining why.

She was usually allowed two or three hours for food shopping so long as she sent them regular updates on her location via WeChat. The first time she went out she saw many things had changed in town too. The cleavers at the butcher's were chained to their chopping blocks. In shops and cafes and beauty salons there were several sticks leant just inside the doors. Big and thick, one for each member of staff. Once or sometimes twice a day, she learned, there came a signal. At the signal the beauticians had to abandon their clients and the waiters their service then line up outside with their stick and run through basic combat drills. Failure to appear or just being late could get you detained. The idea was that if there was a terrorist attack then the shopkeepers would be able to stop the terrorists until the police arrived. Saira heard of one government worker who had kept her stick by her desk instead of by the door, reasoning that any attacker would come from outside and immediately get between her and it. An official saw and for that she had been sent to a camp. Activities against the Party, police had said.

The cafe near Saira's house was still busy but the customers she saw when she walked by looked quiet and guarded. It used to be a place where some people would order tea and some would order beer and no one much cared who did what. Now nearly everyone had alcohol at their tables. Saira saw people on her WeChat feeds who had not drunk before regularly posting smiling pictures of themselves sitting down together with bottles well in shot. Insurance against being suspected of extremism.

She found she was on some kind of blacklist so her business had been shut down and her accounts frozen. Not that she would have been able to restart things. Her local customers and nearly everyone else all knew she had not been on an eighteen-month business trip and were scared to speak with her. The Party turned out to have plans for her time anyway. They made her write out a long statement repeating the things she had told the release committee alongside her imaginary transgressions. A minivan would come in the mornings and collect her and a group of other recently graduated trainees from their homes and take them to villages in the area as part of a cautionary roadshow. Local Party representatives from each village would gather residents together and Saira and the others would read their statements aloud to these coerced gaggles.

"My name is Saira, and I once did not know the Chinese language and had no job and no home," she would start. "But thanks to the generosity of the Communist Party, I was enrolled in a vocational education and training center."

She would go on to explain that there she had learnt to speak and read Chinese as well as many other useful skills to help find work and succeed in the new China.

"I advise all of you to listen to the Party," she would say, "and to follow their instructions exactly."

She could feel judgement from the reluctant eyes on her. They must all know the camps were not as the Party told them but surely assumed that the graduates had done at least something wrong to get themselves sent there. If she had not been arrested herself, she would have thought the same. She knew what people said. There are no waves without wind.

But for Saira, the waves came with no wind at all. The trainees had been taken only for the possibility of a crime.

She was not herself then. There was not a moment she did not feel tired and it was not a normal tired but a bone-deep, unsparing fatigue that the slightest activity inflamed and no amount of sleep dissipated. With it came a haze that settled in her and never left. She would forget the simplest things and wonder how she had not been able to hold them in her head. She thought with unhappy wonder of the woman she had been who would sit down to memorize pages of prose and verse then recite them at will. When she left the house she would find herself confused as to where she was if she did not keep her mind on things. Once or twice she got lost in places she had known better than any other.

Perhaps it was whatever the injections had been and perhaps it was because she lived only a half-freedom beset by two pressing problems. First was the existential issue of whether she would be rearrested. It went from a constant possibility to utter inevitability the more she thought on it because the graduates would not always be useful to authorities. There was also the more urgent question of how to support herself and her mother. One day she asked permission to go to the mayor's office and she spoke with someone there. "My mother is old and unable to work, so I need to," she said, "but you have blacklisted me and blocked my accounts, so I cannot continue to operate my businesses. How am I supposed to look after her?"

Bizarre circumstance led to someone assigning her a position at a security post on the border. Her job was to monitor a section of the vast camera network watching over the no-man's-land between them and Kazakhstan. She never saw anything other than rocks and patrolling guards and the occasional speck of birds circling unknowingly across the frontiers but she started to think of a way across that strip of ground. The idea was vague at first but it solidified as she noted the camera's few blind spots along with the guards' patrol routes. Soon she knew what to do. She would arrive for her afternoon shift with a cigarette lighter, some chocolate and a small knife she could hide in her sock. After dark at just the right moment she would tear out onto the slope from a blind spot and run as fast as she could without ever looking back and hope no guards, bullets or hungry wolves were at her back. Before she was ready, a commissioner visited the border post and demanded to know why there were camp graduates working there. That put Saira back under house arrest with her plan in pieces.

One afternoon she was returning from her permitted supermarket trip with laden plastic bags when a luxury sedan in lustrous black approached and slowed down right by her. It was the kind of car that Party officials drove so she stepped back to let it past but it stopped and she recognized the man driving it. He had lived nearby when she was only a child but she had not seen him for years and heard that he now had a job high up in local government. He greeted her curtly through the window and told Saira to sit in the back. She wavered but opened the door and slid across the leather seats with her bags.

The man drove out of town and wound up into the hills. He said nothing and Saira grew apprehensive and said nothing too. When they were high above the town and well out of sight he pulled over and turned around. "I always liked you," he said. "You were smart and you worked hard. I was proud to see you grow to be a writer and a businesswoman."

Saira said nothing still.

"I know what happened to you too," he said. "And because of it, they will be following you for the rest of your life."

"So," he asked, "if you could, would you want to go to Kazakhstan?"

She decided to trust him. "Yes," she said. "Yes of course."

"But you will not betray me?"

"No, I promise, never."

What she should do, he explained, was write a letter to a certain local government department and say that before she went for vocational training she used to run an export business with many customers in Kazakhstan. "Tell them," he said, "that you had sent a shipment there but not yet received payment and that now you need to go and collect the money. Tell them you need to go for three months to do it. Keep writing to them and don't stop." She nodded and thanked him and he drove her back down into the town and dropped her off out of sight.

She wrote a letter exactly as he had said. Then another and a third. The department people called her in. "Why do you need three months?" they asked. "Can't you handle it in less time?"

"No," she said. "I was in a training center for a year and a half. Do you think they'll have my money ready and waiting for me? It will take time. But if you don't want to let me go, then give me the money they owe me yourselves and I'll tear up my passport right here."

"We will look at your application," they said.

A week, two, nothing. Then it came. They would allow her to leave for forty-five days. Saira went to see them. "Why not three months?" she asked.

"We need you to come back," they said. "In three months you will become a resident of Kazakhstan."

So the visa was issued and along with it the conditions designed to ensure her return. She must not take jewelry with her, they said, not even rings, and she could carry no more than 300 dollars' worth of cash. That was not enough to last her forty-five days, she said, but they replied that the money she was to collect would surely keep her going. They asked her too for a local guarantor to ensure she came back. She said there was only her mother and that her mother was elderly and could not be responsible for her. They had her bank accounts there, she said, and her business too. Everything she had worked for, things she would never abandon. "That," she said, "is my guarantee."

Saira prepared herself. She assembled on her phone the pictures that chronicled her life. In the oldest she is a baby wrapped in white at the center of her solemn family. Then she is a young girl in overexposed monochrome with a cap on her head and a pearl necklace doubled up around her skinny neck. The advent of digital photography and she is a woman but just barely and she is posing in traditional clothing in front of a photoshopped meadow of impossible green. A real meadow this time and she sits in the shade of a white parasol. Wearing tight jeans and a leopard-print top, she stares confidently at the camera by the crook of a wide river. Returned from Urumqi, she sits at her lace-adorned computer monitor. Assured and respected, she speaks at the entrepreneurship forum with those red curtains behind her.

She saved pictures too of the things she was proud of. Books packed onto shelves and piled nearly to where the walls met the ceiling. Her various certificates for expertise and excellence and the award that said WORK TOGETHER TO WIN with hands extending to shake each other around a globe.

Then she searched social media for people she knew from the camp and found pictures of her fellow inmates in the times before. Happy and oblivious in their best clothes with perfect hair and makeup. She searched for the guards and found them with arms around wives and children in restaurants and parks or proudly uniformed at official events. She knew everything would be searched when she left so she downloaded a cloud storage app, loaded the pictures onto the app and deleted them from her phone.

There was an old friend of hers, a writer and a poet. He heard that she was to receive temporary travel permission and seemed to know that she would not be coming back. One day he gave her a sheet of paper with a poem fourteen stanzas long written on it. "Memorize this and rip it up," he said. "That's my wish."

She sat down with it later. It said everything he could or would not say directly. For her and for everyone who could leave.

    A wish
    To my sister Saira
    Spring has come, blue rain has fallen,
    Shaking his head with a willow-poplar face.
    Why, why is the baby bird afraid,
    She flapped her wings and got scared.

It spoke of many things. Of how while she travelled, he would be tending his goats in the mountains. Of the luck he wished for her journey and the life that she would live away from those who had known and cared for her. Of how in Kazakhstan he believed she would one day be thought of like the great poet Fariza Ongarsynova.

She treasured it but no matter how long she tried she could not remember it all. So she took a picture of it, uploaded it to the storage app and burnt the folded paper. Then she made sure she was sure of the login details for the app and deleted that from her phone as well.

She packed on June 10. Not much, only what she could easily carry. Then she passed a terrible day wondering if she would ever see her mother and her sisters again. Whether what she was about to do would hurt them. And she thought too of a saying she had once heard. That it was better to be poor in your own motherland than a sultan in a foreign land.

She was a Kazakh and Kazakhstan was her historic motherland. If she died trying to make it there then she would die a Kazakh. Her mother knew what she was planning but they had said little more about it. "I want you to be safe," she told her mother before she left, "and I want to be safe and to be happy too. I promise not to do anything that will bring you shame." She was sure of herself, but she felt the same pain as she had when she had looked at the faces of the women she was leaving behind in the camp.

25

The U.S. government assesses that since April 2017, Chinese authorities have indefinitely detained at least 800,000 and possibly more than 2 million Uyghurs, ethnic Kazakhs, and other members of Muslim minorities in internment camps.

—US deputy assistant secretary of state for the Bureau of Democracy, Human Rights, and Labor addresses a Senate Foreign Relations subcommittee, December 4, 2018

Winter threatened. The winds grew sharp, snow crept down from the peaks around Almaty and Serikzhan's father developed a dry, persistent cough. No frame-racking paroxysms, no blood. Just a few quick, reflexive exhalations that after three or four minutes came again and gave him no respite. His temperature was normal, the doctors at one Almaty hospital said, and there wasn't any fluid in his lungs either so there was not much to be done. Serikzhan and his sister worried. Their mother had died not long before and they could not lose him too. They bought their father different medicines, and none of them made any difference to the cough. They tried a different hospital and the doctors found nothing either. Then Serikzhan's sister said that a Kazakh doctor from China had been recommended to her who was well known and very experienced so perhaps they could send their father to him. The only thing, she said, was that he was not in Almaty but a small town to the east that was more than eighty miles by road.

Serikzhan drove. His father, his sister and his sister's husband with him in the Nissan. He had been up all night talking with researchers and journalists in the US and spent the morning in the office helping record video testimonies. The strong tea he drank for the journey quickly wore off and he fought to keep his eyes open. They soon hit snow on the highway and followed the furrowed tracks of those before them, slowly, carefully, until at last they approached a small town of gridded streets with fields around and they were parked at a gray clinic by a house on its outskirts.

Serikzhan was spent. "Please take father to see the doctor," he said to his sister and her husband. "If he's from China too, there will not be any issues. I'll just lie down here, I need to sleep half an hour." The three of them headed out into the cold and Serikzhan turned up the car's heater, reclined the seat and closed his eyes. Not five minutes and there came a knocking at his window and a man's voice along with it.

"Serikzhan," the voice was saying. "Serikzhan?"

"Yes, it's Serikzhan," he said, dragging himself back to consciousness.

"Oh come in, come in please," the man said. It was the doctor, a slight man with narrow shoulders and short gray hair that stood on end all over his head. "As-salamu alaykum," he said. "I know you, Serikzhan, I know your work, please come inside."

The doctor had asked Serikzhan's father for his details and because Bilash was not a common surname, he had asked if it was Bilash like Serikzhan Bilash. "Yes," Serikzhan's father had said, "he is my son. He is outside in his car at this moment." And out the doctor had hurried.

The doctor diagnosed Serikzhan's father quickly enough. It was a rare condition, he said, but would require only a series of injections to treat. So Serikzhan bought the medicine, settled up with the doctor and thanked him. They went to leave and the doctor asked to speak to Serikzhan about a problem of his own. His wife had been detained in China, he said, and was being held at a camp in Künes. He did not know how he could save her.

"That's no problem," Serikzhan said. "Just come to our office and record a video testimony." He began to give his practiced instructions on what the doctor should bring. A Chinese passport, a Kazakh passport, whatever identity documents he had of his wife's.

The doctor thanked him but said there was still a problem and that it was a difficult one. "My wife," he said, "she is not Kazakh."

"That too is no problem," Serikzhan said.

"You don't understand. She is Uyghur, her name is Tursunay."

Halmirza explained it all to Serikzhan. Their return to Xinjiang, their confiscated passports, the month she spent in a re-education camp and how she had been taken again and that since then he had heard nothing.

Serikzhan was undaunted. "Uyghur," he said, "what kind of problem is this? You are a citizen of Kazakhstan. And whether she's Uyghur or Kazakh or Mongolian or Tibetan, she is the wife of a Kazakh citizen and you have the right to protect her. Come to our office and record a video explaining it."

Halmirza was still concerned. For Tursunay and for his family still in China. If he recorded a video, he asked, would they be in danger?

Serikzhan had a response ready there too. "All of us have sisters or brothers or parents in China," he said, "but the government will focus on you. They will always threaten you so that you will want to stay quiet. That is how they program you, how they control you. But we must turn against that programming, we must stand up and expose these crimes against humanity. Maybe then the Chinese government will begin to be afraid of us not the other way around."

Halmirza asked the same question over again. Ten times in ten different ways. About his family, about Tursunay. Was Serikzhan sure, was he really sure?

"Yes," Serikzhan said, "I believe it. Hundreds of people have been released after their relatives recorded a video like that. The Chinese government is scared of the world's media, of everything that they are doing being exposed. If you do as I suggest, they will have to release your wife."

Halmirza soon came to visit him at the Atazhurt offices holding a large passport-style picture of Tursunay wearing black with gold hoop earrings. The two of them went over her story again. Chinese officials had already been in touch, he said. A man who said he was with the police had called and asked him if he was already a Kazakh citizen and asked for his passport number. Halmirza answered yes and asked in turn why Tursunay had been arrested but had got no answer.

Serikzhan sat down with Halmirza to record a video. It was the same format as all the others. They sat together behind the desk, Serikzhan in a navy suit, Halmirza in a checked shirt, small even next to Serikzhan, who was not tall. Serikzhan made a brief introduction. "This family, they are separated by Chinese officials in two countries," he said as Halmirza held up his Kazakh national ID. Then he switched to Kazakh and asked Halmirza to address the camera. Halmirza introduced himself then produced the picture of Tursunay and the camera zoomed in on it. Serikzhan took notes as he talked and translated into English, giving Halmirza's name and his national ID number, giving Tursunay's name too and the dates of her travel and detention. He mentioned the calls from the police and how much Halmirza needed his wife.

Serikzhan told him the video would likely be published on YouTube later that night. He asked Halmirza to listen carefully. "This is what will happen," he said. "Tomorrow morning or the day after or the day after that, you will receive a phone call from a Chinese landline. It will be from the Chinese police or from your wife. I'm sure of it, it has happened thousands of times. If it is her, she will ask why you visited a terrorist organization and made a video. She will tell you how happy she is there, that the Chinese government had given her an opportunity to study, to educate herself because her mind had been infected by harmful ideology. She will tell you that she is learning Chinese language and deepening her political education. She might cry, she might shout at you but you must remember that it is not her. The Chinese police will be standing right next to her and the words she speaks will not be her own. If it is only them, the message will be the same."

"Here is what you must say back to whoever it is. You must ask what kind of political education, what kind of language education means that your wife has disappeared for months without even calling. Means she did not have the right to send even a short message to let you know that she was ok. You must insist that you will not stop. Say that you know she is in chains, that she is in a concentration camp. Perhaps again they will say that you should never visit this terrorist organization Atazhurt again. But you must say that on the contrary, you will visit again and again. You must tell them that this organization is in contact with hundreds of members of the foreign media and with human rights groups that you will meet with one by one. And that even more than that, if you get a visa you will visit America and Europe and tell them the whole story too, because you are her husband and you have to have her back."

26

Since 2016, with Secretary Chen Quanguo as the squad leader, the Party Committee of the Autonomous Region has thoroughly studied and implemented Xi Jinping Thought on Socialism with Chinese Characteristics for a New Era, and fully implemented the spirit of the Party's 19th National Congress and the spirit of the Second and Third Plenary Sessions of the 19th Central Committee; resolutely implemented the CCP Central Committee's strategy for governing Xinjiang with Comrade Xi Jinping at the core, closely focused on the general goal of social stability and long-term stability in Xinjiang . . . Party Secretary Quanguo and the Party Committee of the Autonomous Region are loyal, firm, impartial and selfless, with a spirit of "throwing caution to the wind" taking responsibility for the country, and leading the cadres and masses of all ethnic groups in the region. Through more than a year of extraordinarily arduous hard work, the phase-specific goal of "in one year stabilize" has been achieved . . . ensuring that the overall social situation in Xinjiang is stable, the situation is controllable, stability is improving, which made a major contribution to the overall situation of the nationwide counterterrorism struggle, and also created a safe and stable social environment for the reform and development of Xinjiang.

> **—Speech Given While Listening to the Report on Public**
> **Security and Stability Work on the Xinjiang Autonomous Region,**
> **Zhao Kezhi, Chinese Minister of Public Security,**
> **June 15, 2018, via the Xinjiang Police Files**

Guards moved Tursunay to another new cell on another long corridor and things were better than they had been. There were fewer of them in there and they had a bed each. The interrogations stopped and the food was recognizably food but she was still sick and still bleeding and the fear that guards and men in masks

might come for her again was always with her. At night she would lie
there unable to sleep for it and during the day the memories tumbled
in and she shrank back every time the door opened.

There were new one on one sessions where guards and teachers asked them what they had learned from their time in training.
Tursunay gave them the right answers. She questioned nothing and
said nothing other than what was asked of her. On December 25, 2018,
the guards moved around the cells holdings lists of the trainees who
had relatives living abroad. Tursunay's name was on there and she
panicked when she heard. Whatever was happening to those people
might be one of the things that people never came back from. Guards
called her from the cell and she was shaking so much she thought
she might pass out but they only took her to one of the classrooms. A
Kazakh woman and a Chinese woman were waiting there and they
had many things to tell Tursunay. She was to be released, they said,
and when she was, she should say nothing about the training centre
to anyone. They had documents for her to sign that included pages
of confessions and they made her record a video expressing her gratitude to the Party. She knew it was real then but her coming freedom
brought her no happiness when she thought of the women she had
suffered together with who would be going nowhere.

It was snowing when they escorted her through the doors. Gates,
fences, razor wire and outside her sister waiting next to two police
officers and a Party woman. Her sister greeted her with stifled emotion and the officers gave her ID card back to her and they all got
in a car and drove towards a nearby apartment that her sister kept
for when she was working in the area. Tursunay watched through
the window as the flakes settled chill over the fields and she felt only

hollow sadness. They arrived and the officers and the woman told her that they would also be staying that night. Tursunay grew angry but her sister hushed her before she could say much. The apartment was small and they all crammed in side by side when it came time to sleep. The woman was next to Tursunay pressed up against her and soon breathing deeply. Tursunay lay still and awake and then around midnight she saw through hooded eyes one of the men get up and stand as if he was on guard duty.

Party cadres told her where she should rent an apartment and for a while two of them lived with her. One man and one woman. They left during the day but would take turns coming by to see what she was doing every couple of hours. Then they would both come back again in the evening and pass the night. Members of the local neighborhood committee would visit too and sometimes search the apartment. To shop or visit relatives or do anything else outside she had to first apply for permission and once she did leave, she had to send videos showing where she was to the cadres.

She was still weak, still bleeding and in pain. She felt mostly numb then but rushes of nameless emotion overwhelmed her and she would weep without anything setting her off. Noises, footsteps, shadows spooked her and at night when she tried to sleep she kept the light on always. It seemed to her that was all there would be for her until they took her back again. And she did not expect to survive another detention. Two of her brothers turned out to have been taken to the same facility as she had and they had also been released sick. Urinary tract issues apparently. She could not imagine what had been done to them.

There were more rules and there were Chinese classes that she had to go to. Then every Monday morning was the flag raising ceremony.

They had to be in the courtyard outside the neighborhood committee office by seven thirty but Tursunay always arrived early to be safe. She would join the crowd milling around on the hard packed snow, stamping their feet and avoiding eye contact. They would form up into silent rows, exhaled condensation held in the beams of the street-lights, then members of the neighbourhood committee and several policemen would walk into the courtyard and take up their places by the flagpole. Familiar crackly bugles sounded over the speakers and everyone sang "March of the Volunteers" while one of the policemen hoisted the flag. The committee secretary would begin talking and would go on for hours about this and about that and he seemed not to care the ranks he addressed were shivering and unable to move to warm themselves.

The cadres let Tursunay have a phone but she did not try and contact Halmirza. She had been sent to the camp because of her life overseas and to provoke them again would be madness. Then the police told her specifically that she could call him if she wanted to. She was confused as to why that would be so still did nothing. They said it again and asked if she wanted to call from a phone they had that would make international calls. That seemed safer.

He picked up and she could not say a word to him. She just sobbed. "Don't cry," he told her. "You will be free and you will come and join me in Kazakhstan." She did not say anything to that either.

The police came to her once more. You know, they said, you should call your husband again. They took her to same place. This time Halmirza asked why she was crying and asked what had been done to her. She did not answer and he kept asking. "Don't fear for anything," he told her. "I will save you and if they harm you I will sue them and I will never stop." He was insistent and he was angry and the police listening in seemed cowed. "Yes," they said as he spoke. "Yes, yes."

Another time they came and took her to a room in the police station with several televisions in it. They told her to watch one. There she saw Halmirza. He was sitting at a table with another man and he was holding her Chinese identity card and her picture and he was talking but the sound was off so she could not hear what he was saying. She stared amazed. The police asked her if it was her husband. "Oh yes," she said. "Yes that's him, that's my husband." The police took her away again and told her later that she would be permitted to contact Halmirza on WeChat from then on. They spoke and she lied that she was ok.

That spring, the police and the neighbourhood committee secretary and a crowd of others arrived at the apartment unexpected. One of the crowd was carrying a large, professional-looking camera. They would be making a video, the secretary told her, to explain how good her life was. They gave her a sewing machine and a piece of red cloth to stitch on it. They told her to sit down and a woman styled her hair and applied a full face of makeup.

So she sewed and addressed the camera in Chinese and said how thankful she was to the Party and how happy she was. She wanted to cry when she said it and they made her do it again ten times over until she had smiled like they wanted and sounded as grateful as she should.

Ramadan began in May and went unacknowledged because to fast or pray was to be taken but on the 15th day, the committee secretary held a lunch. Tursunay was invited. They all sat down and the secretary paid particular attention to her. He was drinking alcohol as he ate. Something clear from a small glass. He turned to Tursunay and said she should have some. She had never drunk in her life so she told him that she had stomach problems and it would make her sick. He held out a glass and looked at her. "Perhaps," he said, "your ideas have not really been changed."

It burned so badly when took a sip that she almost spat it out but she held it down while the secretary smiled horribly at her and carried on with the meal. Nausea built and soon she excused herself, then went to the bathroom and vomited.

Restrictions loosened and she found that a few other graduates that she had known had also been released. They were able to meet up on a few evenings and the time passed nearly silent. There was no light in any of them anymore, no thoughts of a future. The eyes of one were red and ringed dark, she must not be sleeping. The youngest of them seemed to have begun drinking and not just to keep the cadres away. Another was thinner even than she had been in the camp. So thin Tursunay thought she might be close to death. Tursunay asked if she wanted to go and eat something but she said she could not. Her husband had been taken and she could not find work so any money or food she could get went to her children. Tursunay bought her some *chöchure*, dumpling soup. The woman ate it fast and afterwards she did not look well.

Then authorities gave Tursunay her passport back. It had expired by then but they said that she could renew it and go back to Kazakhstan if she wished. She did not really believe it. Getting a passport had been nearly impossible the first time around and it could only have become harder. They assured her that no problems would be made for her and somehow it happened just as they said. She went bemused from office to office collecting stamps and signatures and soon she had a passport that the cadres made the subject of another video. Then she travelled to Urumqi for the Kazakh visa application. The night train pulled into the smog and icy air in the early hours. There were a few ethnic Kazakhs making the journey for the same reason as her and they spoke and decided that it was so cold that they should take rooms in a nearby hotel until the visa office opened. The Kazakhs checked in easily enough but when the hotel staff examined Tursunay's identity card they turned suddenly rude and told Tursunay to leave and not to come back until she had registered with the local police station. "It's four in the morning," she said. "I don't know where I'm supposed to go. Please just let me check in now and I'll get the letter later." They would not allow that. They did not even allow her to stay in the hotel lobby and it was not until eight that she was admitted shivering to the police station.

She made for the visa office after a few hours' sleep but the first taxi driver she tried was Uyghur and said he could not take her because the office was in an area of town where only Han drivers were permitted. So a Han driver took her instead and she submitted her papers and her passport and she waited.

27

Urgent Action: Human rights defender under house arrest.

Human rights defender Serikzhan Bilash has been under house arrest since 10 March. He is the leader of the human rights organisation Atajurt, which exposes human rights violations against ethnic Kazakhs in China. Serikzhan Bilash is facing charges under Article 174 of the Criminal Code, in an apparent move by the authorities to intimidate and harass him simply for defending human rights. He risks a maximum prison sentence of seven years. He is a prisoner of conscience and should be immediately and unconditionally released.

—Amnesty International, May 8, 2020

They came to the Atazhurt office late in the afternoon of March 9, 2020. A group of men who showed neither identification nor the slightest remorse for their intrusion and busied themselves with silent intimidation. 150 people might pass through the office on a normal day, and these men were like none of them. They were tall and hard-faced. Their bodies were stocky and trained. Their hair was cropped close at the back and sides. They carried matching black Nokias with hands-free earpieces. They sat themselves down on some free chairs and said nothing when Atazhurt members asked if they could help them with anything.

The men showed particular interest in Serikzhan when he went to have a look at them. He thought they might be there to arrest him but they just stayed sitting where they were. Perhaps they had a hidden camera with them, he thought, or were reporting everything they saw back to headquarters. Or maybe they intended only to scare families who might take their cases to Atazhurt.

Serikzhan had someone call the police but the police did not come so they confronted the men again and asked to see their identity cards. "Are you Kazakh?" they asked. "Chinese?" The men held their silence.

When they did leave, it was in a hurry. Fast up out of the office then up one set of stairs and back down another with a few angry Atazhurt people behind them. There were police outside and the pursuers demanded that they stop the men but the police seemed to have an idea who they were and did nothing.

They left behind a stubborn sense of unease. Things had been getting worse lately. Authorities were still refusing Serikzhan's attempts to have Atazhurt officially registered but the previous month they fined him for running an unregistered organization anyway. There was a social media campaign against them too. Slander and lies. The men who had been calling him from withheld numbers to try and get him to stop had started calling his sister and his brothers and his father too. There was not a moment anymore that he did not worry for them and for himself. The incursion was another escalation. He decided to spend the night in a hotel instead of going home. He and Laila had three children by then, all boys, and he could not put them at risk too.

A colleague booked him a room under a false name and the two of them closed up the office then ordered a quick dinner at a traditional place nearby. A group of men walked in while they ate. They were not the same ones from earlier but Serikzhan recognized the hard faces, short hair and dangerous physiques so he paid and left quickly. The hotel was on the same lot as an amusement park to the south, a massive building of concrete and turquoise with a tropical pool and spa. Serikzhan used neither and went straight to his room on the eighteenth floor then fastened the thick security chain and succumbed to a troubled sleep.

He woke in darkness to bodies and voices in the corridor and was fast up and by the door. Whoever it was must have had a key card, because they had the door open already and were scrabbling at the security chain. Thugs come to kill him on the orders of the Chinese government. To shoot him as he lay in bed. It had to be. He squared his shoulder to the door and he cried for anyone who could hear him. He tried in Kazakh and in Russian. "Help." he shouted. "I am innocent, help me." He heard nothing in return and no one came to his aid but the men on the other side gave up on the chain and started kicking the door. Big, heavy blows that Serikzhan knew he could not hold. He looked behind him for a way out but there was only the window and a fall no one could survive. So he kept his shoulder set and fought for the last moments of his life.

The moments were hours. His thoughts came quick and ordered. Laa ilaaha ill-Allah, he repeated to himself, there is no God but Allah, the words that would hasten the passage of his soul to paradise. He saw his childhood, his parents, the school, the mountains. He thought of his own children and how they would grow up without the love of their father. He thought of Laila. He thought of the decisions that had led him there. He thought all kinds of things.

A crash and the security chain tore loose from the frame and there were too many of them for him to stop. The door opened fast and pushed him back across the carpet so the skin ripped from the bottom of his foot with a flash of pain. Then the men were in the room and they were not some rabble of toughs but security officers of some kind with body armor and pistols and long guns and ballistic glasses. "Who are you?" Serikzhan asked.

"We are from the government," they said, "we are National Security," and Serikzhan knew why they'd had a key and why no one in the hotel had answered his calls.

Serikzhan still had a hold of himself and started demanding to know what they were doing. They were arresting him, they said, for harming relations between Kazakhstan and China.

"If you wanted to arrest me," he told them, "you could have come to my house or just called me and I would have visited your office." He knew as he said it that the reason they arrested him like some dangerous terrorist was so that they could say he was one if they ever needed to.

They took his phones and they let him dress but did nothing about his foot so he smeared blood over the bathroom floor as he did. Then they led him downstairs to a waiting car. "Don't worry," he said, "I'm a gentleman, not a terrorist, I won't try to escape." They did not listen and put him in the back of the car with a big man on each side of him.

He would be taken to Astana, they said, and they drove directly to the airport and put him in an empty VIP room there. His throat was dry and his foot was throbbing so he asked for a cup of tea or water. One of them brought him water then a nurse came in to look at his foot. She bandaged it up and it began to feel a bit better.

The entire unit that had forced their way into his room boarded the plane with him and the one he thought was a commander sat close.

Dawn was approaching as they touched down in Astana. Serikzhan saw the commander turn on his phone and look worried at whatever he read there. "Come with me," he said when they had disembarked.

"We need to record you. You must tell social media that you are ok." Serikzhan agreed. It was the only way he would be able to get any message out at all.

"My dear supporters, my followers," he told the camera, "I am safe and I am in Astana, do not worry about me." The commander cut him off there.

They took him to a hulking old building that had once belonged to the KGB and then down underground through windowless corridors. He prepared himself for what was to come. Kicks, baton blows, electric shocks. Perhaps even death. He was scared but he calmed himself and thought of the Kazakh heroes he learned of as a boy. Kenesary Khan, who had fought for freedom from the Russian Empire. Osman Batur, the military leader hanged by Chinese communists. It had been clear for a long time that a day like this would come and he found that the threats and the constant worry of it had inoculated him against the worst of the fear. I am ready, he thought. If I am to die, then let me die.

At first it was only an interrogation room and questioning. "Do you feel guilty?"

"No," he said, "I have done nothing wrong."

"Why do you make these provocations?"

"I don't think I'm a provocateur," he said.

"But why would you put us in danger by destroying the friendship between the Chinese and Kazakh peoples?"

"Why is that a danger?" he asked. "Will China occupy us? All I did was to gather information and publish it."

They put him in a cell with two beds and a hole in the ground for a toilet. There was another inmate in there. A man, they said, who had drunkenly stabbed another man. Serikzhan knew that was a threat and a plausible one. If he turned up dead, authorities could say that he had got into a fight with his cellmate.

It was not until the eleventh that his lawyer, Aiman, finally reached him. She told him about the press release the prosecutor's office had put out stating the exact nature of the crimes he was accused of. It was Article 174 as he had expected, inciting ethnic discord through extremist speech. A guilty verdict could mean ten years in jail. The extremist speech in question turned out to be an address he made during a meeting of Uyghurs in Almaty that February when he had called for an information jihad against China. He had meant by exposing the situation in Xinjiang rather than by picking up a gun and had said so but social media accounts friendly to the Kazakh and Chinese governments had been circulating edited videos of the address that removed that context.

More bad news. Police had raided Atazhurt's office and confiscated computers, notebooks, printers and cameras. The hard drives with all their recordings on them too and whatever paperwork they could stuff into bags. Then they had sealed off the door and denied access to anyone. Serikzhan saw China's hand in all of it.

Aiman told him also of the mad panic after he had been taken. A group of Atazhurt members went to the hotel early and found only disorder and dried blood. They had started to really worry then and made a short video showing the trail of dark red in the carpet and in the bathroom and posted it on their YouTube channel. The stir that caused must have been why Serikzhan had been made to record that video at the airport. He thought it might have saved his life.

Prosecutors brought him in front of a judge who read the charges and ordered that he be held under house arrest and that it had to be in Astana. He moved into a place owned by a friend in a residential quarter of two-story buildings behind concrete walls and metal fences. There were not many other options. By then he had sold his horses, his cows and most of the rest of his assets to keep Atazhurt going.

Armed guards watched over him. Three of them at least and sometimes four or five. They tried to station themselves in the house at first but that was said nowhere in the court order and they eventually retreated outside.

Government men came to him. Often they showed him videos of himself and they seemed to have hundreds of them. Footage in the office shot clumsily between shoulders or at press conferences and events. Footage of him sitting in a herdsman's home in some remote village and telling them that if their family members had been arrested in China then it was their right to ask for help from the Kazakh government. The NSC must have had people on him nearly everywhere he went, watching for something that they could use as a weapon.

One of the government men brought pictures of various members of Serikzhan's family as if to show how easily they could get to them. It was no surprise that they could. They tried to get him to sign things and tell them things and they offered him imminent release if he resigned from Atazhurt.

He always told them no but it was lonely there. Court orders banned him from accessing social media or having a phone of his own. Sometimes he made a fleeting call to Laila on a borrowed handset but they both knew that someone might be listening in so never said anything much.

Aiman brought him news when she had it. On the charges and

on the people who offered to testify against him and the links some of them seemed to have with the Chinese embassy. All the while the courts kept extending his house arrest and Atazhurt switched its operation to campaigning for his release. #FreeSerikzhanBilash was the hashtag. They used it everywhere they could and asked people they had helped to make videos of their own demanding Serikzhan's release and uploaded them to the YouTube channel.

An official indictment on July 16 switched the nature of the charges. He was still accused of extremist speech but without threatening violence and that dropped the maximum sentence to seven years. Not much better. Then came a trial hearing. His supporters gathered in and outside the courtroom. They held up banners with a picture of Serikzhan suited and sombre against a deep-blue background flanked by the golden eagle that topped the Kazakh Eli Monument in Astana's Independence Square.

He addressed the journalists in English during a break and told them he was innocent and had been trying to raise awareness of what could be described as genocide against Kazakhs and Uyghurs and other Turkic peoples. He told them that it was China who was putting him on trial through the hands of Kazakhstan's government. China's soft power and money, he said, was turning Kazakh authorities and intellectuals into Beijing's agents of influence. Then something at last went his way and the judge ruled that because the alleged hate speech had taken place in Almaty, both the trial and his house arrest should continue there.

One of the same men who had visited in Astana kept coming to him back home and talked always of that agreement. It would be a plea deal that would see Serikzhan released in exchange for accepting his guilt on the incitement charges, a fine of roughly 280 dollars and the promise not to lead any form of political group for seven years. "You have no other choice," he told Serikzhan. "Just sign it or we can extend your house arrest month after month after month. Or perhaps it will get worse," he said, and he spoke of men who had been given many years in jail and of the beatings and broken bones they had suffered there.

The next hearing was scheduled for August 16 so Serikzhan had plenty of time to think on it. He made up his mind but told no one and arrived at court well before Aiman. More than two hundred of his supporters had gathered in the street and they chanted for him. Aiman arrived and waited in the courtroom while Serikzhan met with the man who had offered him the agreement and told him he would accept it. He needed freedom. For himself and for Laila and the children. The paperwork required a defense lawyer's signature but Aiman would not sign it when he told her what he planned to do. So Serikzhan gave up her council and asked for another well-known lawyer by name who turned out to be outside in the crowd.

Serikzhan stepped out tired and exuberant and went for dinner with dozens of supporters at a restaurant with low sofas all along the walls. He stood up at the table and told them all that he'd had no choice, that it was for his family's sake. It was that or seven years in jail. But he knew, he said, that the rest of Atazhurt would continue their work undaunted. People applauded when he finished and afterwards a few of them told him it had been the right thing to do.

28

State Councilor and Foreign Minister Wang Yi held talks with Kazakh Foreign Minister Beibut Atamkulov in Beijing on March 28, vowing to promote cooperation in various fields.

Calling Kazakhstan a good neighbor and comprehensive strategic partner of China, Wang said that under the leadership of the first President Nursultan Nazarbayev, Kazakhstan has made well-recognized achievements in national building and is playing an increasingly important role in international and regional affairs . . .

Emphasizing that President Tokayev attaches great importance to the development of relations with China, the foreign minister said that Kazakhstan is willing to work with China to promote the construction of the Belt and Road and strengthen cooperation in various fields.

Atamkulov said Kazakhstan understands and supports the measures taken in Xinjiang to combat terrorism, separatism and extremism and to ensure regional security and stability.

—**State Council of the People's Republic of China, March 29, 2019**

T he road to Khorgos cut through sprawling rectangular lots and warehouses until Saira could see the layers of wire and cameras that was the border then the steppe and scrub and mountains beyond that was no longer China. The checks before she could leave took terrifying hours. She gave officers the passcode for her phone and the login for her WeChat and watched as they looked through the photos, messages and contacts. She signed the papers they gave her. One said she had never been held in a camp and another promised she would say nothing negative about the Chinese government while she was away. Then they abruptly let her go and she hurried and tried to make it seem like she was not towards one of the buses that ferried travellers across the curved strip of no-man's-land. The bus dropped them off before Kazakh passport control and she joined the rough queue that formed there. Her phone lit up. It was WeChat, a video call from her sister. She answered to her sister's face and the shadow of someone next to her.

"Have you passed the Kazakh border yet?" her sister asked. Saira thought the authorities had changed their mind and wanted to come and get her again. "Yes," she said, "yes, yes, I passed already. Speak to you soon." She hung up and turned to the others in the queue, who were nearly all Kazakhs. "Please," she said to them, "I survived the camps and now the police are calling me, can I go ahead of you?" They ushered her forward explaining her situation to those in front and soon a border guard had waved her into the country with little ceremony.

Another queue for another bus. Bound west this time and it was nearly Saira's turn to climb aboard. Then a man's voice was shouting her name. She flinched but kept her eyes ahead, imagining guards hunting for her. The voice shouted closer and she turned with a panic in her. Walking happily towards her was an old customer from Kazakhstan. He must have been overseeing a shipment coming across the border. "Oh Saira, what are you doing here?" he asked. "I haven't heard from you for a long time. How are you?"

He seemed glad to hear she was spending some time in Kazakhstan and he wanted to help. "Do you have someone picking you up? No? I will not let you take the bus. I have my car, let me drive you. Where are you staying?"

She told him she had not yet booked anywhere and he said that was fine, they could organize everything on the way. She gave in to his jovial insistence and he put her bag in the trunk of his car. They drove out through the steppe and dry fields then looped through the region where her great-uncle had lived and perhaps his family still did, then down into the town of Zaysan with its tree-lined yards, shops and hotels. He checked her into one of the hotels. A nice place, the kind she had not seen in a long time. "Ok," he said. "Rest, shower and we'll all go for dinner in a while."

She stood under the warm water and she weighed telling her old customer where she had been. Their relationship had been only professional and this was the same customary hospitality she would have shown him had things been the other way around but he obviously thought that she was still in business. It did not feel right to mislead him but who knew what Kazakhs had heard of the camps. He might assume she was a criminal or perhaps even be scared of her. She would not be able to stand the shame.

She dried off, dressed and started putting on her makeup. Her phone rang. "Are you ready?" he asked. "If you are, I'll send you a driver."

Soon she was walking into a restaurant and on to a long table already laid with the best dishes. He introduced her to other local businessmen and even the mayor of Zaysan. She shook hands and said polite hellos. By the end of the evening it was like things had been before and they were taking smiling pictures and speaking of bright futures and business successes to come.

Her customer called again the next morning with a suggestion that they go to look at a new venture of his by a national park nearby. "I cannot go," Saira said, "and I need to tell you something."

He was as surprised as she had feared but he was not scared. His son's girlfriend was in a camp too, he said, and she had done nothing wrong either. "Look," she said, "let's just say you haven't seen me, and I haven't seen you. We never met, and I'll be on my way."

He would not go along with that. "It was always good to do business with you," he said. "Now I want to help. I'll get you a clean cell phone, lend you some money, and make sure you get to Almaty, then we'll be in touch again. I insist," he said when she tried to refuse, "and I promise you I'll be very upset if you do not let me."

He bought Saira a bus ticket and food for the sixteen-hour journey, and he pressed about 300 dollars' worth of Kazakh tenge on her to cover any urgent eventualities. She would once have spent that much on a business dinner without a thought but now it doubled everything she had. It was enough to get by, enough to save her. He drove her to the bus and he spoke to the driver, telling him to put her into a taxi to her hotel once they reached Almaty.

The city was overwhelming. The noise, the crowds and the skyline all reminded her of Urumqi but she felt no excitement at the discovery. Only worry over what was to come and the idea that Chinese authorities might still try to take her back. She got in touch with a young woman she knew from home who was studying in Almaty and who she had sometimes helped back when she was able. She told the woman that she had been in a camp and urgently needed a way to get citizenship. "Can you help me this time?" she asked. The woman told Saira that getting citizenship cost the equivalent of thousands of dollars and that applications could take as long as a year to process. Even then, she said, the agencies who did all the paperwork did not guarantee it would be accepted.

Saira did not have that sort of money and she needed to move faster. If Kazakh authorities deported her, she was done. She called a TV journalist she knew from home who was now in Astana and who she thought might be better connected. Saira explained herself and asked if there was any other way to secure citizenship.

"My sister," the woman said, "how many times did I have guests from abroad and you treated us all to dinner? How many times did you lend me money and never ask for it back? And when I needed people to interview for work, would you not always help me find them? Now it's my turn. Come to my house, stay here and we'll sort it all out."

The train traced the Kyrgyz border for a time then jutted north along the shores of Lake Balkhash, basin to the Ili and six other rivers. Onward still with the steppe slipping by in the night and at last she was among the curved glass and white tiles of Astana station. Her friend had enlisted another friend's help and together they took Saira to a residency office, where a woman who was also Chinese-Kazakh and seemed to understand Saira's situation told them that she would do her best to get her citizenship accepted in three months. It would cost, she said, less than 500 dollars. The woman asked Saira nothing of her background and Saira was desperately glad of it.

Ten days later she was issued a temporary ID number and proof that her application was being processed. That was good but her friends told her that the city was not safe for her until she had the protection of a Kazakh passport. No parks or malls or anywhere else because Chinese authorities might snatch her up or have someone do it for them. She rented a studio apartment that was only a few cluttered steps from window to wall and because she had no other source of money, she set herself up as a cook making Xinjiang dishes for the many displaced in Astana craving the flavors of home. Most popular was spicy big tray chicken with potatoes and peppers in garlicky chili sauce. Motorcycle-helmeted couriers came every evening and picked up steaming packages of it for delivery all over the city.

Her friends would visit and they introduced her to others. Writers, journalists, poets. They talked and told her about the capital and about how things had been for refugees like them from Xinjiang. They mentioned an organization called Atazhurt that Serikzhan Bilash had founded. The camp guards had lied. Chinese authorities had not captured him at all, they said, and he had been working for years to publicize what was happening in Xinjiang and return detained Kazakhs.

She yearned to be free of the apartment but when she did have to go out, she became easily confused among the commuters and the traffic rushing down the boulevards. If she heard sirens or saw the flashing lights of a police car, her heart would thump because she thought they might be coming for her. It felt worse still when her mother and her sisters began calling and messaging to ask why she had not come back. In them, she felt the Chinese state.

Lonely months passed and winter closed in, colder still than home. The snow fell heavy and the sky was an ice blue and the view from her window perfectly beautiful. Finally a brief notification to say that her passport was ready. She rushed ecstatic to pick it up and sent her friends beaming selfies holding the turquoise cover close to her face.

She sent another picture of it to a local administrative body at home. She was Kazakh now, she said, and legally she had to renounce her Chinese citizenship. "So," she said, "please annul it."

They refused. "You will have to come here yourself for that," they told her.

"I'm not a criminal," she said. "I owe no money in China and I have the right to choose the country in which I live. If you don't do it within three days, I will go and I will speak to journalists and tell them everything that happened to me in the camps."

"Don't do that," they said, replying quickly. "We'll get back to you." Hours later they sent her pictures of freshly stamped paperwork and it was done.

Her friends planned a small gathering for her on December 16. It was a national holiday marking Kazakstan's independence from the collapsing Soviet Union back in 1991. "Let us celebrate your citizenship," they said, "your first Independence Day." Two weeks shy of a year since her release from the camp, they drank tea and ate pastries and deserts. At nine o'clock they watched a crescendo of fireworks burst over the city and drift dimming to the icy ground.

Saira liked Astana very much. The climate reminded her of home, the modernity of it all intrigued her and her friends felt close already. The problem was that Astana was the sort of city where life was good so long as you had money and she had nearly none. Almaty was bigger and built on centuries of commerce. If you wanted to work, to trade, to do business then it had to be there.

She returned and found there was still far too much traffic and too many people. When she walked the streets and crowds closed in around her that familiar claustrophobic panic came fast. It really did feel as hectic as Urumqi sometimes and that was something she no longer missed. Much was different too and she noticed it all. The people there were not like the people at home who seemed always hunched, guarded and careful. As if the heavy workers' clothes of Mao's era had forever formed their bodies. Kazakhs in Almaty were freer in their gestures and their speech, the ways they walked and sat and ate. They had unlearned the communist way of being, or they had never known it at all and she wanted to experience that for herself.

29

The centers provide free education. They employ teachers, legal workers and senior vocational technicians with solid professional knowledge, as well as fulltime
doctors for medical services. The dormitories are fully equipped with radio, TV,
telephone, air conditioning, bathroom and shower. Sports ground and library
have been built. Various extra-curricular activities, such as contests on ethnic
dancing, singing and sports, are organized to help the trainees regain aspiration
for a better life. The trainees' personal dignity and freedom are fully protected.
The centers implement boarding management, under which the trainees can go
home on a regular basis and ask for leave whenever needed. The trainees' right
to use their own spoken and written language in daily life is fully ensured. The
customs and habits of trainees of different ethnic backgrounds are also given full
respect and protection.

After more than two years of practice, vocational education and training in
Xinjiang has scored remarkable achievements. The trainees have gradually broken away from the spiritual control of terrorism and extremism and got to know
what is legal and what is not. They have gained access to modern knowledge and
information, learned basic practical skills and enhanced their employability. Now,
many trainees have graduated from the centers, got stable jobs, and lived a happy
life with better quality.

—Address by Aiken Tuniyazi, member of the Standing Committee
of CPC Xinjiang Uygur Autonomous Regional Committee
and Vice Governor of Xinjiang People's Government, at the 41st
Session of UN Human Rights Council, June 25, 2019

The Chinese border guards looked surprised when Tursunay
showed them her three-month visa and the travel permission
from Künes authorities. Those were not things usually issued to

Uyghurs. They asked if she had been in a vocational education and training centre then took her to a room where a guard strip searched her and cut the heels off her shoes and checked the seams of her jacket and the lining of her bag. The afternoon drew on and took what was left of her strength with it. It was September and she was nearly nine months out of the camp but the pain was still horrible, the bleeding continued and a cough sporadically convulsed her.

Two hours until they let her go and she was exhausted nearly completely. Relief at the sight of the Kazakh border post with the blue and yellow of the flag and the two guards in their peaked teal hats kept her going. "Sister," one of the guards said, it's been some time since you were here. "Welcome to Kazakhstan and enjoy the reunion with your family." Then she was through and there at last was Halmirza and there was his nephew too. Twenty years old now, smiling and running to hold her up as the emotion of it took her. He half-carried her towards the parking spaces where the marshrutkas and informal taxis waited and helped her into the car. They had been so worried, Halmirza said. They had been waiting all afternoon and the guards had told them the bus she had crossed on would be the last of the day.

They took the smooth new Almaty highway and drove out past the dry port where freight trains rolled in slow under the gantry cranes. Then there was only the ridge of the mountains to the right and the river Ili to the left flowing away from her homeland. She looked no longer and drifted into sleep as they lurched around laden container trucks and sparse traffic.

Nearly four hours later and they were driving up and away from the highway into the hills. They stopped at a house she did not recognize because Halmirza had had to sell the one with the garden she had tended to so carefully. She did not much mind and watched exhausted and disinterested as the world lurched around her and people appeared, embraced her and passed away again. She went to bed and she slept again, waking sometimes from the pain and never turning off the bedroom light. She slept through most of the next few days as well, stirring occasionally to move ghostly around the house. It never felt like freedom and she was certain that she would be back in Xinjiang before long. Fear of it was with her still. Sometimes that fear came in a great, suffocating wave and she could only sit and shiver because of it. Sometimes she thought she might be losing her mind completely and semi-conscious, imagined she was in other places, other times.

The messages began then. From one of the same cadres who had watched over her before. How was she, he wondered. Had she reached Kazakhstan safely? He reminded her that she should not meet with strangers or discuss the circumstances of her re-education. She did not want to provoke him so she said she had arrived but that she was very tired and put her phone where she could not see it.

She had to rouse herself eventually. There were things to be done and the most important was to arrange her temporary residency. She queued at an office until a woman told her without bothering to look up that they could not help and that if she overstayed her visa then she would be sent back to China. Tursunay pleaded. Halmirza was a Kazakh citizen, she explained. The woman only became more dismissive.

Tursunay left the office humiliated and panicked, sure the woman would not have been like that with her if she was not Uyghur. Halmirza tried to reassure her. They would try again. There were other people he knew who could help.

One of those people, Halmirza said, was named Serikzhan and he was keen to see her. Halmirza told her about Atazhurt and the videos he had made. There had been more after the one she saw at the police station. In a second he addressed the camera alone just holding his ID and a small picture of Tursunay. In a third he joined a group of families bowed under their worry and grief and spoke in front of a mosaic of pictures of the missing. He had talked about Tursunay's house arrest and about their video calls. How unwell she had looked. How her voice was different, her hair short and her face swollen with what he suspected was edema. He had talked as well about the Chinese official who had been calling to assure him that Tursunay's passport was being processed so he should not worry or make any more noise or appeals. He told her how at Serikzhan's urging he had contacted the police directly after the first call when Tursunay had only cried and he had demanded to know what was wrong with her.

He urged her to visit Serikzhan but she said no. She recoiled from it and she felt the same when Halmirza and the others talked of what was happening in Xinjiang. Repression, they said, genocide. "Why do you speak like this?" Tursunay would ask. "That's not how it is." And she thought of how China would lead the world one day soon and that there was nothing that anyone could do about it. She thought of how even mentioning what had happened to her would be to betray China and sometimes she thought that perhaps what the Party had done had been good and right. So when they sat down for lunch or dinner and the others prayed before and after they ate, as they always had and she had too, it would make Tursunay so uncomfortable that she would stand up and rush into the next room.

"Tursunay," Halmirza, would say to her. "You need to wake up. You know what your people are suffering. How can you face them if you don't speak out? You must support them, help them." She would tell him to stop talking but he would not. "You have faced so much," he would say. "But you are free here and you don't need to be afraid of China anymore."

She would not. She was certain that if she said or did anything at all then her family would be taken or just killed. Still the memories stole on her unexpected and she cried out when they came. Two months of that and of the normalcy around her and she saw how firmly she continued to follow what she had been taught in the camp and that the Party had built another prison within her that she herself maintained. She tore away and allowed back the part of her that had always resisted. She told Halmirza fragments of what had been and grew angry instead of compliant. The anger came in unexpected flashes. If Xi Jinping was on television or someone spoke of the Chinese government. When she saw a plastic stool like the ones they had spent all that time sitting on in their cells she wanted to tear it to pieces.

So they drove to Almaty and to the Atazhurt offices and they talked together with Serikzhan. She recognized him at once from the video. He was warm and friendly and spoke fast and assured. Tursunay liked him. He asked if she would be willing to make a video statement explaining what had happened to her in the camps. It was important, he said, that survivors talked about what was going on for their people and their nation. They were witness to the crimes of the Chinese government that he and the others had been working to expose. Tursunay said no. She was grateful for what he had done but it was too much and too soon and she could not imagine what going public would do to her. "Please don't," she said. "Don't force me to speak out."

Serikzhan had kept out of sight as much as he could since his release, letting others in Atazhurt make public appearances and interviews. He would not keep away completely and he thought Tursunay was important to their cause so he kept asking. Halmirza often called Serikzhan on one of the numbers he rarely gave out. One of what he called his black numbers linked to an unregistered SIM card. Halmirza would apologize when he did and say that he had talked with Tursunay many times and she would not change her mind. Serikzhan invited them to eat at a restaurant near the office and made his case once more. Again Tursunay refused. He got the sense she was scared of publicity and scared of him too because of the things authorities said about him.

Then he invited she and Halmirza to visit him at home. They came, and they talked together longer than they had before. Hours. About Xinjiang, about their lives, about Atazhurt. That persuaded her and Tursunay said she would come and record a video the next day. By the time she and Halmirza had got back to Shelek, she had changed her mind and she called to tell Serikzhan that she was sorry but in fact she could not do it.

Another call and Halmirza told Serikzhan that he and Tursunay had argued. Tursunay had said she had to think of her siblings, and in return he had asked whether she thought she was the only one to have people there. He also had a brother and sister in China, he said, but he had given them up when he recorded that first video because she was his wife and he had a duty to rescue her.

On October 15 Tursunay visited Atazhurt once more. This time

she sat down in the office wearing a dark jacket with a hoodie underneath, her hair swept back by an ornate headband. Halmirza sat next
to her in front of the microphones and two Atazhurt men sat on the
other side.

She talked of her history. The confiscated passports and the first
stint in the Künes facility. Then the next time and how it had been
so much worse. She described the enlarged camp, the huge number of
detainees, the humiliating bathrooms and the armed guards. She told
them about the red songs, that siren drill and the Kazakh women who
had been taken away.

And she left much out. The interrogations and what had happened
in that dark camera-less room. The screams. The women brought
back to the cell catatonic or crying and shaking uncontrollably. She
could not revisit it. Not there with them. She could not bear to have
anyone know at all, especially Halmirza.

"Ok," Tursunay said when they had finished. "Publish it."
Serikzhan scheduled the video to go live that night but Tursunay
called Serikzhan when she got back to Shelek and she was terrified
again. She had changed her mind, she said, please don't do it.

"Of course," Serikzhan told her. He called Galym, Atazhurt's camera operator and editor, and told him to upload the video to YouTube
but to keep it set private so only they could see it.

Serikzhan was up late. He answered messages and emails, he
spoke to a journalist in Canada and then at last he put his phone on
silent and he slept. He woke around ten to dozens of missed calls
from Tursunay and called her back right away. She was terribly upset.
Why, she asked, why had he published her testimony when she told
him not to?

He checked and it was true. Serikzhan got hold of Galym and Galym apologized too because he had been so tired the previous evening that he had forgotten to set the video to private. Serikzhan called Tursunay again and told her that it was going to be taken down again. "I'm sorry," he said, "I made a mistake. It's my fault."

She called him back after an hour. "It's ok," she said, "publish it. The Chinese authorities know. It has already happened. Just publish it."

She should not have answered the call. "How could you do this?" the cadre asked. "How could you turn on your country? What kind of person have you become in Kazakhstan?" He told her that she was responsible for the things that would happen to her relatives.

Tursunay threw her phone away and the fear swallowed her again. She called Serikzhan. "This is bad," she told him. "I'm in danger here. China regrets letting me go, and Kazakhstan is going to deport me."

She knew the power Chinese authorities had in Kazakhstan. Perhaps they would just send police for her. Serikzhan tried to reassure her. "That's not going to happen," he said. "I'll talk to some contacts and call the American consulate to make an appointment with the officials there." They had helped other survivors and escapees before, he said, and perhaps they would again. Tursunay did not know much about the US other than the things the Chinese government said about it but she would hear out anyone willing to help.

The consulate building was a tower of dark glass in a large compound of its own. Tursunay left her phone at the entrance and passed through several layers of security. A neatly dressed American man welcomed her and Tursunay told him much of the same things that she had told Serikzhan. "Be assured," he said through a translator, "you have our support. That doesn't mean that we're going to take you to the US. I can't promise that. But I can guarantee you that they won't deport you to China." The man assigned Tursunay a lawyer too, a Kazakh woman named Aina who he said often worked on human rights cases like hers and could act as a liaison between her and the consulate. Tursunay felt a whisper of relief. She seemed to be useful to the Americans, and they wanted to know what she had to say.

She and Aina went back again to the residency office the next morning. The same queue, the same room, the same woman who had been so rude before but this time the woman's attitude had changed completely. Aina spoke to the woman mostly in Russian but Tursunay had picked up enough to follow some of the conversation.

"Oh, our apologies," the woman said as she flicked through the paperwork. "I didn't know." Why though, she asked Aina after a few moments, did people in America care about this woman so much. Aina told her that Tursunay was a survivor from the Chinese camps so the woman should just do what was asked of her. And like that, Tursunay was granted asylum-seeker status and a three-month visa extension. There would be a court date before her visa expired, Aina said, and they would be able to extend it again. She repeated the words of the consulate man. "Don't worry," she said, "we won't let them deport you."

A reprieve. Tursunay hoped she might start to feel better in Kazakhstan. That her body might heal through distance from the place of her suffering but the bleeding still came and the cough persisted. She slept and felt no more rested. Loud noises made her start, uniforms made her nervous and sometimes when the winds roared around the house she heard the screams and pleas of the women held with her. She veered between better days when she ventured outside in the last of the Autumn sunshine and the ones where she felt irreparably broken.

Towards the end of the year her assurances of safety in Kazakhstan seemed to be evaporating. She was not sure exactly what had changed but Aina no longer seemed confident that her asylum-seeker status would be renewed in the spring. Serikzhan warned her the Chinese government might try and block it and if they did then she would likely be deported the moment it happened. It felt unfair. Kazakh camp survivors were looked after but neither the authorities nor the people seemed to care much about Uyghurs. She and Halmirza did what they could, continuing their involvement with Atazhurt and preparing her case. Aina thought international attention might help her so Tursunay spoke to some journalists and told them about the camp conditions but still kept much of what had happened to herself.

One afternoon Halmirza came back from Friday prayer with an expression on his face she did not like. A man had approached him in the street, he said, a man he had never seen before but who spoke to him by name and told him that both he and Tursunay needed to stay quiet. He brushed it off but something twisted in her and was still there when she went to bed.

She woke from a deep sleep around two in the morning and at first was not sure why. Halmirza was awake too and on his feet over by the window. Then he was shouting. "A fire." he was saying. "Get up, get out of bed." He called through too to his sister and her daughter, who had been staying with them a while.

It was the outbuilding next to the house, he said. He went to the front door to see what was happening but then Tursunay heard him struggling with the door and he shouted that would not open. She was out of bed pulling on clothes and so was her sister-in-law and the girl. They could soon smell smoke seeping into the house and thought the fire would spread with it. Tursunay screamed and Halmirza kept hammering the door with his fists and feet and charging it with his shoulder.

The door opened a crack at last. Enough to see that turns of wire had been wrapped around the outside handle to secure it to the jamb. Halmirza rushed to the kitchen and grabbed a knife and hacked his way through. Then they were out and taking ragged breaths of night air. They called the fire service but by the time the trucks came, the outbuilding was nearly burned out and the flames had happily not spread to the house.

Tursunay called Aina and Serikzhan and told them she thought someone had tried to kill her to stop her from talking. Aina arrived not long after daybreak with the man from the American consulate and a colleague of his she had not seen before. They looked over the scorched cinder blocks and puddles of firehose-drenched soot, they took pictures of the damage and the wire on the door handle and then talked quietly between themselves and told Tursunay and Halmirza that they must move at once.

Aina and Serikzhan helped find them an apartment in central Almaty. It was nice. Airy and on a leafy street near a shopping mall but Tursunay could enjoy nothing. The fear surrounded her and she was getting sicker, her bleeding worse. She did not want to leave the apartment at all and when she did she saw spies and assassins in the faces around her and recoiled from looming shadows. So she stayed in when Halmirza went to run errands and he always called before he came back so she knew it was him at the door. Aina and Serikzhan did the same when they visited and Tursunay would lock up quickly after them.

Often after Halmirza went out someone would ring the apartment doorbell. She never answered or asked who it was and there was no peephole to look out of. So she froze in the middle of whatever she was doing when it happened and made as little noise as possible while her heart hammered away. She would stay that way until she was sure they must be gone. Sometimes there was no bell but she still heard movement outside. Coming and going. Breaths and footsteps. It was almost worse.

A doctor told Tursunay that she would need tests to find out what was wrong then probably surgery to do something about it. She knew she could not go on getting worse but she was afraid that if she was admitted to a Kazakh hospital then Chinese agents would find a way to get to her. The camp guards had asked her about the World Uyghur Congress and she had known nothing of it but an activist named Sedirdin who was a member heard about her case and suggested that she go to Istanbul for the procedure and promised that they would help her secure a visa to do it. Turkey was a country of Muslims far from China. She thought it had to be safer and Serikzhan told her to leave Kazakhstan any way they could.

30

The greatest charm of Xinjiang lies in the multi-ethnic harmony and diversity in cultures. There are 25,000 places for religious activities, including 24,400 mosques. On average, there is one mosque for every 530 Muslims. Xinjiang has a population of 25 million and hosts all 56 ethnic groups in China such as Uygur, Han, Kazakh, Hui, Kirgiz, Mongolia, Tajik, etc. The minority population accounts for 59.9% of the total population. The people of all ethnic groups hold together like pomegranate seeds, cherishing national unity as much as their own lives.

—**Xinjiang: a sweet and peaceful homeland for people of all ethnic groups, Yao Jing, Chinese ambassador to Pakistan, July 5, 2019**

S erikzhan had never intended to abide by anything more than the letter of his agreement with the prosecutor's office. He sat out his probation in Almaty. Then he went back to Atazhurt's headquarters on the first of January 2020 and made a video detailing his plans. He would be getting back to work right there in the office, he said. He would not be in charge, of course, because he could no longer legally lead any such organization but he would work as a translator or a driver or a cleaner. He would do whatever was needed.

An NSC officer called the next day and said two of his people were on their way to Atazhurt's offices so Serikzhan should go with them.

"You began to work," the officer said when Serikzhan arrived at the NSC building, and he was not at all happy about it. It was true, Serikzhan said, and explained that working for a group but not leading it was not forbidden by the agreement. After all, he said, he spoke English and Chinese, he could be very useful to Atazhurt as a translator. The officer looked furious but made some calls and told Serikzhan to go.

The next morning that same officer called and asked Serikzhan to come to see him again. "I'm working," Serikzhan said. "I'm busy, please come to see me at my office." The officer sounded even less happy than the previous day but did not press it, and Serikzhan got back to what he was doing and waited to see what they would try next.

Saira met with Serikzhan not long after arriving in Almaty. He explained that he was collecting testimony and evidence from survivors of the camps and asked if she would tell him about what she had experienced.

She was wary at first. She wanted people to know what was happening in Xinjiang but doing that would make her visible in a way she had not been before. Almaty was close enough to the border that it would be easy for someone to cross from China to get at her if they wanted. Perhaps it would not even be necessary for anyone to cross. She had heard that some survivors and exiles had started working for Chinese authorities in exchange for being able to speak regularly with their families or for the possibility of meeting them at Khorgos. Then there was her mother and her sisters. Criticizing China so publicly risked any further chance of communication with them and might put them at risk too.

Serikzhan tried to convince her. "Please," he said. "Help the world understand what happened in China. People need to know."

Saira thought of the faces of those left behind in her cell and of everything that the guards had said to them about their plans for Kazakhstan. She decided that China's ambition was not just dangerous for her but for the world and she tried to reassure herself about what she was about to do. God knew her intentions were good. She would be judged by those.

She talked Serikzhan through it all before she recorded a video. He listened and asked questions about what she had said and then asked if she was omitting any difficult details. Some kind of sexual violence, for example. "Please tell me if something like that happened," he said. "It's important."

"Nothing did," she said. "You can ask any person in my camp, they will tell you the same."

That was how she learned about the things that had happened at the camps in Ghulja and Kashgar and other mostly Uyghur regions. Trainees there had also slept on concrete floors next to open toilets and sung red songs in cramped classrooms but there had been assaults, rapes and torture far worse than anything that she and her cellmates had endured. She had not believed the guards who told them they should be grateful they had not been sent somewhere else because she could not imagine how it could have been worse. They had not been lying.

She met other survivors and they talked of what had been done to them. There was Baqitali, a thin, nervous man who used to sell vegetables and had been arrested and sent to a Künes camp for planning a trip to Kazakhstan. Guards had beaten him with fists, boots and batons so badly that he signed his name to any confession they put in front of him. He saw men half-paralyzed from the torture there and one whose arms did not work properly after being hung by his wrists for four unbroken days. He saw other men who died from it. Before the camp, he himself had been a strong man, he said. Never sick. It was hard to imagine as he talked hunched over the table and swallowed by his clothes. By the time they let him go he vomited blood most days and could not walk on his own. He had managed to reach Kazakhstan much as she had but had to be hospitalized for months after.

Then she met two brothers of Nurlan, the man who had been taken from her camp and brought back mute and unable to care for himself. The brothers were explaining it all to Serikzhan. Showing him documents and doctors' reports detailing what had been done. She met Tursunay once there too. She seemed withdrawn and unsettled. Like whatever had happened was still right there with her. They exchanged numbers and said they would keep in touch.

Survivors like them formed a network of sorts. Through it Saira learned that more women she had been held with had managed to reach Kazakhstan. The one who had been forced to have an abortion when she was detained was there. So was her husband and they had just had a child. The woman who had been held in a tiger chair for seventy-two hours, she was there too. Saira got in touch to arrange tearful reunions, and they called and messaged each other often. Some of them she introduced to Serikzhan but with a warning. "Make sure not to embellish even the slightest thing when you talk to him," she told them. "I don't know how many years it will take to prove it. five, ten, more. But if one of you lies, it will ruin all the work that everyone has done. It will make everything that everyone has sacrificed worthless."

31

The Chinese government is taking draconian measures to slash birth rates among Uighurs and other minorities as part of a sweeping campaign to curb its Muslim population, even as it encourages some of the country's Han majority to have more children.

While individual women have spoken out before about forced birth control, the practice is far more widespread and systematic than previously known, according to an AP investigation based on government statistics, state documents and interviews with 30 ex-detainees, family members and a former detention camp instructor. The campaign over the past four years in the far west region of Xinjiang is leading to what some experts are calling a form of "demographic genocide."

—Associated Press, June 29, 2020

The Turkish visa came through as promised at the beginning of August. Quickly, electronic, and valid for a six-month stay. Halmirza told her it was good news but Tursunay was so worn out that she could not imagine she would be allowed to leave. Halmirza booked the soonest available tickets to Istanbul and Sedirdin from the World Uyghur Congress arranged for some Uyghurs living there to pick them up from the airport and give them a place to stay while they found something longer-term. So everything was set and then it was not because the night before their flight Halmirza's nephew died suddenly. The nephew who Tursunay had loved so and thought of as a son. Who met her at Khorgos and nearly carried her all the way to the car. Grief overwhelmed her and she wanted to stay. Halmirza had to so that he could help his sister through the miserable drudgery of post-bereavement bureaucracy but he insisted that Tursunay go as planned.

She prepared her bags. One of brown leather containing the few essentials she was strong enough to carry. Two more that were plastic with printouts of tickets and her visa as well as her medical charts that she imagined would ease her passage out of the country. Sedirdin met her and Halmirza at the airport and his presence helped calm her mounting concern. They walked across the terminal hall, bright and nearly empty because so many flights had been cancelled since the Covid-19 pandemic began . Before they parted, Halmirza took a picture. It showed her wan and tired, clutching her bags, with sunglasses on her head, an orange sweater around her waist and a blue surgical mask on her face as pandemic restrictions dictated.

She put her bags through the scanner, emptied then refilled her pockets and reached the passport control booth lightheaded and unsteady. An officer looked at her and took her passport. He opened it and flicked through the pages but instead of stamping it and giving it back to her, he kept it. "Come with me," he told Tursunay. "We need to make some checks." The guard told her to wait just past the booth. Ahead were the gates, screens, seats and contained impatience of the departures area. She could see the planes lined up. Umbilical boarding bridges attached and tended by squat ground-crew vehicles. On one side seemed to be flights for Turkey. On the other, for China. How easy it would be for the guards to send her back. All they need do would be to march her onto one of those Chinese flights and she would be gone and no one would be able to do anything for her. She trembled thinking of it. She called Sedirdin and he promised to inform the Americans and to tell the police that if anything happened to her they would be personally responsible.

The passport officer returned with three more officers and they pressed in around her. One of the newcomers was in charge and it was him who asked the questions. When had she come to Kazakhstan, he wanted to know, why had she stayed and why did she want to go to Turkey now? What was she planning to do when she arrived there and would she be coming back again? Tursunay offered up her talismanic medical records. She explained that if she was not operated on then she could die but that the operation could not be done in Kazakhstan. Standing for so long was sapping what was left of her strength and muddling her thoughts and she could not lie to them. She did not promise she would return but repeated that her husband was staying behind in Kazakhstan and only God knew whether she would be able to come back because perhaps she would not survive the operation. "I'm sick," she told them. "I'm sick and I'm only going where I can be treated." Eventually they grew tired and gave Tursunay back her passport.

The plane came in low over the Black Sea and bumped down into Istanbul's colossal sprawl. Tursunay heard the pilot's announcement but she worried as she moved slowly along the air bridge that she might be somewhere else somehow. Then on the shoulders of the ground staff she saw the same star and crescent as East Turkestan's but against a red background and she was reassured.

The airport was enormous with gleaming new glass-walled corridors stretching right and left under an arched lattice roof. Tursunay followed the other passengers. It was difficult going now she was back on her feet. Consciousness kept ebbing away from her and the bleeding was worse too. She looked around for a bathroom to clean herself up and saw none so she walked on behind the echoing footsteps and rumbling suitcase wheels. There was a man named Abdulrahman who was one of the group waiting to meet her so Tursunay paused and took out her phone to call him but found she did not have signal.

Signs and arrows, a descending escalator and she was nearing the passport gates. She must not have looked well because a man came to her and said something that she only partially understood. "Are you a Turk," she made out, "are you a Turk?" And she knew that the man did not mean was she a citizen of Turkey but was she of the people that stretched from there across sea, mountain and steppe to Xinjiang and that for him that was something good. She nodded and mimed that she needed to use a telephone. The man offered her his and she dialled Abdulrahman and told them she had arrived.

"Welcome," he said. "We're waiting for you outside."

Past passport control and onward through the duty-free shop between the luggage carousels and she found them. Abdulrahman was a burly, kindly man with a bald head and a beard streaked gray. His wife had come with him too. Tursunay thanked them and collapsed into a car seat and they pulled out past blocks of multistory parking and a huge Turkish flag undulating red. Then they were on a many-laned highway and driving fast until they met the edges of a newer suburban district sloping down towards glimmering sea.

She rested and the fear abated but not completely. Turkey's government seemed to her not unlike Kazakhstan's. Chinese money was helping keep the economy moving from what she heard and Uyghur dissidents had been arrested there. So she felt a stab of anxiety when her phone lit up with an unknown number on the third day. She answered to a woman speaking Uyghur. The woman said her name was Gulbahar and that she had heard that Tursunay had reached Istanbul and wanted to call her because she too had survived the camps. Tursunay listened but found she could not speak and then that she was crying because there had been kindness and help and generosity since her release but so few who understood what had happened to her. On the other end of the line she could hear Gulbahar crying too and for a while there was only breaths and muffled sobs.

"You should have come to me," Gulbahar said eventually. "Where are you?" Tursunay told her and Gulbahar turned out to know both Abdulrahman and his wife. Soon they were in the car and on their way to her place.

Gulbahar opened her door and Tursunay took in a stout woman in her fifties with heavy brows and a mole on her right cheek. Again Tursunay could say nothing and they embraced and they wept. There was no need to talk much anyway, Tursunay thought. Pain had bonded them and it was like they could see right into each other.

Gulbahar cooked Uyghur food for her and fetched supplies from pharmacies and supermarkets. "Whatever I can do," she said, "I want to. Please let me help you." She stayed with Tursunay all night. It was solace just to feel her there asking nothing and requiring nothing but Tursunay kept getting weaker and had no appetite even for Gulbahar's kitchen. She ate and she knew it was good but she could not enjoy anything. Neither did she wish to see the sights of Istanbul. Even from a car as Abdulrahman had offered. Not the Blue Mosque or the Hagia Sophia or the Golden Horn in all its beauty. They took her down to the waterfront once and the Sea of Marmaris stretched out before her, the container ships riding at anchor in the blue. "What a lovely day it is," they said, encouraging, but the sunshine did not warm her, the wind was up and there was no beauty for her there. "No," she said. "No, no, let's go back again."

Halmirza arrived and rented a house for them. It was near enough to Gulbahar's but she insisted on staying with Tursunay still and Tursunay was thankful for it. Halmirza's arrival also meant the start of hospital visits and each one was exhausting and complicated by pandemic restrictions. Receptions, waiting rooms, examinations, injections, prescriptions. And for everything an itemized bill for far more than they expected.

Tests were inconclusive, results delayed and soon Tursunay and Halmirza had spent 4,000 dollars or so in Turkish lira and were starting to run low on money. Each day she sunk further. She soon feared she would collapse after only a few minutes on her feet and when she looked down at her body, her bones pressed through her skin. Halmirza went out and bought drugs he hoped might at least stop her from getting worse. They only slowed her decline.

One day Gulbahar went to meet a Uyghur activist named Arslan Hidayat, who was gathering testimony from camp survivors. She brought him back to Tursunay's after a while. A young man with a neat chin-strap beard and cropped hair. She had mentioned Tursunay to Arslan, she said, and he had asked to meet her. Arslan did not hide his shock at her condition and promised to do what he could to help.

A voice message on Tursunay's phone. It was another woman who was a stranger to her. This one said her name was Elfidar Iltebir and that she was with the Uyghur American Association in Virginia. The association had learned about Tursunay's situation, she said, and the community there had gathered 3,000 dollars to help pay for her treatment. "Sorry it's not more, we don't have much," Elfidar said. "But this is just for now. We want you to get better and we want you to come here." Arslan told her that a different American organization, the Uyghur Human Rights Project, would be sending an additional two thousand dollars. Tursunay was overcome. People she had not met in a country she had never been had done so much for her and wished her to join them.

The donations paid for more checkups and tests that led doctors to a diagnosis in early September. Tursunay needed an operation to remove her uterus, they said, and it would cost 10,000 dollars. Tursunay and Halmirza did not have that much but he told her that this was not something that could be delayed. He went to the hospital and he begged the doctors. "Please operate first," he said, "and then I don't care if it's twenty thousand dollars or more, I'll go back to Kazakhstan and sell my property, I'll bring you the money." The doctors told him they must have it up-front before they would do anything.

Arslan called Tursunay about three weeks after they first met. "Sister," he told her, "someone from the US consulate will phone you soon and when they do, you should go to the consulate. They have a visa for you. Once you have it, UHRP will book your flight ticket. Everything is ready." She asked if Halmirza could come too and he said for now it would only be her but that he should be able to join her after she arrived.

Abdulrahman picked them up and forty minutes later they saw a hulking building of pale stone standing citadel-like on a hill of its own behind layers of walls and fencing. They followed a narrower road along one of those walls, residential buildings on their left with peeling paint and laundry strung from balconies. Only Tursunay was allowed inside the consulate. She walked up the path, left to a gatehouse with scanners and security doors and then hesitant along a corridor where another guard directed her to an elevator. More corridors and eventually a room of numbered booths where staff worked behind protective glass. A woman exchanged her passport for a slip of paper and told her to return the next day.

She did as she was instructed and a different woman gave her passport back. She flicked through the pages until she saw it. It took up one whole page. UNITED STATES OF AMERICA, it said, then VISA and her picture and personal details with a picture of a domed building and a statue of a bearded man behind them.

Halmirza and Abdulrahman were waiting anxious by the car. She walked towards them and a spirit of hysterical mischief made her decide to play a trick on them. "What happened?" they asked her. "Tell us, did you get the visa?"

"No," Tursunay said, "not yet, they just asked more questions." The two of them looked so disappointed that they must surely have cared about her more than she did herself but still she said nothing.

They got into the car again and pulled away. Halmirza turned back to Tursunay. "Are you sure there was no news?" he asked. "Please just tell me something."

"No news," Tursunay said, "nothing."

Then Abdulrahman looked at her in the rearview mirror. "Tursunay, are you sure they didn't say anything?" he asked. "All I was thinking of today was that we would celebrate. I was going to take us to a Uyghur restaurant where we could all eat together."

She took out her passport opened it at the visa page and passed it to the front of the car. Abdulrahman noticed it first, looked down for a second and was nearly shouting. "My God, it's a one-year visa. Oh my God," he said, his voice filling the car. He pulled over to the side of the road. "Oh God," he said. "Allahu akbar, Allahu akbar." He and Halmirza were so happy and so joyously relieved that she started to believe it too and the emotion grew too much for any of them and they were all crying and shouting and whooping as the oblivious traffic barrelled past.

Abdulrahman ordered a feast at the restaurant. Tursunay barely ate but the others happily worked their way through dumplings and noodles and rounds of skewered meat. After a while, Halmirza turned earnest to Tursunay. "Can you leave tonight?" he asked. "Tomorrow?" She told him UHRP were going to buy the ticket. "Do not wait a minute more than you have to," he said, "because if you do, you might never leave." And in his relief he began to tell her the things he had been doing when he was out in the city alone. It had seemed so likely that she might die in Istanbul that he had searched for graveyards with available plots so that if it happened she could be buried quickly as Muslim law dictated.

Omer Kanat, UHRP's chairman, called her that night. "Congratulations," he said. "When are you ready to leave?"

Tursunay told him whenever she could and that if they bought her a ticket for the following day then she could leave the following day. "I have nothing here to prepare or to pack," she said. "I am ready." Omer sent the ticket soon after and Tursunay went to bed dazed. After everything, she was still there. Truly, she thought, you can survive anything. While your soul remains, you will live.

They had to park such a distance away from the main airport building that Tursunay was not sure she would be able to walk it. Abdulrahman told her not to worry and fetched one of the luggage carts. She was too tired for dignity and sunk into its uncomfortable angles and tucked in her knees. He pushed her all the way to the gleaming departures floor where they said long goodbyes.

At her gate she grew scared. Perhaps when security checked her boarding pass and her passport they had switched it for a flight back to China. Perhaps it was all just a trick. She fumbled for the pass and it looked ok. She scanned around for people who looked American because a plane full of them would surely not be going to China. There were none. She was early and the gate was mostly empty. A man arrived. Tall and pale with neat gray hair and wearing slacks and a shirt. Unmistakably American. Tursunay showed him her boarding pass then pointed at herself and the gate and to him too and said one of the only words she knew in English. "Washington," she said. "Washington." The man mimed that he too was going there so Tursunay calmed herself and settled back down on a chair from where she could easily see him. As long as she got on the plane with him, then she would be going to the right place.

Airline staff arrived, the gate filled up and Tursunay started to need to go to the bathroom. She held it. There were some not far from the gate but if she moved she might lose track of the American man. A while longer and she could no longer deny her bladder yet still she worried she might lose him. She had an idea. She approached him and put down her bag on the next seat then pointed to the bathroom and him and the bag until it was clear that she wanted him to look after it until she came back. He nodded and she walked off confident that he could not go anywhere.

Her seat was in the middle aisle but no one came to sit next to her and that somehow calmed her. It was surely only with God's help that she had been able to escape the camps at all and here was another blessing to ease her journey. She put her bag on one of the seats and curled up across them. A flight attendant came to her and told her to sit up and put on her seat belt. Tursunay gestured to her stomach and winced to show that it hurt there and that she needed to lie like that. The flight attendant eventually nodded that it was ok, she could stay where she was.

The pain usually brimmed up in her almost unbearably every few hours but she lay there in the ambient light and pressurized air and it never came. The bleeding lessened too. She rested and slept a while and drank something when the flight attendant came to check on her. Night caught up with them somewhere over the Atlantic and it was black out with rain splattering the acrylic windows by the time she felt the plane angle downwards.

A passport control agent at US immigration waved her towards his booth. The agent asked her something in English and Tursunay indicated that she did not understand. He looked at her passport and at XINJIANG in capital letters in the place of birth and place of issue fields then took out his phone, typed something and held it up to her. It was open at a translation app and the text asked in Uyghur who had invited her to America. Tursunay did not know how to answer. Back in Kazakhstan she had seen often that Secretary of State Mike Pompeo had condemned what China was doing to Uyghurs. Genocide, he had called it, crimes against humanity. So that was how she answered. "Pompeo," she said. And the border guard started laughing and called to a colleague, who laughed too. He asked again and showed her that same screen. Again Tursunay told him Pompeo. It was true. The US government was helping her so surely they would understand. She kept repeating Pompeo's name and the guard kept laughing and after a while he gave a thumb's up to say that things were ok.

Omer was waiting for her with his wife, Medine, and Louisa Greve, who headed advocacy for UHRP. Omer was a small bookish-looking man with only a small band of graying hair on the back and sides of his head. Louisa was taller than him with a neat bob. They seemed so glad to see her that they quickly felt not like strangers at all. These were her saviors, she thought. She would always feel close to them.

Omer and Medine said they would be taking Tursunay to a hotel in Virginia. She had expected that she would be in someone's home and she did not want to be alone but Omer said it had to be that way because of the pandemic. Highways led to a succession of narrowing streets until they were checking her into an unremarkable ground-floor room. Tursunay eyed the windows. Anyone determined could get at her in seconds if they wanted. Omer told her not to worry. That they were in America so nothing would happen to her. Then he wrote his phone number in large, clear digits on a piece of paper. Whatever she needed, whatever happened, he said, she should call him and he would be there.

Medine returned with food for her. It was home-cooked chöchure, neat dough parcels of lamb and onion, crimped and curled in broth rich with pepper and cilantro. It would be like that each day, Medine told her. The Uyghur community in DC and Virginia was the biggest in America and they had organized themselves to take turns bringing food and checking in on her.

She came again a bit before lunch the next day. They talked briefly and she produced some more food then said goodbye and closed the door behind her. With no warning, Tursunay's bleeding started again. It was terribly bad. Much worse than before. She panicked and she screamed Medine's name and somehow Medine heard her and hurried back. Medine told her to sit down because it might help slow the bleeding and she called an ambulance.

Tursunay was already faint when they got to the hospital and staff helped her straight to an examination room. Everything was clean and white in there. The walls, the floor, the sheets of the adjustable bed. A nurse came in and put absorbent pads down on the bed and laid out a hospital gown. She told Tursunay through a translator to get changed and to lie down. "No," said Tursunay. "No, no." She was bleeding so much that it would get everywhere and in the hospitals she had visited in Xinjiang she would expect to be punished for that.

"The blood will mess up your bed," she said. "I can't take off my clothes."

"Please calm down," the nurse said. "We need to examine you." Life spilled from her between those gleaming walls and the nurses just kept changing the pads and they were so nice about it and their voices so reassuring. She shivered with a profound chill and someone wrapped her in a thick blanket and she was warm again. Others pricked her skin with needles and began to examine her but still everything was so cosy and comfortable. She wondered if it was because she had been brought there by the American government that she was getting such special treatment. One of the nurses called someone over, a big man. He was just as gentle and kind as the others and helped lift her like a child onto a gurney. They wheeled her away to run more tests, and the corridor lights passed woozily overhead.

32

The Chinese Government has embarked on a systematic and intentional campaign to rewrite the cultural heritage of the Xinjiang Uyghur Autonomous Region (XUAR). It's seeking to erode and redefine the culture of the Uyghurs and other Turkic-speaking communities—stripping away any Islamic, transnational or autonomous elements—in order to render those indigenous cultural traditions subservient to the 'Chinese nation'.

Using satellite imagery, we estimate that approximately 16,000 mosques in Xinjiang (65% of the total) have been destroyed or damaged as a result of government policies, mostly since 2017. An estimated 8,500 have been demolished outright, and, for the most part, the land on which those razed mosques once sat remains vacant. A further 30% of important Islamic sacred sites (shrines, cemeteries and pilgrimage routes, including many protected under Chinese law) have been demolished across Xinjiang, mostly since 2017, and an additional 28% have been damaged or altered in some way.

—Cultural erasure, Tracing the destruction of Uyghur and
Islamic spaces in Xinjiang, The Australian Strategic
Policy Institute, September 24, 2020

The same government men who had plagued his house arrest came to him still. They wanted him to stay quiet and to shut down Atazhurt completely. Serikzhan refused. He was sticking to the terms of the plea deal and thought that protection enough. His visitors did not and some of them began talking of underground cells with no phone calls and no record of arrest. One of them suggested something worse. "We told you over and over to stop and you did not stop," the man said. "So what should we do? Arrest you? That didn't work, and all that publicity would only begin again. Let you go free? That didn't work either. What if there was an accident? What if a Kamaz," he said, talking of the big six-wheeler trucks, "crashed into that little Nissan of yours? That would be that, and your wife and your children would be left crying and alone. Or perhaps it would be them in the car instead, and you left with no one."

"It's up to you," the man said. "You choose." You choose. He said it with complete nonchalance like he was offering Serikzhan options from a cafe menu. Cappuccino or americano, still or sparkling, silence or execution.

President Nazarbayev had at last stepped down, although he remained head of the Security Council and had chosen the man to follow him in Kassym-Jomart Tokayev. Tokayev promised to carry on what Nazarbayev had begun and ruled in much the same way. Things closed in again on Serikzhan. New cases were opened against him. Cars and watchful eyes lingered outside his home. Authorities said he was a terrorist and froze his bank accounts and the bank accounts of his parents after his father died.

In February 2020 police arrested an activist and protester named Dulat Agadil. Dulat had supported Atazhurt since the beginning and had called for an end to pro-China policies and to official silence on the camps. The crowd of plainclothes men that took him arrived at his family home at night. There was video showing them leading Dulat out into the dark towards a waiting car, snow streaking in its headlights.

Authorities announced Dulat's death a few days later and blamed it on suspected heart failure, though he was only forty-three. A forensic exam showed he had been drinking, they said, though those who knew him said he never touched alcohol nor even smoked. And they produced testimony from cellmates who said he had not been touched by the guards, though before they buried him his family found scrapes on his body and dirt on his palms.

So in September Serikzhan fled. To Istanbul with Laila and the boys. Turkey seemed the most sensible choice. It was easy to get to for Kazakh citizens and relatively straightforward to get residency. They travelled light with the reassurances of an Atazhurt member already there who passed on promises made by a liaison to Erdoğan's government. Because their cause was so important to the Turkic world, the liaison had said, the government would furnish Serikzhan and the others with offices to work from. It would fly camp survivors to Istanbul for medical examinations to gather still more evidence and it would donate food, clothes and money to the families of those lost to the camps.

Serikzhan recorded a livestream for his followers not long after he arrived. "I'm so happy," he said. "Turkey is one of the most powerful countries in the world. It will truly help us and we will stop having to beg for money to keep Atazhurt running."

He soon found those promises were for nothing. The liaison stopped talking and the Turkish government that had once spoken out so strongly in defense of Xinjiang's Muslims was buying Chinese vaccines and welcoming Chinese investment.

Serikzhan and Laila did not feel safe there. When he left the house he was sure people were following him and was sure that his communications were being monitored as well. He heard what had happened to Uyghurs living in Istanbul who had refused to be quiet. Police had dragged actvists from their homes or picked them up in the street and sent them to deportation centers. Most were released after weeks or months with warnings not to be so noisy. A few were said to have been sent to Tajikistan and the Tajik government was friendly with China's so would likely pass on any detainees.

One man who had gone to the press and told them he had been coerced into becoming a spy for the Chinese government had been shot in the back and shoulder outside a friend's house. He was lucky to have lived but the police never found who did it. It was easy for Serikzhan to imagine something like that happening to him.

Laila told him to leave and this time to the US. He had an unused visitor visa that was still valid so he would be able to but she did not and neither did the children. "Go," she said. "You must save yourself, your work, your country." He contacted an organization based in Texas named China Aid that advocated for religious freedom in China and had supported a camp escapee's journey to the US. The China Aid people said Serikzhan would have a good case for asylum there and that family re-unification should not take long afterwards. He travelled to Washington DC on January 20, 2021.

China Aid arranged for him to stay in Virginia with Michael Horowitz and Devra Marcus, an older couple who had often helped religious refugees. Things were busy at first. There were journalists who wanted to interview him and officials and activists of various kinds who spoke admiringly of the important work he had done.

He loved Washington DC. It was to him the heart of the democratic ideals he admired and he saw the sights that everyone must in the capital. The White House, the Washington Monument, the Capitol Building. He livestreamed his visit to the Martin Luther King Jr. Memorial to his followers. A great man, he told them, a great, great man. At the Lincoln Memorial, he wandered in the chill with a friend admiring the columns and the murals and the great marble statue. It was a while before he noticed the man walking after them holding a camera with a long zoom lens. The man looked Chinese to Serikzhan and was taking pictures that seemed to be focused not on the memorial but on him. He and his friend turned towards the man and the man busied his lens with the memorial but it soon it swung back their way. It shook Serikzhan. That was not how he expected things to be in America.

He started to notice cars and vans outside Devra and Michael's place. Parked up out on the road. Michael told him not to worry but he did anyway and sometimes at two or three in the morning he would wake up with his heart going hard and head downstairs to make sure the outside doors were locked.

Laila was worried too. She told him she had heard of men making their way around Kazakhs in Istanbul holding pictures of Serikzhan and asking where he was and where his family was. She and the children could not stay there.

Perhaps it was the pandemic or the political upheaval and change of administration in the US but Serikzhan's asylum case seemed not to be moving. Without that no one could tell him how long reunification might take. So they waited and the intimidation kept coming. One day he opened a Facebook message from the head of a Chinese student association in Kazakhstan that threatened his life and the lives of his sons. Then he saw another. A video of a man talking to the camera.

"Maybe you don't want your wife," the man said. "But we do. I'm going to go to your wife in Turkey and if she's short of money, I'll give her some. If she ends up liking me, I can stay there for a few nights."

33

Lie No. 7: Some overseas Uygur people have been claiming "their relatives or friends in Xinjiang cannot be contacted and have gone missing" on overseas media and social media platforms.

Fact check: Xinjiang protects the freedom of travel of people of all ethnic groups, including the Uygurs, and their communication with overseas relatives according to law.

—Verification with relevant departments shows that some allegedly "missing" people, mentioned by the "East Turkistan" separatists overseas, are living a normal life, while other "missing" incident reports are pure fabrications.

—Fact Check: Lies on Xinjiang-related issues
versus the truth, Ministry of Foreign Affairs of the
People's Republic of China, February 5, 2021

September broke the stifling months of summer and the kind of clouds that seem to hold back the dawn were emptying themselves over Istanbul as Adiljan left his apartment for the protest bus. At a little after seven he was sheltering under a bank frontage as commuters crowded by with hoods up and umbrellas in hand on their way to transit stops. He had ignored the weather and dressed in linen slacks, a purple blazer and immaculate light-brown loafers. Under his arm were two placards that he had made to replace the ones confiscated by the police. They also showed Mihribangul and the children and were bent and slightly stained from months of use. Two old and bearded Uyghur men who he knew a little came by. Adiljan shook their hands, then they stood slightly apart from him and talked to each other so that from where he was their mouths moved only with the noise of the traffic.

There had been demonstrations at the Chinese consulate every Friday for months but this would be his first since July. He should have joined them before but guilt and melancholy and thoughts of his family had flooded back after his first spell of energetic protest and they had overwhelmed him. He had been priced out of Zeytinburnu so moved further west and mostly stayed at home scrolling through his phone.

The planned departure time passed and they waited a while longer until the small hired bus arrived with an East Turkestan flag tied to the front and the shadows of passengers peering from its streaked and fogged windows. Adiljan climbed on and put the placards in the rack above a free seat then the driver pulled out into a snarl of rush-hour traffic, brake lights glistening red off the tarmac. Soft chatter swelled from the back. The other passengers were mostly older women wearing black headscarves or full veils and there were a few men in doppas among them. They offered a bag of fresh flatbread up and down the aisle then settled in. Some read, some reclined their seats and slept. One woman firmly wrapped an East Turkestan flag around her face for an eye mask as the sun burned through the receding clouds and the tower blocks and residential districts unfolded ahead. Adiljan watched videos on his phone then dozed too, his head nodding gently with the bus's stops and starts until his placards fell clattering from the luggage rack.

More than an hour later they pulled up at Sariyer marina and the passengers patiently disembarked onto the puddled concrete of the seaward side. A line of bored police by a parked up water-cannon

truck stood across the road at the bottom of the cobbled hill leading to
the consulate and a few plain-clothed officers to one side were failing
to look inconspicuous behind their sunglasses. That puddled concrete
was as far as the protesters were allowed to go now. Far enough away
that the consular staff could ignore them completely.

Another bus spilled its own contingent out onto the pavement and
then there was not quite forty of them in all. The second one was
mostly men. They were somber and middle-aged in shirt collars. And
they were older still with white beards and folding camp stools under their arms. They stood a moment then began unpacking banners
and posters with the ease of frequent practice. Adiljan shook hands
with one of the men then helped another hang bunting of alternating
Turkish and East Turkestan flags from roadside trees. Most of them
had homemade placards of their own missing listing names and their
relation to them. WIFE. HUSBAND. SISTER. BROTHER. AUNT.
UNCLE. IN-LAW.

The morning was starting to warm up and some of them hung jackets, umbrellas and the bag with the remaining bread from branches
too. The women began lining up but Adiljan waited around stiffly
until other men had joined and those that had them had sat down on
their stools before he took a place on the end.

One of the organizers circulated among them holding his phone
up for a Facebook live broadcast and complaining about the small
number of attendees. A mobile PA system shrieked briefly and the
East Turkestan anthem played muffled and overwhelmed by the passing cars. The organizer stopped his broadcast and led chants first in
English and then in Turkish with pictures of his own detained family
members slung around him as a cape.

"Terrorist China." he shouted into a microphone and waited for it to be repeated by the others.

"Fascist China."

"Stop Uyghur genocide."

"Close the camps."

"Release our families."

Adiljan only mouthed along with the English, not confident with the pronunciation.

The group seemed small there, dwarfed by the broad roads and surrounding luxury. Pedestrians in coordinated lycra walked or jogged by with dogs on leashes or phones in hand and eyes elsewhere. The police chatted in groups and rarely looked their way. Occasionally a sign of recognition. A woman waved from the passenger's side of a passing car, a horn beeped and one of a group of young men squeezed between construction equipment in the back of a pickup extended his fist with the pinky and index fingers raised. The salute of the pan-Turkic ultranationalist Grey Wolves group.

Around ten someone distributed bottles of water from a shopping cart and not long after that they packed up and got back on the buses. Adiljan walked home from the drop-off point along the main highway past a scrapyard and an impound lot. His apartment was tucked away in a courtyard with laundry and rugs hanging from the railings and bars on the inward-facing windows. The place was neat and clean, with a mismatched patchwork of worn rugs underfoot and a pair of matted lilac slippers with silvery white bows just by the door that he slipped on as soon as he got in. In the main room was an ornate dresser too large for the apartment and a lace-curtained window that looked onto a wall a few feet away and had done little to alleviate the summer heat. East Turkestan and Turkish flags hung from an exposed water pipe and underneath the boiler was an empty bird cage.

It had once belonged to Adiljan's parakeet, *Aşkım* (my love). The bird had been beautiful. A turquoise chest with white and black wings, a white speckled head and a yellow beak. Adiljan had got into the habit of talking to it when he was lonely and that was often. Then came one cold afternoon at the end of spring when he had forgotten to close the window and returned home to find the bird dead in the bottom of the cage. His fault, he thought, it must not have been able to handle the weather. He had decided to find a new one because he had liked the company but he had not yet done anything about it because he had to be careful with money.

There were not many options for work. His latest venture was selling traditional Uyghur medicine. Herbal cures mostly to men who said they had problems with their kidneys because the climate in Istanbul was so different from Xinjiang. Or to others who were having problems with what they called their private life.

When he had guests, he always apologized about the mess, although there was none to speak of. Sometimes he served the Arabic-style coffee he had been learning how to make from YouTube tutorials. There was seldom cause for it.

Adiljan heard that Abdullah had died back in 2017 but the things Abdullah had set in motion still dogged him. He had told people about what had happened and instead of sympathy, there had been much talk. People asking how a normal Uyghur man could possibly have caught a spy of the Chinese government. He felt their suspicion when he went out to eat or drink tea and some of the people he knew had slowly pulled away. It was the same when he mentioned the Party cadre calling himself Izmet who had contacted him with those pictures and videos of his children.

Others had received the same kind of calls and offers as he had. Nearly everyone it sounded like it but no one wanted to discuss their own experiences so confirming his own had made people wary. Not that he trusted others easily either. The only people who understood him all seemed now like potential spies. There were other Uyghurs in his new district as well as Uyghur restaurants and shops, a community center and a mosque, but he did not spend much time with them. When he prayed it was at the Turkish mosque in a leafy square nearby.

He thought sometimes of applying for asylum in the US or Canada but he did not know if it would be possible and he did not speak any English. To pass the time he had begun reading more and found some comfort in that. Not the same kind of books as had got him in trouble when he was young. Books about history and culture that he downloaded as PDFs. He had made plans to expand his traditional medicine operation and perhaps to set up a shop but the paperwork was intimidating and he would need to find the money for it. So he retreated inward and found little to do other than sit in his apartment with his grief and his guilt and his phone and try to think of a way forward.

34

China Arab TV: On February 2, the BBC revealed the so-called "experience" of a female graduated trainee Tursunay Chavdun in the U.S. and reported that "women suffered systematic rape, sexual abuse and torture in concentration camps of Xinjiang." The spokesman of the U.S. Ministry of Foreign Affairs alleged that "he was deeply disturbed by reports of raping Muslims systematically in Chinese refugee camps," and reiterated that "China has committed crimes against humanity and genocide in Xinjiang." These atrocities shocked people's conscience and must bear serious consequences. What's your comment on that?

Xu Guixiang, the Deputy Director-General of the Publicity Department of the CPC (Communist Party of China) Xinjiang Autonomous Regional Committee: Let me answer first! Here, I solemnly state again that the so-called "crimes against humanity and genocide in Xinjiang" were wantonly fabricated by Pompeo, which is a "lie of the century" as well as the biggest frame-up case in human history. The statement of the U.S. Ministry of Foreign Affairs has severely trampled on international law and norms governing international relations, interfered in China's internal affairs, and hurt the feelings of people of all ethnic groups in Xinjiang. Xinjiang Uygur Autonomous Region and people of all ethnic groups strongly condemn and oppose it.

The so-called "crimes against humanity and genocide" in Xinjiang are totally out of thin air.

—The 4th Press conference by Xinjiang Uygur Autonomous Region on Xinjiang-related Issues in Beijing, the Ministry of Foreign Affairs of the People's Republic of China, February 18, 2021

I t was a long time until Tursunay's strength started to come back to her. Doctors stabilized and discharged her after that first panicked hospital trip but they had agreed with the Turkish diagnosis that her uterus would have to be removed and scheduled the operation for the beginning of October 2020. Before then she was rushed twice more from the hotel to the ER when the bleeding got suddenly worse. The Uyghur community had been wonderful and the women especially. She had at last met Elfidar. Kind and energetic, always busy and always dressed with perfect neatness. Tursunay had begged her to sit and talk with her a while when she visited her in the hotel and Elfidar had, telling her about the community center nearby that held regular Uyghur cultural events and classes for the children on language, traditional dance and music. There was a Uyghur mosque too that was a gathering place for even some of the less-observant families after Friday prayer or during Ramadan.

The operation went well and she moved in with a woman named Hurshide afterwards who had visited her often. Hurshide lived in a big place with her children and young grandchildren and Tursunay was glad to at last be around people. She mostly stayed in bed but Hurshide cooked and checked in on her and the children would come and sit on the bed and steal morsels of the meals that she did not have the appetite to finish. "Let us stay with you Aunty, we want to stay," they would say when Hurshide tried to shoo them out and as tired as she was, Tursunay would smile and let them.

Three days passed like that and then she was sick again but differently. Fever this time and stomach pains and vomiting. Hoshida took her straight back to the hospital and the doctors said that there might be an infection from the surgery that would mean they needed to operate again. They said too that something might be wrong with her lungs that they had not noticed before and they ran tests and waited for the results.

It happened in a moment. The nurses rushed in wearing even more protective equipment than usual and started screening her off from the world. A translator arrived and explained that the tests had shown that she had tuberculosis so she would have to be isolated until it was no longer infectious. Tursunay cried because as one of her ordeals seemed almost to be over another had begun. Treatment was antibiotics and syringes of various other things. So many injections that the veins on her arms were nothing but pricks and bruises and Band-Aids.

The fever persisted until she was too weak to move herself. Nurses did everything for her. Fed her, took her to the bathroom, carefully sponged her body with warm water each day. She thanked them because that was all she could say and when she was alone she prayed for them. The fever eased enough that Tursunay began to worry about Hurshide and her family. Perhaps she had infected everyone in the house. Perhaps Omer and Medine and Louisa. Perhaps the women who had brought her food and sat so patiently with her. All were tested. Hurshide and the children were unaffected and that felt like a miracle. The UHRP people were too but Elfidar and some of the others tested positive and needed a course of treatment.

Doctors discharged her after a week with orders to maintain strict isolation and run a course of pills. The pills were enormous capsules that tasted disgusting and stuck in her throat. She had to take ten of them each day.

She checked into a different hotel and this one had a suite with a kitchenette. A nurse came at eleven each morning to make sure she took the pills and Tursunay planned her day around it. She would rise early to prepare and cook eggs with peppers and tomatoes, then put them aside and pour herself cups of water. The nurse would arrive and Tursunay would choke down five of the pills and gulp the water. Then she would ask if she could take a minute and she would eat a mouthful of eggs. The eggs always tasted awful with the pill residue still in her mouth but they helped her face the rest of the dose.

Three months and the doctors told her she was no longer contagious so she could see anyone she liked. She was still weak but with a clarity she had nearly forgotten. Clear enough that she began to think about what would come next. Halmirza rarely contacted her by then and she no longer expected him to join her. It was as if he had discharged his responsibilities towards her and with them any thoughts of a life together. Tursunay could accept that.

Some of the UHRP members had suggested that she might speak with the media about her experiences once she felt ready. The phone calls, the harassment and the arson had all worked to quiet her but time and distance lent her courage. She thought often too of the women and men still detained in the camps who had been broken as she had been. Who'd had their health destroyed and their minds with it. In her dreams she saw them and in quiet moments she heard their voices.

Early in 2021 she told UHRP that she would do it and this time decided she would tell them everything. Her first interview was with the BBC. They came to her and Zubayra, who worked with UHRP, translated. Tursunay dressed carefully in dark clothes and a chiffon headscarf and sat down with the journalists when they arrived. They asked questions now and again and for her to identify images and footage of the camp but it felt like a natural conversation so she kept on talking until it was nearly all out. They took pictures of her too. Sitting at the table and on the sofa framed by curtains.

The report published on February 2. It mentioned other women too but at the top of the page was a close-up of Tursunay's in profile, sunlight on her face, the rest of her in shadow.

"Their Goal Is to Destroy Everyone: Uighur Camp Detainees Allege Systematic Rape," the headline read.

People started calling first thing in the morning. Zubayra checked on her but so did many others she knew and they were all shocked and tearful at what they had read. Soon she heard that someone from the US State Department had talked about the article, decrying the genocide and Chinese crimes against humanity.

She was sickened by the enormity of it. How could she look people in the face when they knew what had happened to her? And what about Halmirza? The idea of what he and his family would think if he saw it nagged at her but she heard nothing from him. Perhaps he had not noticed.

Ten days later the Party held a press conference in Beijing. There were around thirty people there. Party officials who were mostly men and several Uyghurs described as graduated trainees. They sat on leather chairs around an open wooden conference table with a microphone and light-pink name card at each place. All wore surgical masks and took them off only when it was their turn to talk.

The first question was from the *People's Daily*. It asked how the graduate trainees came to have been influenced by religious extremism and how they finally rid themselves of it with the help of the vocational education and training centers. One of the officials was ready right away and said that a twenty-eight-year-old graduate from Aksu would answer.

A young man with a short haircut and new suit stood up. He introduced himself and talked blankly about how his so-called friends had convinced him of the pleasures of a paradise where he would have seventy-two beautiful wives and endless money but that this paradise could only be entered through jihad and killing unbelievers. He explained he had obtained a fake passport so he could travel abroad to wage holy war but was caught trying to leave the country. Authorities had offered him time in a vocational education and training center instead of prison.

There, he said, he studied the Chinese constitution, laws, regulations and deradicalization until he knew what was right again. He deeply regretted his behavior and how close he had come to falling into an abyss of evil. The vocational education and training center, he said, had taught him marketing management. So after graduating from the center he had found a real estate job with satisfactory income then got married and bought a car. "We are grateful," he said, "to the vocational education and training centers."

More questions followed. From the state broadcaster CGTN. From Xinhua. And eventually from Associated Press of Pakistan because it was run by the Pakistani government and so was reliably friendly. The answers were all prepared and the Party men either read from notes or called on another of the graduates to explain how they too had been led astray and infected with religious extremism but were grateful to the vocational education and training centers. The women trainees stressed that some of them had since had children since graduating so any allegations of sterilization were nonsense.

A reporter from China Arab TV asked a question about the BBC report on Tursunay and the comments that US official made afterwards. The reply came from a regional Party press officer. He condemned the American's comments then spoke of Tursunay specifically. In exchange for her refugee status, he said, she had been willing to become an actress and had been manipulated by anti-China forces and at their bidding fabricated her experience in the vocational center. Why else, he asked, when she had spoken to press in Kazakhstan would she not have mentioned sexual assault or beatings?

He had a graduate ready to add to that, a woman. She said she solemnly stated that no female trainee had been sexually abused in a vocational education and training center. "We want to tell those rumor-mongers in the BBC," she said, "that if you continue to humiliate us female trainees, we will hold you accountable through legal channels."

Tursunay avoided all of that as much as she was able but she knew her interview had bothered Chinese authorities and thought that perhaps it could prevent what had happened to her happening to someone else. That made her braver. She would speak out and she would tell the truth as loudly and as often as she could.

So she did an interview with CNN later in the month and the attacks on her continued. At one foreign ministry press conference a spokesman held up a grainy picture of her face on a clipboard and said she spread lies and rumors. "Considering her character," he asked, "should we just believe her when she accuses the vocational education and training centers of carrying out systematic sexual abuse against women?"

He held up another picture. Of Zumrat Dawut, who had survived the camps and also found refuge in Virginia. She too had talked to journalists and so she too was a target.

Tursunay's recovery was quickening by then and the first signs of spring were starting to appear. "Walk," her doctors urged, "you need to regain your strength." She paced deliberate circles in her room first and soon she was venturing a little way outside. Everything was a little more alive each time she did. Flowers and leaves budding, the grass greener, the sun warmer on her skin. She would walk and admire it and take pictures on her phone of the things she saw that pleased her. A particularly well-formed tree. The light playing on a new flower. A perfect sunset.

35

148. The information currently available to OHCHR on implementation of the Government's stated drive against terrorism and "extremism" in XUAR in the period 2017–2019 and potentially thereafter, also raises concerns from the perspective of international criminal law. The extent of arbitrary and discriminatory detention of members of Uyghur and other predominantly Muslim groups, pursuant to law and policy, in context of restrictions and deprivation more generally of fundamental rights enjoyed individually and collectively, may constitute international crimes, in particular crimes against humanity.

—United Nations Human Rights Office of the High Commissioner, OHCHR Assessment of human rights concerns in the Xinjiang Uyghur Autonomous Region, People's Republic of China, August 31, 2022

Marine Park in Brooklyn, and Serikzhan followed the asphalt paths between the oaks and lindens and Japanese zelkovas. Shouts and thwacks echoed from the basketball and tennis courts blending with the lively racket from the playground. All around were joggers and sightseers, picnickers and dog walkers out enjoying the summer warmth and acres of green. Serikzhan had been trying to lose weight lately and came to the park with thoughts of joining a basketball game but settled on walking as briskly as he could. A phone call waylaid him and he slowed to a stroll. It was only after pocketing his phone again that he became aware of a persistent presence behind him and stopped and turned. A man was there and the man stopped when he stopped. The man was certainly Chinese, Serikzhan thought,

and he had the body of a wrestler. The man did not move and kept
his fixed eyes right on Serikzhan with a look so horribly implacable
that Serikzhan started fast away. The man started walking too and
kept easy pace thirty or forty feet back. Serikzhan took a right and
the man did as well. He took a left and so did the man. He started to
walk even faster and so did the man and when he glanced back the
man was still there and his eyes still held him. This man was not like
the man with the camera in Washington DC, there was no pretense
with him. This man might mean violence. Serikzhan kept moving and
called a friend who lived nearby. It was an emergency, he said, and he
needed a ride. He started to run when he saw the car on the edge of
the park a few minutes later.

Time to calm himself and he saw that if the man had wanted to
attack him he could have. That was not the point of it. The point was
to deliver a threat. We know where you live and where you are any
time at all. We can reach you anywhere.

It should not have been a shock. Things had been quieter since he
moved from Washington DC but not so much that he felt safe enough
to keep an address for more than a month or two. Moving around
like that was not much of a way to live but it bothered him far more
that he was still alone. China Aid had arranged an immigration lawyer but he and Laila were still waiting for reunification papers and
there was little progress even with his asylum claim. At least she and
the children had left Istanbul. It happened because there had been
protests in Kazakhstan nearly a year after he reached the US. They
began as outcry about increased gas prices and soon coalesced with
broader anger at the inequalities and indignities the government up-
held. There was violence in Almaty and the security forces returned it

many times over. More than two hundred were killed and thousands arrested. Tokayev called the protesters bandits and terrorists and said that he had ordered troops to shoot to kill and give no warning first.

Serikzhan had been loud with his support for the movement and his condemnation of Tokayev. The government response to him had been so furious that even Turkey had seemed too easy to reach for the NSC. He and Devra and Michael and the China Aid people formed a plan. Laila would struggle to travel alone with three young children and all of their luggage so Devra and Michael flew to Istanbul and accompanied them on a flight to the Netherlands. Laila and the children claimed asylum when they landed and Dutch police arrested Devra and Michael for helping them. Human trafficking, they said. Three days later the two of them were back in the US and told Serikzhan it was an honor to have helped.

There was nothing much for him after that but to wait. His Kazakh bank accounts remained frozen while cases against him continued in absentia. He tried to give his brother power of attorney to sell the Nissan or at least add himself to the insurance but even that turned out to be impossible.

Every day around noon he recorded a livestream. He spoke about the things he always had and more besides. It was no longer only about saving Kazakhs from Chinese camps for him but saving all Kazakh people from their leaders. He spoke of the problems he saw in Kazakhstan and criticized religious extremism alongside blind obedience to the state. He spoke of the values of democracy and freedom of speech and equality as well as the importance of thinking independently and escaping the influence of Chinese and Russian propaganda.

He said Tokayev was a lackey of Russia and of China and that

Kazakhstan should part with every piece of its Soviet history and become a truly independent country. "Do not have your children study Russian, because that is the language of corruption and dictatorship," he told his followers. "Have them study English, French or German instead."

Sometimes he talked about life in America too. "Do not listen when Russian propaganda speaks of perverts and degenerates in the West," he would say. "Yes, in America, a man may love a man but he may also love a woman. Each person can choose to do as they will because that is freedom."

Tens of thousands watched him most days. Not just Kazakhs but Uyghurs, Uzbeks and Kyrgyz as well, whose languages were close enough to his for general comprehension.

The streams lasted hours at a time. He was animated then. Forceful and confident in his cause and himself. Afterwards that spirit sometimes left him and he thought about the way things had ended up. There were moments he felt lucky. He was not dead, he was not in prison and he and Atazhurt had done so much and done it well. He would look at the hundreds of messages of thanks from camp survivors and their families and know that it had been his duty to expose the crimes of the government that had once been his.

Then came moments where he thought himself the unfortunate man of an unfortunate nation and days at a time passed in deep depression. He had thought that the thousands of hours of testimony and the images and video that Atazhurt gathered would mean the democracies of the world would find a way to stop it all. Lately he worried that he had been wrong and that the Kazakhs were alone and the Uyghurs alone and the ethnic Kyrgyz and the Hui too.

Politicians in the US and Europe and Canada and the United Kingdom had made grand speeches condemning the Chinese government and its genocide. Journalists had written all about it on their websites, their newspapers and magazines. And yet there had been no progress and no real support for those millions arrested, beaten, raped or sterilized. For the families split forever apart. Perhaps they were only a political game to those politicians and the public's memory was short. Perhaps he had been childish to think otherwise and the democratic ideals that he spoke of on his livestreams were hollow, the Western promise hypocritical. Or perhaps he was wrong about all of that and something would change. He hoped he was.

Days like those he wanted to give up everything for his family. Family should always come first. Children should. And he had missed so much of his own children's lives. Birthdays, outings, first days at school, countless tiny moments of joy. All lost forever to him. He looked at pictures of them and they were so different from how he remembered. He thought of Laila and her face and her smell no longer came easily to him.

Then there were the circumstances he had left his brothers and his sister in. He had discovered that National Security watched them always. Plainclothed men with cameras followed them every time they left their houses and lingered outside whichever cafe, shop or restaurant they visited. The same men followed their spouses too. Once his brother had been parked by the side of the road and a bus had plowed into his car. He had been unhurt but Serikzhan remembered the National Security man telling him that one day a Kamaz might crush his Nissan and he saw a warning.

He longed for Almaty. He returned to its avenues and trees and parks often in his dreams and remembered life as it had been when he was just a businessman. He had everything then. Money enough and a circle of people he loved and cared for. He could do what he wanted and go where he wanted. There had been no court cases, no ceaseless fear of arrest or attack.

Even in the US he felt it. National Security and the Chinese government were on him still and he thought Russia might be too. The online campaign never stopped. An anonymous, organized network of social media accounts said he was FBI or CIA then called him a traitor and said that traitors should be executed. For a time they tried suggesting that he was secretly Hui and so had no standing to comment on anything Kazakh.

Members of Atazhurt still in Kazakhstan were slowly falling away. One who had been with them since the beginning called Serikzhan and told him that he wanted to resign his role and return to academia. Serikzhan asked why and the man said that because of his involvement with Atazhurt the threats from National Security were constant and his son had recently been fired from a government job. Serikzhan understood. "Of course," he said, "you have done so much and worked so hard. Go and finish your studies."

Another Atazhurt member arrived in New York. Serikzhan and he drank cappuccinos in cafes not far from the water and sometimes drove out to the Poconos and Bear Mountain State Park at the weekends where the peaks reminded him of home. There were plenty of other Kazakhs, Kyrgyz and Uzbeks where they were but it was difficult to trust new people. Serikzhan saw how China's reach had turned Uyghurs to suspicion of each other and he saw it happening to Kazakhs as well.

He kept on with his livestreams and his social media posts and he felt even more exposed. Sympathetic organizations asked to meet with him and he refused because he was afraid to. He worried about being tailed and sometimes wore a mask and a baseball cap and sunglasses when he left the house. He would sit looking unconcerned on the subway ride home right until the doors were about to close at some intermediate stop and then jump up and out of the train watching to see if anyone did the same. Then he would change directions and do it again and another time. Sometimes he saw the same person one too many times in the street and began to panic. He would tell himself not to be so sensitive, that it was surely just someone who lived nearby but he found he was unconvincing.

His concern grew unbearable after he heard of attacks against other exiled Kazakh activists. "I'll be here," he told people when making plans for the days to come, "unless a Chinese spy or the Russian KGB or Kazakh intelligence have me shot." He smiled when he said it but it was not a joke, not really.

His phone rang one day as summer settled over the city and the dew point crept up. No caller ID. He answered. A man's voice, speaking English with a heavy Russian accent. "Is this Serikzhan Bilash?" He said it was. "Shut up," the man said, "just shut up."

36

On 31 August, the Office of the High Commissioner for Human Rights (OHCHR), in disregard of China's solemn representation, insisted on releasing the so-called "assessment" on Xinjiang, China. We firmly oppose this so-called "assessment" which is not mandated by the Human Rights Council, smears and slanders China, and interferes in China's internal affairs. It seriously violates the purposes and principles of the Charter of the United Nations, and undermines the credibility and impartiality of the OHCHR.

The so-called "assessment", based on presumption of guilt, uses disinformation and lies fabricated by anti-China forces as its main sources, deliberately ignores authoritative information and objective materials provided by the Chinese government, maliciously distorts China's laws and policies, denigrates the fight against terrorism and extremism in Xinjiang, and turns a blind eye to the tremendous human rights achievements jointly made by people of all ethnic groups in Xinjiang. Its content is completely contradictory to the end of mission statement made by the High Commissioner after her visit to China. It exposes the deep-rooted bias against and ignorance on China of some people in the OHCHR.

The so-called "assessment" is purely a farce plotted by some Western countries and anti-China forces. They have been consistently pressing the High Commissioner and the OHCHR, and demanding the release of a so-called "assessment" on Xinjiang, so as to bring ammunitions to their political manipulation of Xinjiang-related issues. It is completely a politicized document that disregards facts, and reveals explicitly the attempt of some Western countries and anti-China forces to use human rights as a political tool.

—**Chinese Mission to the UN spokesperson Liu Yuyin's remarks on the so-called "assessment" on Xinjiang issued by the Office of the United Nations High Commissioner for Human Rights (OHCHR), September 1, 2022**

One day in late February 2023, Tursunay woke at her apartment in suburban Virginia, the lamps she still could not sleep without weak in the daylight. She walked through to the open-plan kitchen and the macrame-clothed table just big enough for three pushed up against the floor-to-ceiling window. She passed time there first thing each day, enjoying the stillness and the exiled night. The view was of parked cars and other houses. Clapboard walls, green grass, the morning reflected in windshields and after a time the calming mundanity of people leaving for work or corralling sleepy children for the school run. In summer it was all verdant foliage and welcome shade but the trees were still mostly bare save for sparse leaves of red and tired green that had survived the winter and a few optimistic buds daring the forecast cold snap.

The apartment had been empty when she moved in nearly two years earlier. Just plain walls and laminate flooring really but she had immediately liked the way the sun streamed in. She'd had nearly nothing with her and one of the Uyghur women who lived nearby had brought her some bedding. Tursunay laid it out on the floor but another woman soon arrived and walked around with a critical eye.

"Oh, we will have to have curtains here," she had said, "and to get you a bed. Here we'll have some shelving and here we'll repaint."

Elfidar had visited. Zubayra too and many more who were new to her. They all helped furnish. Bringing something new or something cast-off, clubbing together for a bigger item. It was so organized that she'd had to buy nothing and do nothing for herself. Through them she had met other camp survivors like Zumrat and like Mihrigul, who sometimes visited after she had dropped her two young children at school. Mihrigul was cheery and excitable and still noticeably traumatized by her ordeal. She was only a little over a decade younger than Tursunay but a full head smaller and said sometimes that Tursunay felt like a mother to her. They hugged when she came by and if Tursunay was cooking then Mihrigul would help, the two of them standing side by side at the worktop deftly pulling and folding dough into laghman, chopping peppers, potatoes or onions and chatting about this and that.

Tursunay would have been content just to live in safety and peace but that community gave her a sense of love that was unreserved and open. Love that she had never experienced in Kazakhstan when life had been consumed by the duties Halmirza's family expected of her and she had still felt lonely in a house full of them. And in the end, Halmirza had divorced her from afar. She had not been particularly upset because she no longer had the energy or desire to perform the traditional duties of a wife. The time when she was able to support another had passed and now she needed the support of others. Perhaps he had realized that.

The apartment felt like hers now. There were lace curtains at the windows and white faux-leather chairs around the table. There were books on the shelves alongside sheafs of paper and plastic tubs of vitamins. Because she still altered and made clothing sometimes, there were piles of fabric and a newish sewing machine with cotton spooled on top. And because she liked it, there was a gilt frame on one wall holding a printed oil-paint study of a vase of flowers.

That day stretched ahead of Tursunay uneventful until a late afternoon protest planned outside the Chinese embassy over in DC. It was the one organized by a local Jewish group that said they would not hold their peace as genocide unfolded and it had taken place the third Thursday of every month for the past two years.

She had stuck to her resolution of doing anything that might help and her only consistent longing was to see justice visited on the Chinese government. If she died the day after that came to pass then she would happily die.

One of those things had been to testify to the House Committee on Foreign Affairs. She did it via video link. "I am not asking for sympathy for myself," she told them. "I am asking governments around the world to wake up and save the millions of my people who are still suffering today in my homeland."

She had done much the same at another committee hearing and travelled to DC too. She had met Nancy Pelosi; Sophie Richardson of Human Rights Watch; Kelley Currie, the ambassador-at-large for the Office of Global Women's Issues; and lots of men in suits whose names she had forgotten. They had shaken her hand and said how good it was to meet her and how brave she was and it had felt like they meant it.

The attacks had continued. There had been more press conferences with Party men brandishing her photograph. Articles in the Party newspapers called her and Zumrat and Mihrigul liars every so often. She expected it but she worried for her family.

Government media had begun publishing more videos and pictures from Xinjiang lately. People were happy in them. They wore garish versions of traditional clothing and they danced and sang for the entertainment of visiting tourists so that their culture was reduced to an theme park version of itself. Tursunay read that some of the more overt security measures had been scaled back and some of the camps had closed but she was sure it was because people there had been brainwashed as she had been and lost sight of any idea of freedom. Repress enough people for long enough and checkpoints, body scans, travel restrictions and arrests all become utterly routine. There were times that she wished she had never properly woken from it herself. Perhaps then she would have been something close to happy because the real suffering had come after her escape when she realized what was happening to the people she loved and how little she could do to save them from it.

So she did not try to contact her brothers or her sisters because it would certainly have made things worse and they existed for her in a state of limbo. They might be fine or they might be detained. And if they were, then it could have been her speech that sacrificed them. That was a calculation nearly all Uyghurs living abroad had to make. Among the community in Virginia was the knowledge that talking about Xinjiang carried with it the near certainty of being contacted by Chinese authorities. Mihrigul had also testified and spoken with journalists and someone had thrown a rock through her window afterwards. She moved to a different address and a note threatening her children was pushed under her door. She still thought she saw people following her in malls and parking lots and supermarkets. Elfidar had been subjected to an organized cyber campaign that posted her family's personal information online so often that she installed CCTV around and inside her house. Another activist was attacked in the street after an online dispute with a Chinese student association. Untold others who posted on Twitter or Facebook about detained relatives had received calls, texts and voice notes from police back home and from embassy employees. Occasionally even from the relatives themselves. The message was always the same. Think of your family and stop what you're doing. It often worked.

There were members of the diaspora who stayed away from even the community center.

Tursunay had chosen her path and she attended every protest and event she could. Earlier in the month she had passed a cold afternoon in DC's Lafayette Square at a gathering organized by the East Turkistan Government in Exile. She stood in her turquoise baseball cap with the crescent moon and star as part of a small group by the dulled bronze statue of Andrew Jackson on his rearing horse. "We will now face the White House and chant," one of the Government in Exile men had said, and they repeated the familiar refrains of Uyghur protest. "Fascist China," they shouted. "Terrorist China. Go home China. Take China to the ICC." A much better attended and amplified demonstration being held by supporters of the Ethiopian Orthodox Church on the other side of the square largely drowned them out. They stopped and another of the Government in Exile men spoke to a local journalist while the sun emerged to shine thinly down and a middle-aged man wearing a shocking-pink helmet rolled past on a single-wheeled hoverboard.

The following week they had gathered by the low wall at the bottom of Capitol Hill. There was a foot-high stage set up in the clipped grass with a PA speaker on each side and a banner displaying a 32 by 90 grid of ID pictures of the missing strung between wooden poles. More than two dozen people had turned up and that had made it one of the larger protests. Omer, Louisa and Elfidar were there. Adalet too. Adalet taught dance at the community center and came to most of the protests with her five-year-old daughter Erden'ay and a large photograph of her husband, who was trapped in China. There were speeches from various attendees and Tursunay had stood with her arms crossed and shivered while passers by took sidewalk selfies with what was visible of the Capitol dome from behind a scaffold of repair work.

For the Chinese embassy protest, Tursunay wore that same turquoise baseball cap and her black long-sleeved t-shirt that read.

STOP

UYGHUR

GENOCIDE

The script red then white then red.

The sun had slunk below the horizon by the time they made their way along the brick sidewalk towards the embassy and the sodium-vapor globes of the street lamps were tainting the sky a gentle blue. The building rose formidable ahead. Five angular stories of pale and expressionless stone. All of it was secured behind thick walls, anti-climb fencing and pillars topped with cube-shaped orange lamps of their own.

It was the usual crowd again. Louisa and some others from UHRP, Elfidar, the older Jewish couple who helped organize the protest and who Tursunay knew but could never speak to properly because they had no common tongue. Adalet was there with Erden'ay. Both of them wearing matching faux-fur gilets and Erden'ay light-up Velcro sneakers.

They stopped on the corner by a diamond yellow crossing sign and a ribbon of grass still recovering from the winter. A dark-uniformed Chinese guard stood a few more feet uphill next to a double-lane gate into the compound. He watched them from behind a surgical mask.

They began setting themselves up. Some of the placards they unpacked were a job lot professionally printed and worded like Tursunay's t-shirt. One attendee had made his own, coloring in CHINA CAN'T HIDE UYGHUR GENOCIDE with felt tip in a handwritten bubble script. Adalet's placard had a studio portrait of her and her husband in matching traditional clothing.

More people arrived until there was a little over a dozen of them, including an older man in a doppa and a couple with an infant in a stroller. The guard at the gate began taking pictures of them on his phone but that was normal. Sometimes staff took pictures through the windows too as surveillance or as intimidation. Tursunay did not care anymore.

They gathered with their signs and posed for pictures to be posted on campaign social media accounts. Then they stood in a circle and took turns to read aloud the names of detainees and the non-Uyghur attendees stumbled over the unfamiliar spellings. Erden'ay held the poster of her father for a while but grew bored and began weaving between the adults and through a world of her own, LEDs twinkling at her feet. If Adalet's attention was elsewhere then Tursunay kept a careful eye on the girl. Extending an instinctive hand if she got too close to the road, smiling reassuringly, tousling her hair.

The embassy gate had been still but as the work day ended it began swinging open to allow a series of BMW, Mercedes and Lexus SUVs to leave the compound. All with diplomatic plates and the shadows of faces behind tinted glass looking out at the gathering or fixed firmly ahead.

The others talked and Tursunay stood silently on the edge of the group and eyed the increased traffic. Then she broke off from them a few steps and moved slightly uphill and towards the gate. She looked straight at each vehicle that emerged from the compound, staring into those opaque windows and holding up her placard where they could read it. She rotated her body as they rolled past so they would keep seeing her, keep reading it and so they would notice the flag on her cap and how she did not falter at the sight of them.

The older man in the doppa stepped over to join her. "Stop Uyghur genocide," he yelled in English at each passing SUV and the words tumbled angry from him. "Go home China, go home China."

Tursunay just kept her eyes on the gate and moved closer again, right to the edge of the curb. She confronted them like that whenever she could, sometimes turning to the masked guards too, though they would never acknowledge her presence. She did it because they no longer scared her and because it was as close as she could get to conveying a message to the people who had gone so far to deny her existence.

Look at me, she wanted to say to them. I am a camp survivor and the things that happened to me are real. I am a witness to horror and to genocide and I am here. Go and tell your government that. Tell your families and friends. Because by seeing me you should understand and you should be ashamed. Standing there in silent confrontation, she said none of it aloud and the SUVs passed by implacable into the dusk.

37

"In the process of Chinese-style modernisation, we will better build a beautiful Xinjiang that is united and harmonious, wealthy and prosperous."

—President Xi Jinping speaks in Urumqi following a brief on the work of the Party committee and Xinjiang government, August 26, 2023

The calls from home got more frequent after Saira began talking about the camps and the threats more explicit. Police or some other part of the security apparatus would go to her mother's house or sometimes to one of her sister's and then the WeChat calls would start. She could always hear the Party's words in their voices. She should stop what she was doing, they said. She should not speak against China. She should think of her family.

"I'm here legally," Saira said to them for the people listening. "China gave me permission to leave. I'm not a bird who can cross the border as I please." It was true but she felt that familiar pang of guilt and of grief as she said it. She felt it too whenever she thought of her mother alone in the house and worried about how she was coping and what might happen to her. She missed her and missed home so much that some days it was all she could think of. She found it maddening that anyone could take a flight from Kazakhstan to Japan or America or wherever else they chose in just a few hours but the Chinese border was less than two hundred miles away and neither she nor her mother could ever cross it.

She became entangled in melancholy some days. Her family, her homeland, her hopes for the future. All of it the Chinese state had taken from her. The businesses she had built and the money she had earned. That was all gone too. They had stolen her past along with the essence of herself. The things she had done, the places she had been and even the books she had read had all become hazy and difficult to call forth. She tried again to sit down and memorize prose and poems by favorite writers but the words slipped away a moment after reading no matter how many times she repeated them.

The Saira who could do that and could do so many other things was gone. She had always thought you could read everything about a person from their eyes. When she looked at those old pictures of herself posing in a meadow or sitting at her computer or speaking at a conference, she saw a spirit burning behind hers that was gone when she looked in a mirror.

Starting again in Almaty with nothing and no one was much more difficult than it had been in Urumqi. She remembered the times she had told her friends that she did not need a husband or children because she could leave a legacy of her own through her writing and felt it vain nonsense. Too late she realized that one should never speak without thinking. It seemed as if God had heard her and decided to teach her a lesson by making sure her words came true.

Her friends persisted in trying to introduce her to men. One of them they described as a Chinese Kazakh divorcee with shared custody of his daughter. He asked her out on a date and then asked again but she turned him down. "You're always so picky," her friends said, "and look where it got you. In your forties and still not married." So she gave him a chance. It went well enough but a woman knocked on her door a few days later and said she needed to talk to her about this man. He was not divorced, the woman said, and their Chinese marriage had never been annulled.

More months passed and the moments when she appreciated the little freedoms that were hers again came more often. She chose her seat in a restaurant or took a taxi to wherever in the city she wished. She felt the sun on her face and sat down on park benches as the birds she had longed to hear flitted between the trees. She noticed the opportunities of life in Kazakhstan. Little things sometimes. Adults rarely exercised back home but in Almaty it seemed that people looked after themselves better. They jogged, they played sports. It was not the hated physical education classes and the camp calisthenics but something different. Sociable and healthy. Joyful even. Perhaps it was not overly late for her to try something new.

She thought of searching for her grandfather's brother, who must surely have been long dead but perhaps had children. Friends told her of a government program where relatives split apart by borders could supply personal details and researchers would look through records for possible matches then make a connection if they found one. Saira liked the idea but was apprehensive somehow and never got around to it. It was the same with returning to writing. After so long away the task became too vast to imagine.

Perhaps it was the sense of insecurity. The occasional WeChat calls and messages continued but she heard of much worse from others. The arson attack at Tursunay's place. Serikzhan's arrest and flight. Baqitali, the vegetable seller she met who had been held in Künes, had testified at a gathering of evidence and testimony in the United

Kingdom called the Uyghur Tribunal. Afterwards he had been threatened by the NSC and attacked in the street by a group of men who told him to keep his mouth shut. She kept hearing more stories like that in Almaty and the protection of her new passport no longer felt absolute. When she saw groups of Han Chinese people in a shop or cafe or in the street, she flinched and moved tables or made for somewhere crowded in case they were following her or plotting some operation to take her back to a camp.

There were other, more mundane difficulties. Prices for even basic goods were high and kept getting higher and she could no longer work on cross-border trade as she had. She wondered about finding a way to live abroad. Somewhere safer and further away. She spoke with Tursunay and people in the US but it was hard to get an American visa. She read about Canadian plans to admit ten thousand refugees from Xinjiang and thought that could be her chance. It seemed to her that the world owed the survivors who had spoken out. If they had not done what they had and sacrificed what they had then other countries might not even have known about the genocide. Kazakhstan's ban on dual citizenship made her hesitate. Her passport was an official link to her historical motherland and meant she could at least be close to home. She could not give that up easily.

At a party halfway through 2022, her friends got back to suggesting men for her. There was one who was part of their circle. Such a nice guy, they said. Really, she should meet him. He too had once been married and in that marriage had two daughters. One who was then age seven and another who was four. It had turned out that the younger of the two girls was not his. His wife left him when he found out and took the four-year-old but left the older girl with him. "Come on," Saira said. "Please don't introduce me to another divorcee, not after last time." Her friends gave him her number anyway and he soon messaged asking if she'd like to meet. She did not reply.

Not too long after that she was talking to one of those friends and the friend brought up a suggestion that Saira had once made. The suggestion had been that Kazakhstan should make it legal for men to have more than one wife so as to maintain population growth. Her friend was married and found the whole thing hilarious. "Why don't you become the second wife for my husband then?" she said. "But only on the condition that you and my husband can make the money and I will spend it. Oh, and you can cook as well," she said. "I will only have fun." It was a joke but there was something about her tone that infuriated Saira. "You're not looking for a second wife," she replied. "You're looking for a slave. Watch," she said. "By January next year I will be married and I will be happy."

That night, she dreamt that she was given a present of white shoes. In her understanding of these things, such a dream meant that you would soon find a husband. So if you had a suitor then you should give them a chance. The second divorcee messaged her the following day. He said that he sensed that she was not interested in dating him and that was fine but why not at least meet. If she did not want to take it any further then perhaps they could at least be friends.

She agreed quickly enough. They sat down together in a cafe and she examined him for the warning signs that her grandmother had taught her. He sat upright and met her gaze easily. His shoes were clean, his trousers pressed and the ratio between his fingers and his palms was not skewed too far one way or the other. Everything was just about how it should be, she thought, and her friends had not been lying, he was nice. For hours they told each other of their lives. She spared him little and he was open with her too about the end of his marriage and about his economic prospects. He drove a taxi, he said, and that was not much of a living but he made enough to get by.

It felt so abruptly right that Saira went further. She told him that she had determined to marry by the beginning of the coming year and that was not too far away. "Look," she said, "the camps damaged me in ways that I will always carry with me. I'm always nervous, I forget things, I get lost in the streets and I'd need you to take me from place to place sometimes."

"Ok," he said. "I understand."

"They gave me injections of who knows what, and I may not be able to give you another child," she said.

"I know," he said.

"I'm still being watched, still being pressured. They could try and take me anytime. They might even try and threaten you."

"I'd look after you," he said.

"Ok," she said eventually, surer of herself and of him. "I know your story and you know mine, and if you want to be with me, we should marry no later than December. If you don't, then get lost."

"I want to marry and I care for our nation like you do," he said. "So if you'll help give my daughter a proper upbringing and teach her to love our motherland, then I'll be happy."

The ceremony was on the twenty-sixth of December, 2022, and it was simple and happy. She moved into his place on the edge of Almaty afterwards. It was not much bigger than hers had been and it took an hour to get into the city center when the traffic was bad and the traffic was often bad. Saira still liked it. It was comfortable and not far from the mountains and she made it hers too with the few things she had. On one bedroom wall she hung a landscape of verdant green that reminded her of the meadows back home.

His daughter was shy at first but she and Saira got used to each other and got to like each other too. He did the things he had promised. When she arranged to meet with other survivors and human rights organizations, he drove her across town. When she felt anxious and disoriented, he stayed with her. He made little enough money from the taxi that she felt she had to find work as well but he told her he did not want her to give up on the things she had always hoped for. "I wish I could take better care of us all," he would say, "and earn enough for us to live comfortably. Perhaps then you could write the story of your life. Everyone would read it and it would be translated into different languages and sold all over the world."

ACKNOWLEDGMENTS

My unending gratitude to the people who entrusted their stories to me. Each relayed and relived the hardest moments of their lives in patient, precise detail at my request and I can never thank them enough for it.

I am indebted to so many others besides. To Zubayra Shamseden and to colleagues who must go unnamed, whose careful and sensitive translation I often relied on.

To the strangers who welcomed me into homes and offices, classrooms and mosques, to gatherings of remembrance and of celebration. To the members of myriad organisations who were so generous with their time and space, in particular Elfidar Iltebir of the Uyghur American Association.

To my agent George Lucas of Inkwell, to Carl Bromley who saw the book I hoped to write and provided such thoughtful feedback on my drafts. To copy editor Theresa Cameron, as well as to Philip Velinov, Mike Lindgren, and everyone at Melville House who helped make sure this book became a book and got it out into the world.

To the outlets that allowed me the luxury of time and column inches to report on these issues, especially *Harper's*, which first published a story featured here in expanded form, and *National Geographic*.

To Danya for a place to stay in DC, to my family for their ever-present support, to Lisen for everything.